Light on the Old Testament from Babel

The Ancient Near East: Classic Studies

K. C. Hanson, Series Editor

Albert T. Clay
Light on the Old Testament from Babel

Albert T. Clay
The Origin of Biblical Traditions

Leonard W. King
Legends of Babylon and Egypt in Relation to Hebrew Tradition

Friedrich Delitzsch
Babel and Bible

George Smith
Assyrian Discoveries

George Smith & A. H. Sayce
The Chaldean Account of Genesis

Light on the Old Testament from Babel

Albert T. Clay

New Foreword and Bibliography by
K. C. Hanson

PUBLISHERS
Eugene, Oregon

LIGHT ON THE OLD TESTAMENT FROM BABEL
The Ancient Near East: Classic Studies

Copyright © 2006 Wipf & Stock Publishers. All rights reserved. Except for brief quotations in critical publications or reviews, no part of this book may be reproduced in any manner without prior written permission from the publisher. Write: Permissions, Wipf & Stock, 199 W. 8th Ave., Eugene, OR 97401.

ISBN: 1-59752-717-3
ISBN 13: 978-1-59752-717-0

Cataloging-in-Publication data

Clay, Albert Tobias, 1866–1925
    Light on the Old Testament from Babel / A. T. Clay.—2d ed. New foreword and bibliography by K. C. Hanson.

    The Ancient Near East: Classic Studies

    ISBN: 1-59752-717-3
    ISBN 13: 978-1-59752-717-0

    Includes bibliographical references, illustrations, and indexes.
    xxx + 437 p.; ill.; 23 cm. Includes bibliographical references, index, and maps.

    1. Bible—Antiquities. 2. Bible. O.T.—Antiquities. 3. Assyriology. 4. Cuneiform inscriptions. 5. Iraq— Antiquities. 6. Assyro-Babylonian literature— Relation to the Old Testament. I. Hanson, K. C. (Kenneth C.). II. Title. III. Series.

    BS1180 .C6 2006

Manufactured in the U.S.A.

To
Charles Elvin Haupt, D.D.
in gratitude and affection

Contents

Series Foreword / ix
Foreword by K. C. Hanson / xiii
Select Bibliography / xvii
Preface / xxxi
List of Illustrations / xxxiii

I   Introductory Remarks / 1
II   The Great Antiquity of Man / 23
III   The Babylonian Creation Story / 59
IV   The Babylonian Deluge Story / 77
V   The Tower of Babel and the Babylonian Temple / 89
VI   The Fourteenth Chapter of Genesis / 125
VII   Babylonian Life in the Days of Abraham / 145
VIII   Code of Hammurabi / 201
IX   Moses and Hammurabi / 223
X   The Name Jahweh in Cuneiform Literature / 235
XI   The Amarna Letters / 251
XII   Babylonian Temple Records of the Second Millennium before Christ / 283
XIII   The Assyrian Historical Inscriptions / 313
XIV   The Neo-Babylonian Historical Inscriptions / 361
XV   Babylonian Life in the Days of Ezra and Nehemiah / 390

Series Foreword

The archaeological discoveries of ancient cities and texts in Mesopotamia, Egypt, and Syria-Palestine began in earnest in the nineteenth century and only accelerated in the twentieth and twenty-first centuries. A few of the most significant early explorations and excavations make the point:

- In 1838, Robinson explored and inaugurated the geographical study of Palestine, especially exploring Jerusalem, including Hezekiah's Tunnel.[1]
- Funded by King Friedrich Wilhelm IV of Prussia, Richard Lepsius discovered several monuments from the Old Kingdom of Egypt during his three-year expedition (1843–1845).[2]
- The earliest treasures of Assyria were excavated by Layard at Calah (Nimrud) and Botta at Nineveh (the Kuyunjik mound in Mosul) in the 1840s.[3]

---

[1] Edward Robinson and Eli Smith, *Biblical Researches in Palestine and in the Adjacent Regions: A Journal of Travels in the Year 1838*, 3 vols. (Boston: Crocker & Brewster, 1841).

[2] C. R. Lepsius, Denkmäler aus Aegypten und Aethiopien, 12 vols. (Berlin: Nicolaische Buchhandlung, 1849–56).

[3] Austen Henry Layard, *Nineveh and Its Remains*, 2 vols. (New York: Putnam, 1849); idem, *Discoveries in the Ruins of Nineveh and Babylon* (New York: Harper, 1853); Paul Émile Botta, *Monument de Ninive* (Paris: Imprimerie Nationale, 1849–50).

- Sir W. K. Loftus carried out the earliest explorations of Ur (Tell Muqqayyar) in 1849. But it was Sir C. Leonard Wooley who did the systematic excavations (1922–34).[4]
- Charles Warren surveyed the topography of Jerusalem and the temple mount in 1867 and 1870.
- The ancient Egyptian sites of Tanis and Gizeh were ex-plored by Sir Flinders Petrie in the 1880s.[5]
- The University of Pennsylvania began excavations of Nippur (southeast of Baghdad) in 1889.[6]
- Under the auspices of the Deutsche Orient-Gesellschaft (German Orient Association), Koldewey excavated Babylon (part of modern Baghdad) from 1899 to 1918.[7]

The remains of ancient societies often require decades to unearth, but much longer to interpret and understand. The methods of archaeology have progressed dramatically in recent years. Archaeologists have continuously refined their tools, methods, and techniques. Today archaeology is characterized by pottery identification, classification, and cataloging; disciplined excavation of "squares"; use of sophisticated electronics, such as GPS, infrared, and

---

[4] C. L. Wooley, *Ur Excavations*, 10 vols. (London: Oxford University Press, 1927–74).

[5] W. M. Flinders Petrie, *Tanis*, 2 vols. (Egypt Exploration Fund, 1880–1888); idem, *The Pyramids and Temples of Gizeh* (London: Field & Tuer, 1883).

[6] Clarence S. Fisher, *Excavations at Nippur* (Philadelphia: Babylonian Expedition of the University of Pennsylvania, 1905).

[7] Robert Koldewey, *The Excavations at Babylon*, trans. Agnes S. Johns (London: Macmillan, 1914).

computer-aided design; and the integration of multiple methodologies, such as epigraphy, art history, physical anthropology, paleobotany, and climatology. The interpretation of ancient Near Eastern history and cultures has also progressed. An increasing number of documents has been unearthed. The vast document collections from Tel el-Amarna, Nippur, Mari, Nuzi, Ebla, Ugarit, and the Dead Sea caves are just some of the more spectacular examples. These provide an enormous amount of detail about the royal administrations, business transactions, land tenure systems, taxes, political propaganda, mythologies, marriage practices, and much more. And things that sometimes seem unique about one culture at first look often fit into larger patterns of relationship when the surrounding cultures are better understood.

The Ancient Near East: Classic Studies (ANECS) reprints classic works that have brought the results of archaeology, textual, and historical investigations to audiences of scholars, students, and the general public. While the discussions continue and the results of earlier investigations are continuously reexamined, these classic works remain of interest and importance.

—K. C. Hanson
Series Editor

Foreword

Albert T. Clay (1866–1925) began his career as Assistant Professor of Semitic Philology and Archaeology at the University of Pennsylvania; and he was simultaneously the Assistant Curator of the Babylonian Section of the Department of Archaeology. He then took a teaching position at the Chicago Lutheran Seminary for just a few years before going to Yale University as the William M. Laffan Professor of Assyriology and Babylonian Literature. He authored and edited numerous works, both translations of ancient documents and historical analyses. In addition to the present volume, Clay's works include the following:

With H. V. Hilprecht. *Business Documents of Murashu Sons of Nippur Dated in the Reign of Artaxerxes I (464–424 B.C.).* Babylonian Expedition of the University of Pennsylvania. Series A: Cuneiform Texts 9. Philadelphia: Department of Archaeology, University of Pennsylvania, 1898.

Business Documents of Murashu Sons of Nippur Dated in the Reign of Darius II (424–404 B.C.). Babylonian Expedition of the University of Pennsylvania. Series A: Cuneiform Texts 9. Philadelphia: Department of Archaeology and Palaeontology of the University of Pennsylvania, 1904.

Documents from the Temple Archives of Nippur, Dated in the Reigns of Cassite Rulers. 2 vols. Philadelphia: University Museum of the University of Pennsylvania, 1906.

Legal and Commercial Transactions Dated in the Assyrian, Neo-Babylonian and Persian Periods, Chiefly from Nippur. Philadelphia: Department of Archaeology, University of Pennsylvania, 1908.

Amurru, the Home of the Northern Semites: A Study Showing that the Religion and Culture of Israel Are Not of Babylonian Origin. Philadelphia: Sunday School Times, 1909.

Babylonian Business Transactions of the First Millennium B.C. Babylonian Records in the Library of J. Pierpont Morgan 1. New York: n.p., 1912.

Business Documents of Murashu Sons of Nippur Dated in the Reign of Darius II. Publications of the Babylonian Section 2.1. Philadelphia: University Museum of the University of Pennsylvania, 1912.

Personal Names from Cuneiform Inscriptions of the Cassite Period. Yale Oriental Series 1. New Haven: Yale University Press, 1912.

Legal Documents from Erech, Dated in the Seleucid Era (312–65 B.C.). Babylonian Records in the Library of J. Pierpont Morgan 2. New York: n.p., 1913.

Miscellaneous Inscriptions in the Yale Babylonian Collection. Yale Oriental Series: Babylonian Texts 1. New Haven: Yale University Press, 1915.

The Empire of the Amorites. Yale Oriental Series: Researches 6. New Haven: Yale University Press, 1919.

Neo-Babylonian Letters from Erech. Yale Oriental Series: Babylonian Texts 3. New Haven: Yale University Press, 1919.

With Morris Jastrow, Jr. *An Old Babylonian Version of the Gilgamesh Epic: On the Basis of Recently Discovered Texts.* Yale Oriental Series. Researches 4/3. New Haven: Yale University Press, 1920.

A Hebrew Deluge Story in Cuneiform: And Other Epic Fragments in the Pierpont Morgan Library. Yale Oriental Series: Researches 5/3. New Haven: Yale University Press, 1922.

Babylonian Epics, Hymns, Omens, and Other Texts. Babylonian Records in the Library of J. Pierpont Morgan 4. 1923. Reprinted, Ancient Texts and Translations. Eugene: Wipf & Stock, 2005.

The Origin of Biblical Traditions: Hebrew Legends in Babylonian and Israel. Lectures on Biblical Archaeology Delivered at the Lutheran Theological Seminary, Mt. Airy, Philadelphia. Yale Oriental Series. Researches 12. New Haven: Yale University Press, 1923.

The Antiquity of Amorite Civilization: An Answer to a Paper by Professor Barton Read before the American Oriental Society. New Haven: n.p., 1924.

Letters and Transactions from Cappadocia. Babylonian Inscriptions in the Collection of James B. Nies, Yale University 4. New Haven: Yale University Press, 1927.

Clay was named President of the Society of Biblical Literature in 1920. And he was the founder and curator of the Yale Babylonian Collection. He was on the original committee formed by the Archaeological Institute of America to establish a school of archaeology in Baghdad, which became a part of the American Schools of Oriental Research. Clay was then named the first Annual Professor of the school in 1923–24.

—K. C. Hanson

Select Bibliography

Batto, Bernard F. *Slaying the Dragon: Mythmaking in the Biblical Tradition.* Louisville: Westminster John Knox, 1992.

Beaulieu, Paul-Alain. *Legal and Administrative Texts from the Reign of Nabonidus.* Yale Oriental Series: Babylonian Texts 1. New Haven: Yale University Press, 2000.

Beckman, Gary. *Old Babylonian Archival Texts in the Yale Babylonian Collection.* Catalogue of the Babylonian Collections at Yale 4. Bethesda, Md.: CDL, 2000.

Bergmann, E., et al., editors. *Codex Hammurabi.* 2 vols. 3d ed. Pontificio Instituto Biblico Scripta 51. Rome: Pontifical Biblical Institute, 1950–53.

Beyerlin, Walter, editor. *Near Eastern Religious Texts Relating to the Old Testament.* Translated by John Bowden. Old Testament Library. Philadelphia: Westminster, 1978.

Bezold, Carl, and E. A. Wallis Budge. *The Tell el-Amarna Tablets in the British Museum.* London: British Museum, 1892.

Bienkowski, Piotr, and Alan Millard, editors. *Dictionary of the Ancient Near East.* Philadelphia: University of Pennsylvania Press, 2000.

Bottéro, Jean. *Mesopotamia: Writing, Reasoning, and the Gods.* Translated by Zainab Bahrani. Chicago: University of Chicago Press, 1992.

Buccellati, Giorgio, and Robert D. Biggs. *Cuneiform Texts from Nippur: The Eighth and Ninth Seasons.* Assyriological Studies 17. Chicago: University of Chicago Press, 1969.

Chavalas, Mark W., and K. Lawson Younger, editors. *Mesopotamia and the Bible: Comparative Explorations.* Grand Rapids: Baker Academic, 2002.

Clay, Albert T. *Babylonian Epics, Hymns, Omens, and Other Texts.* 1923. Reprinted, Ancient Texts and Translations. Eugene: Wipf & Stock, 2005.

———. *Documents from the Temple Archives of Nippur, Dated in the Reigns of Cassite Rulers.* Philadelphia: University Museum of the University of Pennsylvania, 1906.

———. *Miscellaneous Inscriptions in the Yale Babylonian Collection.* Yale Oriental Series: Babylonian Texts 1. New Haven: Yale University Press, 1915.

———. *Neo-Babylonian Letters from Erech.* Yale Oriental Series: Babylonian Texts 3. New Haven: Yale University Press, 1919.

———. *A Hebrew Deluge Story in Cuneiform: And Other Epic Fragments in the Pierpont Morgan Library.* Yale Oriental Series: Researches 3. New Haven: Yale University Press, 1922.

Cole, Steven W., and Peter Machinist, editors. *Letters from Priests to the Kings Esarhaddon and Assurbanipal.* State Archives of Assyria 13. Helsinki: Helsinki University Press, 1998.

Cooke, Stanley A. *The Laws of Moses and the Code of Hammurabi.* London: A. & C. Black, 1903.

Craig, James A. *Assyrian and Babylonian Religious Texts.* 2 vols. Assyriologische Bibliothek 13. Leipzig: Hinrichs, 1895–97.

———. *Cuneiform Texts from Babylonian Tablets, etc., in the British Museum.* Parts 1–30. London: British Museum, 1896–1912.

Dalley, Stephanie. *Myths from Mesopotamia.* Oxford: Oxford University Press, 1989.
———. *Old Babylonian Texts in the Ashmolean Museum: Texts from Kish and Elsewhere.* Oxford Editions of Cuneiform Texts 13. Oxford: Clarendon, 1991.
Davies, W. W. *The Codes of Hammurabi and Moses.* Cincinnati: Jennings & Graham, 1905.
Delitzsch, Friedrich. *Babel and Bible.* Translated by Thomas J. McCormack. 1902. Reprinted, The Ancient Near East: Classic Studies. Eugene, Ore.: Wipf & Stock, 2006.
Dougherty, Raymond Philip. *Records from Erech: Time of Nabonidus (555–538 B. C.).* Yale Oriental Series: Babylonian Texts 6. New Haven: Yale University Press, 1920.
Driver, G. R. *Letters of the First Babylonian Dynasty.* Oxford Editions of Cuneiform Texts 3. Oxford: Clarendon, 1924.
———, and John C. Miles. *The Assyrian Laws.* Ancient Codes and Laws of the Near East. Oxford: Clarendon, 1935.
———, and John C. Miles. *The Babylonian Laws.* Rev. ed. 2 vols. Ancient Codes and Laws of the Near East. Oxford: Clarendon, 1960–68.
Evans, Carl D., William W. Hallo, and John B. White, editors. *Scripture in Context: Essays on the Comparative Method.* Pittsburgh Theological Monograph Series 34. Pittsburgh: Pickwick, 1980.
Fales, F. M., and J. N. Postgate, editors. *Imperial Administrative Records.* State Archives of Assyria 7. Helsinki: Helsinki University Press, 1992–.
Foster, Benjamin R. *Before the Muses: An Anthology of Akkadian Literature.* 3d ed. Bethesda, Md.: CDL, 2005.
———. *From Distant Days: Myths, Tales and Poetry from Ancient Mesopotamia.* Bethesda, Md.: CDL, 1995.

——, Douglas Frayne, and Gary Beckman. *The Epic of Gilgamesh: A New Translation, Analogues, Criticism.* Norton Critical Edition. New York: Norton, 2001.
Frankfort, Henri. *The Problem of Similarity in Ancient Near Eastern Religions.* Oxford: Clarendon, 1951.
——. *The Art and Architecture of the Ancient Orient.* 5th ed. New Haven: Yale University Press, 1996.
Gaster, T. H. *Thespis: Ritual, Myth and Drama in the Ancient Near East.* Rev. ed. Garden City, N.Y.: Doubleday, 1961.
George, A. R. *The Babylonian Gilgamesh Epic: Introduction, Critical Edition, and Cuneiform Texts.* 2 vols. Oxford: Oxford University Press, 2003.
Glassner, Jean-Jacques. *Mesopotamian Chronicles.* Writings from the Ancient World 19. Atlanta: Society of Biblical Literature, 2004.
Gordon, Cyrus H., and Gary A. Rendsburg. *The Bible and the Ancient Near East.* 4th ed. New York: Norton, 1997.
Grayson, A. Kirk. *Assyrian and Babylonian Chronicles.* Texts from Cuneiform Sources 5. Locust Valley, N.Y.: Augustin, 1970.
——. *Assyrian Royal Inscriptions.* 2 vols. Records of the Ancient Near East. Wiesbaden: Harrassowitz, 1972–.
——. *Babylonian Historical-Literary Texts.* Toronto Semitic Texts and Studies 3. Toronto: University of Toronto Press, 1975.
——. *Assyrian Rulers of the Third and Second Millennia BC (to 1115 BC).* Royal Inscriptions of Mesopotamia: Assyrian Periods 1. Toronto: University of Toronto Press, 1987.
——. *Assyrian Rulers of the Early First Millennium BC I (1114–859 BC).* Royal Inscriptions of Mesopotamia: Assyrian Periods 2. Toronto: University of Toronto Press, 1991.

Gunkel, Hermann. *Creation and Chaos in the Primeval Era and the Eschaton: Religio-Historical Study of Genesis 1 and Revelation 12*. Translated by K. William Whitney Jr. Biblical Resources Series. Grand Rapids: Eerdmans, 2006.
Hallo, William W., James C. Moyer, and Leo G. Perdue, editors. *Scripture in Context II: More Essays on the Comparative Method*. Winona Lake, Ind.: Eisenbrauns, 1983.
Hallo, William W., and William Kelly Simpson. *The Ancient Near East: A History*. 2d ed. Fort Worth: Harcourt Brace College, 1998.
Hallo, William W., and K. Lawson Younger Jr., editors. *The Context of Scripture*. Vol. 1: *Canonical Compositions from the Biblical World*. Leiden: Brill, 1997.
———. *The Context of Scripture*. Vol. 2: *Monumental Inscriptions from the Biblical World*. Leiden: Brill, 1999.
———. *The Context of Scripture*. Vol. 3: *Archival Documents from the Biblical World*. Leiden: Brill, 2002.
Harper, Robert Francis. *The Code of Hammurabi*. Chicago: University of Chicago Press, 1894.
Heidel, Alexander. *The Gilgamesh Epic and Old Testament Parallels*. 2d ed. Chicago: University of Chicago Press, 1949.
———. *The Babylonian Genesis*. 2d ed. Chicago: University of Chicago Press, 1951.
Hess, Richard S., and David Toshio Tsumura, editors. *I Studied Inscriptions from before the Flood: Ancient Near Eastern, Literary, and Linguistic Approaches to Genesis 1–11*. Sources for Biblical and Theological Study 4. Winona Lake, Ind.: Eisenbrauns, 1994.
Hilprecht, H. V. *Expedition of the University of Pennsylvania: Old Babylonian Inscriptions*. Vol. 1. Philadelphia: University of Pennsylvania, 1893.

———. *The Earliest Version of the Babylonian Deluge Story and the Temple Library of Nippur.* The Babylonian Expedition of the University of Pennsylvania 5/5. Philadelphia: University of Pennsylvania, 1911.

Hincke, W. J. *A New Boundary Stone of Nebuchadrezzar I from Nippur.* Philadelphia: University of Pennsylvania, 1907.

Hunger, Hermann, editor. *Astrological Reports to Assyrian Kings.* State Archives of Assyria 8. Helsinki: Helsinki University Press, 1992.

Irvin, Dorothy. *Mytharion: The Comparison of Tales from the Old Testament and the Ancient Near East.* Alter Orient und Altes Testament 32. Neukirchen-Vluyn: Neukirchener, 1978.

Jastrow, Morris Jr., and Albert T. Clay. *An Old Babylonian Version of the Gilgamesh Epic: On the Basis of Recently Discovered Texts.* Yale Oriental Series: Researches 4.3. New Haven: Yale University Press, 1920.

Jeremias, Alfred. *The Old Testament in the Light of the Ancient East.* 2 vols. Translated by C. L. Beaumont. Edited by C. H. W. Johns. Theological Translation Library 28–29. New York: Putnam, 1911.

Johannès, Francis. *Neo-Babylonian Tablets in the Ashmolean Museum.* Oxford Editions of Cuneiform Texts 12. Oxford: Clarendon, 1990.

Johns, C. H. W. *The Oldest Code of Laws in the World: The Code of Laws Promulgated by Hammurabi King of Babylon BC 2285–2242.* New York: Scribner, 1903.

Kataja, L., and R. Whiting, editors. *Grants, Decrees and Gifts of the Neo-Assyrian Period.* State Archives of Assyria 12. Helsinki: Helsinki University Press, 1995.

Kwasman, Theodore, and Simo Parpola, editors. *Legal Transactions of the Royal Court of Nineveh.* 2 vols. State

Archives of Assyria 6, 14. Helsinki: Helsinki University Press, 1991–2002.
King, Leonard W. *The Letters and Inscriptions of Hammurabi*. 3 vols. Luzac's Semitic Texts and Translations 2, 3, 8. London: Luzac, 1898.
———. *The Seven Tablets of Creation*. 2 vols. London: Luzac, 1902.
———. *Records of the Reign of Tukulti-Ninib I*. Studies in Eastern History 1. London: Luzac, 1904.
———. *Chronicles Concerning Early Babylonian Kings*. 2 vols. London: Luzac, 1907.
———. *Legends of Babylon and Egypt in Relation to Hebrew Tradition*. 1916. Reprinted, The Ancient Near East: Classic Studies. Eugene, Ore.: Wipf & Stock, 2006.
Kuhrt, Amélie. *The Ancient Near East, 3000–332 B.C.* 2 vols. Routledge History of the Ancient World. London: Routledge, 1995.
Lambert, W. G. "Myth and Mythmaking in Sumer and Akkad." In *Civilization of the Ancient Near East*, edited by Jack M. Sasson, 3:1825–36. New York: Scribner, 1995.
Lange, Armin et al., editors. *Mythos im Alten Testament und Seiner Umwelt: Festschrift für Hans-Peter Müller zum 65. Geburtstag.* Beihefte zur Zeitschrift für die alttestamentliche Wissenschaft 278. Berlin: de Gruyter, 1999.
Lau, Robert J., and Stephen Langdon. *The Annals of Ashurbanipal (V Rawlinson pl. I-X)*. Semitic Study Series 2. Leiden: Brill, 1903.
Leick, Gwendolyn. *Who's Who in the Ancient Near East*. London: Routledge, 1999.
Liverani, Mario. *International Relations in the Ancient Near East, 1600–1100*. Studies in Diplomacy. New York: Palgrave, 2002.

Livingstone, Alasdair, editor. *Court Poetry and Literary Miscellanea*. State Archives of Assyria 3. Helsinki: Helsinki University Press, 1989.
Lubetski, Meir et al., editors. *Boundaries of the Ancient Near Eastern World: A Tribute to Cyrus H. Gordon*. Journal for the Study of the Old Testament Supplement Series 273. Sheffield: Sheffield Academic, 1998.
Luckenbill, Daniel David. *The Annals of Sennacherib.* 1924. Reprinted, Ancient Texts and Translations. Eugene: Wipf & Stock, 2005.
———. *Ancient Records of Assyria and Babylonia*. 2 vols. Chicago: University of Chicago Press, 1926–27.
Lutz, Henry Frederick. *Early Babylonian Letters from Larsa*. 1917. Reprinted, Ancient Texts and Translations. Eugene: Wipf & Stock, 2005.
Luukko, Mikko, and Greta van Buylaere, editors. *The Political Correspondence of Esarhaddon.* State Archives of Assyria 16. Helsinki: Helsinki University Press, 2002.
Malul, Meir. *The Comparative Method in Ancient Near Eastern and Biblical Legal Studies*. Alter Orient und Altes Testament 227. Neukirchen-Vluyn: Neukirchener, 1990.
Matthews, Victor H., and Don C. Benjamin. *Old Testament Parallels.* 2d ed. New York: Paulist, 1997.
McEwan, Gilbert J. P. *Late Babylonian Texts in the Ashmolean Museum*. Oxford Editions of Cuneiform Texts 10. Oxford: Clarendon, 1984.
Michalowski, Piotr. *Letters from Early Mesopotamia.* Writings from the Ancient World 3. Atlanta: Scholars, 1993.
Moran, William L. "The Gilgamesh Epic: A Masterpiece from Ancient Mesopotamia." In *Civilization of the Ancient Near East*, edited by Jack M. Sasson, 4:2327–36. New York: Scribner, 1995.

Nissinen, Martti. *Prophets and Prophecy in the Ancient Near East.* Writings from the Ancient World 12. Atlanta: Society of Biblical Literature, 2003.

Otzen, Benedikt et al. *Myths in the Old Testament.* London: SCM, 1980.

Parpola, Simo. *Letters from Assyrian Scholars to the Kings Esar-haddon and Assurbanipal.* 2 vols. Alter Orient und Altes Testament 5/1-2. Kevelaer: Butzon & Bercker, 1970–83.

———. *The Correspondence of Sargon II.* 3 vols. State Archives of Assyria 1, 5, 15. Helsinki: Helsinki University Press, 1987–2001.

———. *Neo-Assyrian Treaties and Loyalty Oaths.* State Archives of Assyria 2. Helsinki: Helsinki University Press, 1988.

———. *Letters from Assyrian and Babylonian Scholars.* State Archives of Assyria 10. Helsinki: Helsinki University Press, 1993.

———. *Assyrian Prophecies.* State Archives of Assyria 9. Helsinki: Helsinki University Press, 1997.

Peet, T. Eric. *A Comparative Study of the Literatures of Egypt, Palestine, and Mesopotamia: Egypt's Contribution to the Literature of the Ancient World.* Schweich Lectures 1929. London: Oxford University Press, 1931.

Piepkorn, Arthur Carl. *Historical Prism Inscriptions of Ashurbanipal.* Assyriological Studies 5. Chicago: University of Chicago Press, 1933.

Postgate, J. N. *Early Mesopotamia: Society and Economy at the Dawn of History.* London: Routledge, 1992.

Pritchard, James B., editor. *Ancient Near Eastern Texts Relating to the Old Testament.* 3d ed. Princeton: Princeton University Press, 1969.

Radau, Hugo. *Early Babylonian History*. 1900. Reprinted, Ancient Texts and Translations. Eugene, Ore.: Wipf & Stock, 2005.
Reynolds, Frances. *The Babylonian Correspondence of Esarhaddon, and Letters to Assurbanipal and Sin-Sarru-Iskun from Northern and Central Babylonia*. State Archives of Assyria 18. Helsinki: Helsinki University Press, 2003.
Rogers, Robert William. *History of Babylonia and Assyria*. 2 vols. 2d ed. New York: Eaton & Mains, 1900.
———. *The Religion of Babylonia and Assyria, Especially in Its Relations to Israel*. New York: Eaton & Mains, 1908.
———. *Cuneiform Parallels to the Old Testament*. 2d ed. 1926. Reprinted, Ancient Texts and Translations. Eugene, Ore.: Wipf & Stock, 2005.
Roux, Georges. *Ancient Iraq*. 3d ed. New York: Penguin, 1993.
Saggs, H. W. F. *The Might That Was Assyria*. Great Civilizations Series. London: Sidgwick & Jackson, 1984.
———. *The Greatness That Was Babylon: A Survey of the Ancient Civilization of the Tigris-Euphrates Valley*. Rev. ed. Great Civilizations Series. London: Sidgwick & Jackson, 1988.
———. *Civilization before Greece and Rome*. New Haven: Yale University Press, 1989.
Sasson, Jack M., editor. *Civilizations of the Ancient Near East*. 4 vols. New York: Scribners, 1995.
———. "King Hammurabi of Babylon." In *Civilization of the Ancient Near East*, edited by Jack M. Sasson, 2:901–15. New York: Scribner, 1995.
Schmidt, Brian. "Flood Narratives of Ancient Western Asia." In *Civilization of the Ancient Near East*, edited by Jack M. Sasson, 4:2337–52. New York: Scribner, 1995.

Smith, George. *Assyrian Discoveries: an account of explorations and Discoveries on the site of Nineveh, during 1873 and 1874*. 1875. Reprinted, The Ancient Near East: Classic Studies. Eugene, Ore.: Wipf & Stock, 2006.

———, and A. H. Sayce. *The Chaldean Account of Genesis*. 1881. Reprinted, The Ancient Near East: Classic Studies. Eugene, Ore.: Wipf & Stock, 2004.

Snell, Daniel C. *Life in the Ancient Near East, 3100–332 B.C.E.* New Haven: Yale University Press, 1997.

Starr, Ivan. *Queries to the Sungod: Divination and Politics in Sargonid Assyria.* State Archives of Assyria 4. Helsinki: Helsinki University Press, 1990.

Stephens, Ferris J. *Votive and Historical Texts from Babylonia and Assyria.* Yale Oriental Series: Babylonian Texts 9. New Haven: Yale University Press, 1937.

Tadmor, Hayyim. *The Inscriptions of Tiglath-pileser III, King of Assyria: Critical Edition, with Introductions, Translations, and Commentary.* Publications of the Israel Academy of Sciences and Humanities, Section of Humanities. Jerusalem: Israel Academy of Sciences and Humanities, 1994.

Thomas, D. Winton, editor. *Documents from Old Testament Times.* Ancient Texts and Translations. Eugene, Ore.: Wipf & Stock, 2006.

Toorn, Karel van der. *Family Religion in Babylonia, Ugarit, and Israel: Continuity and Changes in the Forms of Religious Life.* Studies in the History and Culture of the Ancient Near East 7. Leiden: Brill, 1996.

Tremayne, Arch. *Records from Erech: Time of Cyrus and Cambyses (538–521 B.C.).* Yale Oriental Series: Babylonian Texts 7. New Haven: Yale University Press, 1925.

Van de Mieroop, Marc. *The Ancient Mesopotamian City.* Oxford: Clarendon, 1997.
——. *Cuneiform Texts and the Writing of History.* Approaching the Ancient World. London: Routledge, 1999.
——. *A History of the Ancient Near East, ca. 3000–323 BC.* Blackwell History of the Ancient World. Malden, Mass.: Blackwell, 2004.
——. *King Hammurabi of Babylon: A Biography.* Blackwell Ancient Lives. Malden, Mass.: Blackwell, 2005.
Walls, Neal H. *Desire, Discord, and Death: Approaches to Ancient Near Eastern Myth.* ASOR Books 8. Boston: American Schools of Oriental Research, 2001.
——, editor. *Cult Image and Divine Representation in the Ancient Near East.* ASOR Books 10. Boston: American Schools of Oriental Research, 2005.
Walton, John H. *Ancient Israelite Literature in Its Cultural Context: A Survey of Parallels between Biblical and Ancient Near Eastern Texts.* Rev. ed. Library of Biblical Interpretation. Grand Rapids: Zondervan, 1989.
Weisberg, David B. *Texts from the Time of Nebuchadnezzar.* Yale Oriental Series: Babylonian Texts 17. New Haven: Yale University Press, 1980.
Whiting, Robert M. *Old Babylonian Letters from Tell Asmar.* Assyriological Studies 22. Chicago: Oriental Institute, 1987.
Yamada, Shigeo. *The Construction of the Assyrian Empire: A Historical Study of the Inscriptions of Shalmanesar III Relating to His Campaigns in the West.* Culture and History of the Ancient Near East 3. Boston: Brill, 2000.
Yaron, Reuven. *The Laws of Eshnunna.* Jerusalem: Magnes, 1969.

Young, Gordon D. et al., editors. *Crossing Boundaries and Linking Horizons: Studies in Honor of Michael C. Astour on His 80th Birthday*. Bethesda, Md.: CDL, 1997.

Preface

A considerable portion of the material of this publication formed the basis of lectures delivered at Winona Bible Conference, Mt. Gretna Chautauqua, Pocono Pines Assembly, and other institutions and churches, besides those given on Sunday afternoons in Houston Hall under the auspices of the Christian Association of the University of Pennsylvania.

In addition to the discussion of the cuneiform inscriptions in these lectures, which bear more particularly upon the Old Testament, several chapters (VII, VIII, XII, and XV) have been included on life in ancient Babylonia. Besides facts published by others, these chapters include a presentation of certain discussions of general interest which I have published in a more technical form in the series: "The Babylonian Expedition of the University of Pennsylvania." These chapters, however, also contain much material that appears for the first time.

The scholar whose privilege it is to labor upon the ancient records of the past cannot but feel under deep obligations, not only to the explorer who by his unselfish devotion and sacrifice has unearthed them, but to the men who have made possible by their generosity and intelligent interest this opening up to the light of day of these remains of ancient peoples in the land of primitive civilization—

apparently the cradle of the universe. To these I desire to express my gratitude, and also to those who in any way have aided me in the publication of these lectures, notably Mr. William H. Witte, Assistant in the Babylonian Section of the Department of Archeology of the University of Pennsylvania, a great many of whose photographs are used to illustrate these lectures; to Mr. Clarence S. Fisher, the architect of the Nippur excavations, for the excellent plan of the Temple Ekur; to my friend, Mr. Hermann Faber, Professor of Art; and also to The Sunday School Times Company for their kind cooperation in securing typographical accuracy for these lectures.

—Albert T. Clay

List of Illustrations

Amraphel of Genesis in bas-relief / 128
British Museum; photo by Mansell & Co.

Arab workmen digging tablets / 57
Photo by Haynes

Aramaic endorsements on documents of Murashu Sons / 402
Museum, University of Pennsylvania

Archaic arch of Nippur / 35
Photo by Haynes

Ashurbanipal as the high priest or canephorus / 355
From the catalogue of the British Museum

Asphalt spring near Hit / 94
Photo by Haynes

Baby rattles in terra-cotta / 195
Museum, University of Pennsylvania

Belshazzaar, Chronicle recording the death of / 374
Delitzsch-Hagen, *Beiträge zur Assyriologie*

Besieging a walled city, The Assyrians / 315
British Museum; photo by Mansell & Co.

Brick-makers in Egypt, from a mural painting of a tomb / 273
From Ball, *Light from the East*

Brick-stamps of Sargon I and Naram-Sin / 118
Museum, University of Pennsylvania

Bronze head from Fara / 54
Possession of H. V. Hilprecht

xxxiv

Case tablets of the Cassite Period, containing seal impressions / 173
Museum, University of Pennsylvania

Cattle and sheep leased by Temple officials, Records of / 297
Museum, University of Pennsylvania

Centaur, The earliest known form of the / 174
Drawn by the author

Creation epic of the Babylonians / 68
From King, *Seven Tablets of Creation*

Cyrus, Cylinder of / 383
British Museum; photo by Mansell & Co.

Cyrus, Portrait sculpture of / 385
From Lindl, *Cyrus*

Darius, Cylinder-seal of / 387
British Museum

Deed with an Aramaic endorsement / 395
Museum, University of Pennsylvania

Deluge tablet of the Babylonians / 79
British Museum; photo from a cast

Dog and her puppies in terra-cotta / 391
Museum, University of Pennsylvania

Door-socket of Gimil-Sin found at Ur of the Chaldees / 198
Museum, University of Pennsylvania

Dragon of Babylon in tiles / 381
Delitzsch, *Babel und Bibel*

Dragon of Nippur / 380
Constantinople Museum; photo by Haynes

Dungi and Kuri-Galzu, Inscription / 286
From Hilprecht, *Old Babylonian Inscriptions*, Part I

Entemena, Silver vase of / 53
From Heuzey, *Découvertes en Chaldée*

xxxv

Esarhaddon holding biblical Tirhakah and Baal with thongs / 353
Berlin Museum

Evil-Merodach, Tablet dated in the reign of, biblical / 370
Museum, University of Pennsylvania

Excavations in the Temple Court at Nippur / 27
Photo by Haynes

Excavations in the Temple precincts to virgin soil / 36
Photo by Haynes

Excavations showing pavements of different ages / 29
Photo by Haynes

Excavations within the Temple Area at Nippur / frontispiece
Photo by Haynes

Fall of Man, So-called Babylonian scene of the / 83
British Museum; photo by Mansell & Co.

Fight of Marduk and Tiamat / 65
From Ball, *Light from the East*

Furnace of the time of Abraham / 192
Photo by Haynes

Garden scene of Ashurbanipal / 357
British Museum; photo by Mansell & Co.

Gilgamesh epic, Seal impression with scene from / 86
Museum, University of Pennsylvania

Gimil-Sin, Door socket of / 198
Museum, University of Pennsylvania

Grinding corn in the Arab camp at Nippur, a woman / 144
Photo by Haynes

Gudea, Stone vase of / 113
Museum of Constantinople; photo by Haynes

Gudea, Statue of / 161
From Heuzy, *Découvertes en Chaldée*

Hammurabi, Clay cone of, referring to his buildings / 130
Museum, University of Pennsylvania

Hammurabi, Code of / 203
Louvre in Paris; cut loaned by Professor Max Kellner

Heads of dolerite statues found at Telloh / 159
From Heuzy, *Découvertes en Chaldee*

Home scene in the Arab camp at Nippur / 282
Photo by Haynes

Hunting scene of an Assyrian King / 359
British Museum; photo by Mansell & Co.

Images, or household gods, of Bel and Beltis / 194
Museum, University of Pennsylvania

Incantation bowls in Hebrew and Mandaic / 409
Museum, University of Pennsylvania

Jehu paying tribute, Bas-relief depicting / 323
Photo from a cast

Jeweler's guarantee concerning the setting of an emerald / 412
Museum, University of Pennsylvania

Kudur-Mabug, Bronze canephorus dedicated to Nana by / 134
Berlin Museum; photo from cast

Labels or tags in clay / 157
Museum, University of Pennsylvania

Lease of fish-ponds / 415
Museum, University of Pennsylvania

Lion of Babylon in tiles / 366
From Delitzsch, *Babel und Bibel*

Lugal-kigubnidudu, Votive slab of / 45
Museum, University of Pennsylvania

Lugal-zaggisi, Inscription of1 / 39
From Hilprecht, *Old Babylonian Inscriptions*

Marble head, Early Sumerian / 37
Photo by Haynes

Marduk and Ramman / 367
Report of the *Deutschen Orient Gesellschaft*

Merneptah, Stele of, mentioning Israel / 277
From Petrie, *Six Temples at Thebes*

Merodach-Baladan, Boundary stone with the picture of, biblical / 340
Berlin Museum

Models of different systems of drainage at Nippur / 191
Made by C. S. Fisher; Museum, Univ. of Pennsylvania

Moon-god Sin, Seal cylinder impression of Ur-Engurd / 199
Photo by Mansell & Co.

Mound covering Nippur Tower / 107
Photo by Haynes

Multiplication table: 18 x 1 = 18 / 189
Museum, University of Pennsylvania

Musicians, Bas-relief in stone depicting / 165
From Heuzy, *Découvertes en Chaldee*

Nabonidus, Cylinder of, containing a prayer for Belshazzar / 372
British Museum; photo by Mansell & Co.

Nabopolassar, referring to Tower of Babel, building inscription of / 122
Museum, University of Pennsylvania

Nebuchadrezzar, Inscribed brick of / 363
Museum, University of Pennsylvania

Nebuchadrezzar, referring to the Tow of Babel, Cylinder of / 368
Museum, University of Pennsylvania

"Ninib" in Aramaic, Name of / 400
By the author

Original tablet illustrating the impressing of the stylus / 170
Museum, University of Pennsylvania

xxxviii

Pavements laid by Ashurbanipal, Kadashman-Turgu and Ur-Ninib / 29
Photo by Haynes

Payments made to temples in Nippur, Records of / 311
Museum, University of Pennsylvania

Payments of Temple stipends / 305
Museum, University of Pennsylvania

Payments to priests showing check marks, Records of / 309
Museum, University of Pennsylvania

Pithom, the store-city, Map of / 269
From Naville, *The Store-city of Pithom*

Plan of buildings in Tablet Hill / 183
By C. S. Fisher

Plan of Ekur at Nippur / 114
By C. S. Fisher

Prayer of Nazi-Maruttash / 287
Museum, University of Pennsylvania

Putting out the eyes of a prisoner / 365
From Maspero, *The Passing of the Empires*

Receipts & records of payments belonging to the Temple archives / 307
Museum, University of Pennsylvania

Reference cylinders from the Temple school of Nippur / 185
Museum, University of Pennsylvania

Release given for and on account of a claim for damages / 426
Museum, University of Pennsylvania

Sargon II and his officer / 336
From Price, *The Monuments and the Old Testament*

Sargon I, Door socket of / 31
Museum, University of Pennsylvania

Seals and Seal-cylinders / 172
Museum, University of Pennsylvania

Sennacherib, Cylinder containing the annals of / 345
From the catalog of the British Museum

Sennacherib seated before Lachish / 350
From the catalog of the British Museum

Sennacherib, Storming of Lachish by / 349
From Ball, *Light from the East*

Shalmaneser II, Black obelisk of / 320
British Museum; photo from a cast

Sheep's liver in terra-cotta, Design of a / 11
From *Cuneiform Texts*, British Museum vol. XV

Shrine of Bel / 103
Museum, University of Pennsylvania

Sisiktu marks instead of seal impressions / 176
Museum, University of Pennsylvania

Sixty-year lease of lands and buildings / 411
Possession of H. V. Hilprecht

Statues in dolerite from Telloh / 163
From Heuzey, *Découvertes en Chaldée*

Stylus, Beveled end / 169
Made by the author

Stylus, Square end / 169
Made by the author

Tablet and envelope / 177
Museum, University of Pennsylvania

Tablet written with beveled end stylus / 170
Made by the author

Temple of the moon-god Sin at Ur of the Chaldees / 197
Photo by the Wolfe Expedition

Temple school of Nippur / 181
Photo by Haynes

xl

Temple stipends, document recording payments of / 301
Museum, University of Pennsylvania

Temple stipends, Transliteration of document / 302–3
From Clay, *Documents from the Temple Archive of Nippur*, Vol. XIV

Thothmes III / 272
From Maspero, *The Struggle of Nations*

Thumb-nail marks instead of seal impression / 175
Museum, University of Pennsylvania

Tiglath-pileser or Pul before a besieged city / 328
British Museum; photo by Mansell & Co.

Topographical map of the environs of Nippur / 293
Museum, University of Pennsylvania

Topographical map of Nippur / 111
Photo by Haynes

Tower of Babel, Simpson's picture of the / 101
From Ball, *Light from the East*

Tower of Ekur, the Temple of Bel at Nippur / 107
Photo by Haynes

Ur-Engur, Stamped brick of / 105
Museum, University of Pennsylvania; photo by Haynes

Ur-Enlil, Votive slab of / 41
Original in Constantinople Museum

Ur-Nina, Votive slab of / 40
From Heuzey, *Découvertes en Chaldée*

Urumush, Marble vase of / 46
Museum, University of Pennsylvania

Vase fragments, Pre-Sargonic / 39
Museum, University of Pennsylvania

Water buffalo used in irrigating machines / 420
Photo by Haynes

Water-wheel or *na'ura* in Babylonia / 424
  Photo by the Wolfe Expedition

Water-wheel, illustrating ancient irrigating machines, modern / 422
  Photo by Wolfe Expedition

Wine jar lined with bitumen / 427
  Museum, University of Pennsylvania

Winged bulls from the palace of Sargon / 335
  British Museum; photo by Mansell & Co.

Zebu, called the ox by the ancient Babylonians / 226
  Photo by Haynes

Excavations within the Temple Area at Nippur.

I

INTRODUCTORY REMARKS

Why is there such an intelligent interest displayed in these days in Oriental excavations? Why are such immense funds expended, and such sacrificing efforts put forth, in digging up the ruin-hills of the past to find perchance the remains of a wall, an inscribed object, or a potsherd? Why does archeology, or the study of the material remains of ancient times, possess a charm for so many? And why do people delight in having opened up vistas of the past through the discoveries of what is left of bygone civilizations?

A desire to have more knowledge concerning biblical matters has been responsible, in most instances, for the work of opening up the mounds which cover the remains of ancient activities. It was felt that the Babylonians, Assyrians, Egyptians, and other nations, having thrived in the days of Israel, and having come into close relation with the Hebrews, should have left that which would throw light upon the Old Testament. Broader questions, such as the interdependence of national ideas and customs, were scarcely thought of. The question uppermost in importance was whether points of contact could be found, and the Bible verified; and every scholar who has worked upon material from which there was a possibility that such revelations might come forth, has longingly searched for the desired data. And when we glance over the trophies gained by sacrifice, industry, patience, and skill, we must exclaim: What a change has been wrought within a few decades by the explorer, the excavator, the archeologist, and the philologist!

Not many years ago little was known of extra-biblical history of the age prior to the days of Greece and Rome. The conception of these times was largely based upon the Old Testament and the uncertain myths and legends which have been preserved by the Greeks and Romans. These furnished all the knowledge which we possessed of the early history of man. But now we have original sources. The resurrection of ancient cities, and the decipherment and interpretation of that which has been unearthed, has enabled us not only to reconstruct ancient history, as well as the background for the Old Testament, but to illustrate, elucidate, substantiate, and corroborate many of the narratives of the early Scriptures. This, in truth, is one of the greatest achievements of the last century.

The right interpretation of the Old Testament, of course, is the greatest service rendered by the monuments, but the average Bible student has regarded the confirmation of the Scriptures as being, perhaps, of greater importance. Corroborative evidence of a contemporaneous character has been in the highest degree welcome, especially because of the declarations made by the skeptic or by the destructive critic. Immense results in this line have been achieved. Episodes which have been affirmed to belong wholly to the realm of fiction, or which have been regarded as mythical or legendary in character, are now proved to be historical, beyond doubt. Many theories, even those put forth by careful and conservative students, have been modified, and many supposed inconsistencies have been satisfactorily explained. Some theories growing out of alleged results achieved by certain scholars, being no longer tenable because of their ephemeral character, have completely disappeared. In short, while some scholars have endeavored to show portions of the Old Testament wholly fictitious, many of their theories, by the help of archeology and philology, can now be shown to be wholly fallacious. On the other hand, there has been much grasping after verifications by some which, in many cases, have turned out to be illusory; and as a result, their supposed confirmations, having been popularized and widely circulated, have done more harm than good.

There is scarcely a period of Old Testament history that has not received some light through these researches. It is as though additional chronicles of the kings of Israel and Judah have been found. The bare outlines of ancient history preserved in the Old Testament are clothed in such a way as to offer pictures realistic in the extreme. Episodes, passages, words, receive new meanings. Acquaintance with the religious institutions of the nations with whom Israel came in contact has offered a better understanding of Israel's religion; and incidentally many questions, as, for example, their besetting sin—proneness to idolatry—receive new light. In short, the study of the life and customs of these foreign peoples shows certain influences that were felt in Israel; and with this increased knowledge we naturally gain a more intelligent understanding of the Old Testament.

While these researches have caused many difficulties to vanish, the fact must not be lost sight of that they have given rise to new problems. While, also, much contemporary evidence has been produced which corroborates the historical character of portions of the Old Testament, certain discoveries have given a totally different conception of other portions, forcing us to lay aside a number of antiquated views, and to reconstruct our ideas on many important questions. Old interpretations which have been copied or revised by a succession of commentators, and have been handed down from century to century, disappear; and that which approaches nearer to the truth becomes known. This increased light is, of course, heartily welcomed by the biblical student, and is regarded as being of inestimable value, as it makes possible a better understanding of the Scriptures.

Introductory Remarks

Perhaps the most fascinating feature of the results gained through these studies is the retrospective glances afforded into the early doings of man. While we are disappointed in not being able to reach still nearer the primitive beginnings, our knowledge of the history of man has been projected backward several thousand years, and is attended by many surprises. We find that cultured peoples antedated Israel by millenniums; and that instead of Abraham's descendants belonging to the dawn of history, they lived in the late pre-Christian period. Instead of Israel being an all-powerful nation of antiquity, we find that, with the exception of the time in the days of David and Solomon when the borders of the nation were temporarily extended, it scarcely can be classed with such world-conquering powers as Babylonia, Assyria, Egypt, Persia, and other nations. Yet, while Israel politically is not to be compared with some of her illustrious neighbors, intellectually and spiritually the nation is found to stand in a unique position.

Another important result is the new historical geography which has been reconstructed, with its thousands of additional data. Hundreds of important points have been located definitely, whose provenience previously could only be surmised, or for which no reasonable position could be assigned. As a result, the number of places and rivers in the Old Testament concerning which nothing is known at the present time is comparatively small. By our knowledge of the nations surrounding Israel, its historical setting is worked out in a remarkable way. The improved perspective for many of the episodes gives them a totally different aspect. Peoples of whom we have had little or no knowledge are again introduced into the galaxy of nations. We become familiar with their language, their religious institutions, their local habitations, their conquests, and even their every-day life. Personalities loom up among their leaders which appear to be equal in greatness with those familiar to us in modern history.

One of the most important results obtained is the knowledge that Israel enjoyed—in common with other peoples—certain social, political, and religious institutions, as well as rites and customs. This knowledge, at first thought, is disturbing to some, especially when told that that which has been regarded as peculiarly Hebraic in character had its origin in antiquity. To cite a single example, circumcision was practised long before the patriarchs. Professor W. Max Müller has recently ascertained that the Egyptians circumcised at least 2500 B. C.

After some reflection this truth, instead of causing apprehension, enables us to understand how it was possible for the leaders of Israel to influence the people. It is impossible to imagine how unheard-of rites and ceremonies could have been introduced in Israel, even though one divinely sent advocated their practise. With some, also, it cannot be inferred that the leaders directly borrowed these rites and customs from their contemporaries, especially in view of the injunction they received: "After the doings of the land of Egypt, wherein ye dwelt, shall ye not do: and after the doings of the land of Canaan, whither I bring you, shall ye not do; neither shall ye walk in their statutes" (Lev. 18:3). The people were required to shun the practises of these peoples; but what shall be said concerning such customs, manners, and traditions, that for centuries during the patriarchal period had gradually crept into the Hebrew life and remained with it? By making use of customs with which they were acquainted, and giving them a significance that conveyed the truth which the leaders desired Israel to have, the success attending their practise is comprehensible. This becomes clearer when we take into consideration the intellectual status of the people, and the fact that, as far as we know, there were no efforts put forth to elevate them prior to the leadership of Moses.

The people of Israel, we must remember, developed into a tribal nation in a land which was enriched by the traditions and civilizations of peoples living there at least several millenniums before them. This land was a highway between two continents—a bridge or a path of communication between the civilizations of the Tigro-Euphrates valley and the Nile; and at the same time it was the outlet to the

Mediterranean Sea from the Great Arabian peninsula. Its position, surrounded by influences from three continents, had a peculiar effect upon the land. The varied topography of the country offered accommodations for peoples who preferred either an alpine or a tropical climate. Petty principalities existed, having little or no connection with each other. As a result, the land prior to the days of Israel, with the exception of the Phœnician cities, did not, as far as we know, develop or enjoy a pronounced type of culture, as did other nations about it. Although many antiquities of the early period have been found through the excavations in Palestine, there is little or nothing to show that an indigenous art existed, as is found, for instance, in Egypt or in Babylonia. Centers may be found, after excavations have been more extensively conducted in Palestine, which will bring to light a highly developed cult that will surprise us; but the indications of such, thus far, are lacking. Practically the only indigenous literary heritage that we possess of the early period in the history of the land, besides some of the Amarna tablets, is what is contained in the Old Testament writings. Notwithstanding this lack of evidence of an advanced civilization, it seems reasonable to conjecture that there did exist a civilization of no mean order; and also that the Israelites were influenced more by the life surrounding them in Palestine than from any other quarter.

Abram's home was the city Ur in Southern

Introductory Remarks 9

Babylonia. His direct descendants obtained their wives in that part of Syria or Armenia which in certain periods was embraced by Babylonia. They even regarded themselves as Arameans. In later years an Israelite, in presenting his first-fruits, said: "An Aramean ready to perish was my father" (*i. e.*, Jacob, Deut. 26:5). Further, it is not improbable that Abram or his ancestors had originally migrated from Syria to Ur, and belonged to the Western Semites who had congregated in Babylonia in great numbers during the first dynasty (see Chap. VII). Although centuries of nomadic life in the West, where the family developed into a nation, would imply that the people were greatly influenced by their environments, it is reasonable to suppose that they had also preserved traditions and customs belonging to their Eastern home. To Babylonia, therefore, we also look for influences which have molded to a certain extent the thought and life of Israel. This seems natural, especially when we consider that the scenes of the events recorded in the Old Testament as having taken place prior to Abram are pitched in that region from which the father of Israel came.

More striking than all else are the inscriptions which record the creation and deluge legends of the Babylonians (see Chaps. III and IV) as well as those which throw light on the story of Babel (Chap. V). The Hammurabi Code, which antedates the Mosaic, has the same underlying spirit of retaliation (see Chap. IX). This, however, seems to be common to all ancient as well as modern Orientals. Divination, for example, by inspecting the livers of animals offered on the altar of the gods, seems to be Babylonian[1]. This fact throws light on Ezekiel 21:21, where we read: "For the king of Babylon stood at the parting of the way, at the head of the two ways, to use divination: he shook the arrows to and fro, he consulted the teraphim, he looked in the liver." The reason why the Hebrews were prohibited from using a portion of the liver of the sacrificial animal (see Exod. 29: 13; Lev. 3: 4; 9: 10, etc.) was doubtless a protest against its use for divination purposes[2]. The words Joseph put into the mouth of his steward: "Is not this that [the cup] in which my lord drinketh, and whereby he indeed divineth?" (Gen. 44:5), are doubtless also Babylonian, and perhaps have some connection with their "Becherwahrsagung." Naturally, this may have been practised as well in Egypt.

It is possible to find certain ceremonials in the Babylonian ritual which have their parallel in the Old Testament[3]. As, for instance, the Babylonian set before his deity twelve loaves of unleavened

---

[1] See Jastrow, *Die Religion Babyloniens und Assyriens*, Vol. II, Chap. 20, for a full exposition of liver divination among the Babylonians.

[2] See Professor Moore's article in Nöldeke, *Festschrift*.

[3] See Haupt, Babylonian Elements in the Levitic Ritual, Journal of Biblical Literature, Vol. for 1900, p. 55ff.

Introductory Remarks 11

showbread, again thirty-six, or seventy-two; in other words, multiples of twelve. In Leviticus

Design of a sheep's liver in terra-cotta, with the surface divided into compartments, and inscribed with miscellaneous omens, prepared for instruction in divination methods in the Temple schools. Found near Bagdad.

twelve loaves were laid before Jahweh. Although it is not mentioned in the Old Testament, Jewish traditions unanimously affirm that the bread was unleavened, the same as in Babylonia. With them the number twelve represented the tribes; and the offering was made "on behalf of the children of Israel, an everlasting covenant." (Lev. 24:5ff.)

A ritual tablet[1] shows that the Babylonian sprinkled the blood of the lamb which was killed at the gate of the palace "on the lintels, on the figures flanking the entrances, and on the doorposts at the right and left." This act is recognized as having its parallel in the passover rite of the Hebrews. Yet, as the late Dr. Trumbull has shown,[2] the passover is based upon the ancient threshold covenant, which goes back to a very great antiquity, and which was practised by other ancient peoples as well as by the Babylonians. For Israel this old rite received a new significance. It was to be observed thereafter as a memorial of the deliverance of Israel from bondage.

The Babylonian priest required certain parts of the sacrifice for himself, which we know was the custom also among the Hebrews (Deut. 18:3). The parts that were retained by the Babylonian differ from those kept by the Israelite priest. This custom, however, is known to have been practised also by other peoples. Another similar feature of the

---

[1] See Haupt, Babylonian Elements in the Levitic Ritual, Journal of Biblical Literature, Vol. for 1900, p. 61.
[2] Threshold Covenant, p. 208ff.

Introductory Remarks 13

Babylonian sacrifice was the requirement that the animal be without blemish. Also, the poor man was permitted to make an offering of less value than the wealthy, the same as provided for in Israel.

Many other interesting suggestions have been made from time to time which cannot be subjected to an adequate test by reason of the fact that too little is understood either of the rite or custom itself, or that with which it is compared, but which can be said to lie within the range of possibility. For instance, the Hebrew *ḥoshen mishpāt,* "breastplate of judgment," in which the *Urim* and *Thummim* were kept, has been compared with the Assyrian *takâlta sha pirishti shamê u erṣiti,*[1] which is translated, "the pouch of the mystery of heaven and earth." Besides there being great uncertainty as regards the meaning of *takâlta,* which is recognized, there is the mere resemblance of the idea of a "sacred pouch" containing perhaps that which is indicative of the deity's will, upon which the oracle is based.

Any suggestion which will open up avenues of thought and investigation whereby a better understanding of biblical matters is acquired, must be heartily welcomed. But, after all that is known up to the present time has been gathered together, and its importance properly estimated, we are

---

[1] See Haupt, Babylonian Elements in the Levitic Ritual, Journal of Biblical Literature, Vol. for 1900, p. 59.

14   Light on the Old Testament

impressed with the fact that there have been many extravagant statements made, and there is not such a great deal, after all, that Israel was directly indebted to the Babylonians for, beyond the stories in Genesis of the times prior to Abram, and also certain customs which belong to the period after the Babylonian exile.

There are those who greatly overestimate the influence of Babylonia upon Israel. They say that practically everything belonging to the functions of the priest has come from this source; that "if we want to trace the origin of the late Jewish ceremonial of the Priest Code we must look for it in the cuneiform ritual texts of the Assyro-Babylonians." To substantiate such extreme views, and to make them intelligible, it will be necessary to produce many additional facts.

Professor Zimmern,[1] and others identify the Hebrew cherubim with the Assyrian bull colossi. This, however, rests only on supposed fancied resemblances. It is limited to both having wings in common, and the fact that the bull-gods were the guardians of temple gates, while the cherubim were placed eastward of Eden. Beyond these resemblances all other details are different. As has been said:[2] "If the idea of the cherubim was borrowed

---

[1] *Die Keilinschriften und das Alte Testament*, p. 529 f.
[2] Foote, The Cherubim and the Ark, Journal of the American Oriental Society, vol. xxv., p. 285.

Introductory Remarks 15

from the Babylonians it must be admitted that it had become so thoroughly Hebraized as to be no longer recognizable."

It has been stated again and again that the Babylonians observed the seventh day, which they called the Sabbath, as a rest day. The proof for the assertion was found in a syllabary which explains the words *ûm-nûḫ libbi*," day of rest of the heart," by the word *sha-bat-tum*. This has generally been regarded as being the origin of the Hebrew Sabbath. But it has since been ascertained[1] from a list, which gives the Sumerian and Babylonian days of the month, that *shabatti* or *shapatti* was the Babylonian name for the fifteenth day of the month. This word does not have anything to do with the Hebrew *shabât*, "to rest," but is explained as a synonym of the Babylonian *gamâru*," to complete."

But the Babylonians did observe the seventh, fourteenth, twenty-first, twenty-eighth, as well as the nineteenth day of their lunar month. It was UD.ḪUL.GAL or *ûmu limnu*, "the evil day." Upon this day the Hebrew Sabbath may in some respect be based. It was, however, not observed every seventh day like the Hebrew Sabbath, for some months had thirty days. It was not a day of rest for the common people, but was observed, as far as we know, only by the king and his officials; when they were prohibited from eating meat that had

---

[1] See Pinches, The Old Testament, etc., p 526ff.

touched the fire; when they could not change their garments, dress in white, offer sacrifices, mount a chariot, pronounce judgment, or the physician touch a sick man. The day was unauspicious for doing business. In the night, the king made his offering to the gods, when they were appeased. While the Babylonians observed such a day, we cannot therefore, agree with those who claim that we owe the blessings contained in the Sabbath (Sunday) rest to the ancient Babylonian civilization, as their day was observed quite differently. If the idea of the rest-day was taken over from the Babylonians, like other institutions whose origin can be traced among peoples prior to Israel, it received an entirely different character. The Israelites themselves, in explaining its origin, we must keep in mind, made it coincident with the last creation day (Gen. 2:3).

Politically, Babylonia has played an important rôle in Palestine. The earliest reference to the Westland which has been found in the inscriptions is on the votive vases of Lugal-zaggisi, about 4000 B. C. He informs us that he conquered the land, and extended his dominion unto the Mediterranean Sea (see page 138). Sargon I, about 3800 B. C., conducted several campaigns in this region, when he completely subjugated the people. He erected his image on the shores of the Mediterranean. Narâm-Sin, about 3750 B. C., marched against Midian and the Sinaitic peninsula. In the latter region he developed the famous copper mines.

Introductory Remarks

Gudea, about 3000 B. C., imported diorite from Sinai, and other kinds of stone from the Amorite land, besides cedars from Lebanon; which facts show at least close relations with that part of the country.

In Abraham's time, we learn that Elam claimed suzerainty over the land. Kudur-Mabug, the prince of Emutbal, a part of Elam, used the title, "Prince of Amurru" (Palestine). When Hammurabi conquered Larsa and Elam he assumed this title. Ammi-ditana, one of his successors, continued to enjoy it. Then the curtain falls, and the next we learn about the country from extra-biblical sources is more than five centuries later, in the Tel el-Amarna period, when the land is found to be under Egyptian control (see Chapter XI). With the predominant political influence of Assyria and Babylonia in the first pre-Christian millennium, all are familiar.

Recognizing the fact that Palestine during millenniums had been subject frequently to the nations of the East, that Hammurabi had been a remarkable administrator, and that his efforts as a legislator were such that the code he promulgated continued to be effective in Babylonia for many centuries, we should naturally suppose that he had also established his laws in all the countries over which he ruled, even though some were far removed from his seat of government. As far as is known, this does not seem to have been the case, at least with

Syria. Further, the influence which Babylonian culture exerted in Palestine, as it becomes known through the Amarna tablets, and in fact through all sources of the early period, to be explicit, was meager. In these letters a place near Jerusalem is mentioned, which was known as Bēth-Ninib "House of [the Babylonian god] Ninib;" and an individual was named Abdi-Ninib. The Babylonian god Nergal figured prominently as the god of disease and death in a letter written in Alashia (presumably Cyprus). Then also the god Baal and the goddess Ashirta of the Phœnicians are to be identified originally with Bêl and Ishtar of the Babylonian pantheon, while, doubtless, Mt. Sinai and Mt. Nebo obtained their names from the gods Sin and Nebo.

These facts would not enable us to prove an extensive influence upon Palestine from Babylonia. Moreover, the gods of Egypt, Syria, and Mitani are also mentioned in these letters. In short, Babylonia for many centuries, as well as Egypt for a shorter period, exercised control over Palestine, and exacted tribute; but these nations do not seem to have made any efforts to reorganize the country politically, or to establish their own cultures in the land. The use of the Babylonian as the diplomatic language of the Canaanite princes does not necessarily prove any extensive influence in that region, as some scholars have claimed, because the same language was used throughout Western Asia and

Introductory Remarks 19

Egypt at that time for the same purpose. French may be the diplomatic language spoken in modern Bagdad and Constantinople, but its use for that purpose would not prove that France exerted any special influence in those quarters. Naturally, the use of Babylonian in the Amarna age points to an extended control and political influence which Babylonia exercised over a great territory at some previous period. On the other hand, when we consider the influence that was exerted by the land of the Amorites (which included Palestine) upon Babylonia, we might claim the reverse to be true. Even the chief god Amurru was introduced into the Babylonian pantheon, as was the worship of Addu, and other gods, as is shown by their nomenclature, an example of which is the Palestinian Dagon in Ishme-Dagan, an Assyrian ruler's name.

The influence of Babylonia upon Palestine is not to be minimized, but it has been greatly exaggerated by some scholars with reference to the culture of the Hebrews. We are not justified in generalizing so freely because of certain things, as, for instance, similar laws which are found in the Hammurabi and Mosaic codes, which are based on common Oriental law, or are to be explained as interesting coincidences (see Chap. IX); or because of the similarity of the creation and deluge stories of the Hebrew and Babylonian; or, for instance, because some weights and measures are found to be similar, which was due to the influence of the

Babylonian trader. As shown, there are rites and ceremonies which have their parallels in the Assyro-Babylonian rituals. Further, in the customs of the late period, after the Hebrews had been in exile, there can be no question that considerable influence was felt from that quarter; to mention a single illustration, the substitution of the Babylonian names of the months for their own. But as has also been shown, there is no justification for the extravagant assertions concerning the Hebrew culture as a whole, which have been made in some of the recent *Bibel und Babel* literature.

It is to be regretted that we know so little of early Palestine and Phœnicia, the countries which have directly influenced the Israelites. It is claimed by some that the plan of Solomon's temple and its ornamentation followed Phœnician models. Yet some declare that it is little more than a reproduction of a Babylonian sanctuary. It might be interesting to see the proofs for these claims, inasmuch as there is very little known of Babylonian fanes.

We must remember that Israel lived in Egypt for nearly five centuries during the period of the nation's infancy. Although separated from true Egyptian life, and under military control, it is natural to suppose that a certain percentage of the people came into contact with the residents of the Nile valley. What is recorded in the Old Testament concerning Egypt is found to be a faithful picture. Other influences, as yet unrecognized, may have come from that direction. But after taking into consideration all the supposed influences now known from that quarter, we must remark that they are exceedingly slight.

Some may also be looked for from Hittite sources. The people of Heth had important settlements in Palestine at a very early date. The Syrians from Damascus, a very ancient center, also influenced the people of Palestine for centuries. What future excavations of the ancient cities of the East will reveal along this line of investigation, no one can surmise. The indications are that very interesting parallels in cultures will be found; and the fact will be recognized that Israel had much in common with other nations, even with those whose antiquity was much greater, and that the ordinary influences of nations, especially of the greater upon the smaller, will be recognized. But beyond that which belongs to common Oriental culture which has been handed down from time immemorial, little direct borrowing, it seems to me, will be found to have been done. In other words, such direct and wholesale dependence upon the Babylonians as has been claimed by some will not be proved.

On the other hand, when we consider the light thrown upon the Hebrew records from Babylonian and Assyrian sources by reason of political and social contact, we have something of a more positive character with which to deal. And it must be a source of gratification to many to know that the ruin-hills of the past have yielded so many things to prove that much which the skeptic and the negative critic have declared to be fiction is veritable history. Archeology must ever be given the greatest credit for having come to the rescue. When we reflect that wherever in the Old Testament reference is made to contact with foreign powers, and we have been able to delve among the contemporaneous records of those powers in nearly every instance, as will be seen in the succeeding chapters, reference to such contact with Israel has been found—truly every lover of the old Book **must rejoice.**

II

THE GREAT ANTIQUITY OF MAN

The Babylonian legend, as handed down by Berosus the Greek historian, claims four hundred and thirty-two thousand years for the period prior to the deluge, during which time ten kings ruled; in other words, each king ruled on an average forty-three thousand two hundred years. All are more or less familiar with the claims of modern scientists that the period for the existence of man on earth covers many thousands of years. In the discussion contained in the following pages on the antiquity of man, only that is taken into consideration which archeology has revealed.

For many years it has been known that Egypt flourished centuries prior to Abraham; that it had an amazingly high civilization, which was old in his day; and that its political institutions were already greatly advanced. Few, however, appreciated the extent of Egypt's development, especially with respect to its great antiquity. The general public did not readily accept the conclusions arrived at by Egyptologists, but continued to accept Ussher's chronology, or other systems which were based upon the Septuagint, as being more or less correct. All this is now changed. Babylonian archeology throws light upon the subject, and not only is the great antiquity claimed by Egyptologists confirmed, but our vista of this early age is enlarged in a manner surprising in the extreme. Nations and peoples of those times are restored to history. Thousands of inscriptions are brought to light, by the help of which a knowledge of the life and customs of the people prior to Abraham's day is unfolded before our eyes, changing our entire conception of those distant times, and revealing a civilization which had advanced in an astonishing degree, centuries before the patriarch. Instead of possessing only the names of a score or more of individuals between Adam and Abram, as are found in Genesis, many thousands become known. In a single document,[1] for instance, written two thousand years before the patriarch, about five hundred names are given. And yet the great work of excavating the cities of ancient Babylonia is only in its infancy.

Nearly a quarter of a century ago, De Sarzec's excavations at Telloh revealed statues and inscriptions (see page 158) belonging to an age antedating by many centuries the old date of the deluge. A decade since, on the basis of the excavations by the University of Pennsylvania at Nippur, a still greater antiquity was definitely fixed for the early history of man. And not very long ago Dr. Banks, who excavated at Bismya for the University of

---

[1] The Obelisk of Manishtusu, see page 46.

Chicago, in the reports of his field work claimed even a greater antiquity for what he found. In the upper stratum of this city the remains of a very early period were brought to light, showing that the city had been destroyed perhaps in the early part of the third millennium B. C., and that it had never been rebuilt. He informs us that beneath the ancient temple were various strata, the lowest of which he dates several millenniums earlier than the oldest date hitherto claimed for any Babylonian ruins. Whether his conclusions will stand the test, after further investigations have been made, remains to be seen. In addition to important explorations conducted years ago by Loftus, Taylor, and Rassam in Babylonia, the German Oriental Society has devoted five years to systematic excavations at Babylon, Fara, and Abû-Hatab, where important results were obtained.[1]

In determining the great antiquity of man in Babylonia prior to the days of Abraham, important lessons are taught by the University of Pennsylvania excavations of the various strata of the mound which covers the temple of Bêl at Nippur. It has been said that twenty-one different strata can be traced with certainty in the temple area. This does not mean strata in the sense of so many cities, but

---

[1] For the past two years the Society, under the directorship of Professor Frederick Delitzsch, has carried on excavations in Assyria where many antiquities of the last two pre-Christian millenniums have been found.

different levels at which objects have been found. The fact is that while a number of pavements intersect the mound of the temple, and several closely defined strata are perceptible, we cannot speak of so many cities, as for instance is done with reference to the ancient biblical Lachish, where Bliss found eight distinct towns, one superimposed upon the other. At Nippur there was a continued occupation, as far as is known, from the earliest period until the latest. The city was without doubt destroyed at times, but the buildings were restored and enlarged, especially those in connection with the temple. In short, the mounds of Nippur, formed through the accumulations of débris, and rising on an average of sixty feet above the plain, show a number of distinct strata with their respective antiquities. These mark different epochs, and represent millenniums of building operations.

When the excavators sent out by the University of Pennsylvania approached Nippur, in 1889, the high conical mound, rising about ninety feet above the plain, was at once recognized as covering the temple tower. In the uppermost stratum, the remains of the late occupation of the city were found. In this stratum were disinterred many Hebrew antiquities, such as inscribed incantation bowls (see Chap. XV). Below this lay a large fortress which had been built upon the temple and ziggurrat in the age following the Babylonian period, presumably by the Parthians or Romans. In the

View of the Excavations in the Temple Court at Nippur, showing the pavement of Ur-Engur, 2700 B. C.

ruins of this building are found some walls which indicate a slightly earlier construction, showing that the structure had been restored. The work of Ashurbanipal (668–626 B. C.) lies several feet beneath this fortress. In the temple court this famous Assyrian ruler laid a pavement of burnt bricks, a good many of which were stamped with his titles. Two feet below this pavement another was discovered. This was laid by Kadashman-Turgu, about 1325 B. C. Descending below this, another was found which belonged to Ur-Ninib, about 2550 B. C. Only two and a half feet of débris exist between the pavements of Kadashman-Turgu and Ur-Ninib, although that amount represents a period of about twelve hundred years. Two feet below the pavement of Ur-Ninib, the excavators found one laid by Ur-Engur, whose date is fixed at about 2700 B. C. But how do we arrive at the date approximately assigned to this royal builder?

Assuming that Amraphel, the contemporary of Abraham, is to be identified with Hammurabi, 2100 B. C. (see page 130), and knowing that he was the sixth king of his dynasty, and also that the number of years his predecessors ruled was one hundred and twenty, we have the date for the beginning of the first dynasty of Babylon. It was contemporaneous with the second dynasty of Ur, or Larsa dynasty, which lasted several hundred years. This followed in order the dynasty of Isin, and the first dynasty of Ur. The number of years or cen-

Pavements laid by Ashurbanipal, Kadashman-Turgu and Ur-Ninib.

Workman removing the pavement containing bricks with the titles of Sargon and Narâm-Sin.

30   Light on the Old Testament

turies assigned to these dynasties, from the number of known rulers, and the length of their respective reigns, cannot be fixed. Although it is assumed that some of these dynasties were partially contemporaneous, a reasonable conjecture is that five or six hundred years intervened. While several of the dynasties are comparatively well represented by known kings, the names of a number of additional rulers must be forthcoming before this period between Ur-Engur (approximately 2700 B. C.) and Hammurabi (2100 B. C.) is completely filled out.

Below the pavement of Ur-Engur, Director Haynes found another. The bricks used in its construction were laid in two courses, and bore the legends of Sargon I, 3800 B. C., and his son Narâm-Sin (see illustration page 118). We again inquire, How is this date arrived at?

Hormuzd Rassam, in 1881, discovered at Abu-Habba a cylinder of King Nabonidus (555–537 B.C.), the father of Belshazzar, with whose zeal for archeological investigations we are familiar. It contains an account of his restoration of Ebarra, the temple of Shamash at Sippara, which Nebuchadrezzar and others before him had rebuilt, but which had fallen into ruins. He says: "While I caused the god Shamash to go forth from within it [and] caused him to dwell in another sanctuary, I tore down that temple; and looked for its old foundation-stone. I excavated eighteen cubits of earth, and the foundation-stone of Narâm-Sin,

The Great Antiquity of Man

the son of Sargon, which no other kings among my predecessors had seen for 3200 years, the god

DOOR-SOCKET OF SARGON, FROM NIPPUR.

Inscription reads: Shargâni-shar-âli (Sargon), son of Itti-Bêl, the mighty king of Accad and the dominion of Bêl, the builder of Ekur, the Temple of Bêl in Nippur. Whoever removes this inscribed stone, may Bêl and Shamash tear out his foundation and exterminate his posterity.

Shamash, the great Lord of Ebarra, the temple, the dwelling place, the delight of his heart, showed me." Adding the 3200 years to 550, which is about the time this inscription was written, we arrive at the date 3750 B. C. for Narâm-Sin, and about 3800 B. C. for that of his father Sargon.

Efforts had been made to show that these kings were mythical personages, created by the priests of the late period. Curiously enough, at the very time this theory appeared in print, Doctor Haynes, at Nippur, like Nabonidus of old, stood upon the temple pavement of Narâm-Sin.

A number of Assyriologists accept the date 3800 B. C., while others are very reluctant to admit such a great antiquity for these Babylonian rulers. Professor Winckler has endeavored to bring Sargon's date down to 3000 B. C., while Doctor Lehmann corrects Nabonidus' figures, and makes the inscription read 2200 years instead of 3200. This would make Sargon's date 2800 B. C.

There is this to be said, however, with reference to the 3200 years of Nabonidus, before we draw our deductions from the facts. Doctor Haynes reported that the pavement of Ur-Engur rested immediately upon the two-course brick pavement of Narâm-Sin. Ur-Engur's pavement consisted of several layers of worked clay, about seven feet in thickness, on the top of which was a course of burnt bricks. No débris, therefore, intervened between the pavement of Ur-Engur and that of Narâm-Sin, although the uppermost courses of each were in some places as much as eight feet apart. Mr. Fisher, the architect of

The Great Antiquity of Man 33

the last expedition, claims that other constructions of Ur-Engur also rest immediately upon those of Sargon and Narâm-Sin. These facts would seem to support the theory that a thousand years do not intervene between the two rulers. And yet on the other hand, as noticed above, only two and a half feet of débris exists between the pavement of Ur-Ninib (about 2550 B. C.) and Kadashman-Turgu (about 1325 B. C.), a period of about 1200 years. For many centuries the pavement of Ur-Ninib may have been kept clear. Perhaps after some years of neglect, or after some catastrophe, the pavement within the temple area was lost sight of, and then began the slow process of trampling the accumulated dust and dirt into the ground floor. The gradual rise of every ancient city is a well-recognized fact. In Babylonia mud bricks were largely used for houses and other building operations. The walls from time to time were plastered. As the mud washed down, it caused the level of the court or sidewalk gradually to rise. It is well known that the level of the streets and alleys rises more rapidly than the ground floors of the houses, owing to the fact that the floors are swept, and little attention is given to the streets. In consequence, upon entering a house in the East of to-day, one is frequently forced to step down into it. And when the floors become too low the roof of the house is removed, the rooms filled in, the walls raised, and the roof replaced.

In the temple court, where brick pavements were laid by certain builders, and dirt was allowed to accumulate, the level rose, but only after the pavement had disappeared from view. If Ur-Ninib's pavement had been kept clear for the greater part of the period following him until Kadashman-Turgu's time, the same might be said for the entire period between Sargon and Ur-Engur.

It is claimed by some that because of the difference in the writing, paleographical reasons may be added to prove that at least a thousand years intervened between these two rulers. Such arguments are exceedingly precarious, as the character of the writing is practically the same. Then also the list of rulers known to the present time between Ur-Engur and Sargon is small, if more than a thousand years intervened. Much more is known of the preceding and subsequent periods. If a millennium did intervene, this age remains the least known of any from 4500 B. C. down to the Christian era. Moreover, instead of correcting Nabonidus, or guessing at the length of this period, it is perhaps better to retain the date 3800 B. C. for Sargon until more light is thrown upon the subject, which we may expect almost any day.

On the third campaign, the indefatigable excavator Haynes descended through Sargon's and Narâm-Sin's pavement. Several feet below he came upon a curb, about twenty inches high, which may have served as an enclosure for the so-called

The Great Antiquity of Man 35

altar,[1] which was found on the same level. At a distance of twelve feet below Sargon's pavement, he found a vaulted arch of burnt bricks, which was built in a wall as a protection to pipes which passed beneath it.[2]

The Archaic Arch of Nippur.

---

[1] See Hilprecht, Old Babylonian Inscriptions, Vol. I, part 2, page 24. Later it was regarded as a crematorium. See Explorations in Bible Lands, page 458.

[2] See *ibid*, page 20. Also Fisher, Transactions, Department of Archeology, Vol. I, part 3.

36   Light on the Old Testament

In descending to virgin soil, the excavator found large urns, drains of various kinds, hundreds of vases filled with ashes, pottery, etc. Between Narâm-Sin's pavement and virgin soil, he reported thirty feet of débris. This represents the accumu-

Excavations in the Temple precincts to Virgin soil.

lations of ages, and prompted Haynes to write in one of his reports to the committee: "We must cease to apply the adjective 'earliest' to the time of Sargon, or to any age or epoch within a thousand years of his advanced civilization." In other words, he found that instead of Sargon and Narâm-Sin

The Great Antiquity of Man 37

being mythological characters, or even belonging to the dawn of civilization, they are representatives of a highly developed culture. This was one of the great archeological surprises of recent decades.

It is impossible to estimate the length of the period represented by the thirty feet of accumulation between Narâm-Sin's pavement and virgin soil. If the rate of accumulations was the same as the period subsequent to Narâm-Sin's time, it should be between two and three millenniums. Naturally, this may be an extravagant conjecture, but nevertheless, there is every reason to believe that the period is an indefinitely long one.

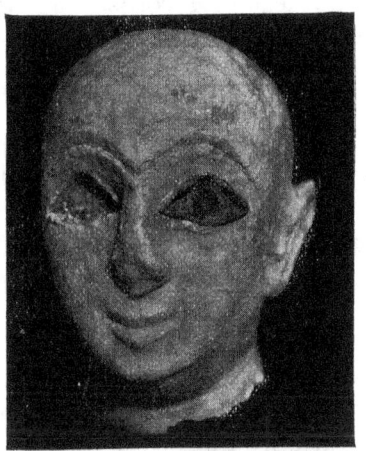

Early Sumerian Marble head from Nippur.

What kind of a civilization is represented by the antiquities which belong to the period prior to Sargon? At Nippur the objects of special value, belonging to this time, are mostly inscribed votive vases, all of which were found in a fragmentary condition. Noteworthy among the very oldest might be mentioned several fragments of a white calcite stalagmite vase, bearing an inscription of

Enshagkushanna. The first reads: "To En-lil (*i.e.*, Bêl), king of lands, En-shag-kush-an-na, lord of Kengi king of . . . ." The second reads: "To En-lil, En-shag-kush-an-na, the spoil of Kish . . . .," and a third: " . . . . The spoil of Kish, wicked of heart he presented" (see illustration No. 2 on page 39). The fragmentary legend records the fact that this ruler had conquered Kish, and from the spoil he presented this vase to his deity at Nippur.

Two fragments (which fit together), of a vase of the same material, also found in the temple area, contain the following inscription of Urzage (formerly read Urshulpauddu): "To En-lil (*i.e.*, Bêl) king of countries, and Nin-lil (*i.e.*, Bêltis), the queen of heaven and earth, *nun-ba-she-na-ni*, the consort of En-lil. Ur-zage king of Kish, king of . . . . has presented it" (see illustration No. 3).

Following or preceding these rulers there is a clearly established line of kings known through the excavations of the French at Telloh: Lugal-shag-Engur, Ur-Ninâ, Akurgal, Eannatum, Enannatum I, Edingiranagin, Entemena, and Enannatum II, Urukagina, etc.

Art treasures belonging to these rulers are now preserved in the Louvre at Paris. Among other inscriptions of Ur-Ninâ, who devoted considerable time to the building of temples, shrines, and storehouses, there is an interesting slab about eighteen

Fragments of Votive Vases (Pre-Sargonic): 1. Lugal-zaggisi; 2. Enshagkushanna; 3. Ur-zage; 4. Entemena.

inches in length. A hole was cut in the center, presumably for the purpose of hanging it upon a peg on the wall. In order to express his sovereignty, Ur-Ninâ is represented as a giant, while his eight sons and servants, who are about him, are depicted

Votive Slab of Ur-Ninâ of Lagash. 18⅛ in. wide.

as dwarfs. He is dressed like a priest or temple servant, with short hair, and naked above his waist, in order to express humility in the presence of his god. Upon his head he holds a reed-basket. Behind him, in the lower half of the slab, his cupbearer is in the act of pouring out wine. The beginning of the inscription is on his head, as if it represents what he has to say. Besides giving his title, and the names of temples which he built, the name of each son is inscribed on his respective skirt.

Votive Slab of Ur-Enlil of Nippur. 8½ in. wide.

Belonging to this age, or perhaps an earlier, is a small limestone slab, somewhat similar, which was found at Nippur. In the upper division, Ur-Enlil stands before his deity with a libation vase in one hand and an offering in the other. The scene was duplicated by reversing the figures.

The inscription reads: "To Ninni-Edin, Ur-Enlil the chief merchant, has presented it." In the lower division besides two figures there is a sheep and a goat. One of the figures carries a square basket on his head, and the other a stick in his hand. The late Professor Cope of the University of Pennsylvania regarded the goat as a domestic hybrid, and the sheep as the uriel, now known in Eastern Persia, and considered that the animal locomotion as indicated by the incised lines is remarkably well executed; and yet the slab belongs to this early age.

The fifth son of Ur-Ninâ who was Akurgal, according to the arrangement on the slab, succeeded him. He is not represented as yet by any inscriptions. Eannatum, his brother, followed his reign. The inscriptions of this powerful successor record a dispute concerning the boundary between Shirpurla and Gishkhu, a neighboring city. The famous stele of vultures commemorates the treaty which ensued. It received its name from the fact that at the top of the stone there are carved in relief, vultures carrying away parts of dead bodies, after the battle which terminated the dispute. Eannatum was a mighty conqueror. He does not seem to have inherited the peace-loving spirit of his predecessors. In a lengthy inscription he tells of the many peoples he subjugated, and the cities he destroyed; among which are Elam, Erech, Ur, Larsa, Gishkhu, Kish, and many others, a number of which have not as yet been identified.

The Great Antiquity of Man 43

Entemena continued this warfare, having difficulties on account of the same boundary and the uprising of the subjugated. In lengthy, grandiloquent records he recounts his victories, and mentions his great deeds.

It seems that Bêl, whose seat of worship was at Nippur, was a favored deity of these Shirpurla rulers; at least they considered that it was he who gave the power into their hands to accomplish their feats. It is therefore quite proper that we should expect to find some token of their gratitude in Bêl's sanctuary. Among the discoveries in the temple area were two fragments (see illustration page 39, No. 4) which read: "Entemena, the Patesi of Shirpurla, to whom power was given by Bêl, who was nourished with the milk of life by Ninkharsag . . . . of Bêl, a large vase from the mountains he brought to Dungur, the lord of the foundation of heaven . . . . ." Other fragments of the same king were found in later excavations.

Urukagina, king of Shirpurla, is represented by four or five inscriptions which the French found in the ruins of that city, now called Telloh. The country seemed to be at peace in his day. He showed his piety and devotion to the gods by building temples, shrines, palaces, and granaries in order to store up the abundance of the land.

A contemporary of this Telloh ruler, as Thureau-Dangin, the savant of the early Sumerian inscriptions has shown, is Lugal-zaggisi (about 4000 B. C.), whose vase fragments (see illustration, page 39, No. 1) have been found at Nippur. In his inscription[1] he informs us that he was the son of a priest; that Bêl had granted him the kingship of the world; that he had made him the spiritual head of all the peoples of his kingdom; that he had conquered the land from the rising of the sun (Persian Gulf) to the going down of the sun (Mediterranean Sea, see page 138). He recounts his restoration of certain cities, well known in later inscriptions, as Ur, Larsa, etc., and closes with a prayer to Bêl, to whom he dedicates the vase.

At Nippur, fragments representing quite a number of additional pre-Sargonic kings were found. Some of these contain only a few lines of inscriptions[2], but from which additional names of rulers and persons are obtained: Utug, Ur-Mama, Lugal-kigubnidudu, Lugal-kisalsi, Abaranna, Lugal-ezen, Aba-Enlil, and others. Exactly in what order these names are to be placed, or whether some of them should be placed before Urukagina, remains at present uncertain.

---

[1] From a large number of fragments, small and large, Professor Hilprecht copied this inscription of about one hundred and forty short lines. See Old Babylonian Inscriptions, Vol. I, part 2. Thureau-Dangin published the first complete translation of it in *Révue Sémitique d'Epigraphie et d'Historie Ancienne*, 1897, page 263 ff.

[2] Old Babylonian Inscriptions, Pl. 46 f.

The Great Antiquity of Man 45

The inscriptions of another king of Kish, which were discovered at Nippur and Telloh, deserve mention in this connection. Some of the vases

STONE VOTIVE SLAB.
Inscription: "To Bêl, Lugal-kigubnidudu has presented it." Diameter, 10 in., thickness, 2⅜ in.

are more than half preserved. Some bear very brief legends, as for instance: "Urumush (or Alu-sharshid), king of Kish;" or again: "To the god

Bêl, Urumush, king of Kish, has presented it." The longest of these inscriptions reads: "To Bêl, Urumush, king of Kish, presented it from the spoil of Elam, when Elam and Barakhse had been subjugated."

Here might be mentioned also the remarkable block of granite known as the Stele of Manishtusu, which was found by de Morgan at Susa, and translated by the indefatigable Father Scheil. It has about two thousand lines of inscription. Manishtusú, who lived shortly before or after Sargon I, purchased a large estate for his son Mesilim. A present was given the seller, as well as the price which was paid. This custom still prevailed in Neo-Babylonian times. In the transaction, the land was estimated at corn value, and the price of corn was fixed according to the silver standard. A regular system of weights was in existence, which was based on the sexigesimal system. Besides a regular judiciary, which was already in existence, over forty professions are mentioned. In all, about five hundred names appear on the stone.

We have thus briefly mentioned the pre-Sargonic

Marble Vase of Urumush.

The Great Antiquity of Man 47

inscriptions, from the earliest found at Nippur, which was perhaps that of Enshagkushanna, to that of Manishtusu which was found at Susa. Whether the Esar[1] statue, found at Bismya, is older, as has been claimed, remains to be determined. Professor Barton of Bryn Mawr published some years ago what is known as the Blau monument. It antedated everything else then known. Recently he deciphered tentatively an archaic tablet belonging to the E. A. Hoffman Collection of the General Theological Seminary, New York, which he regards as being still older; but perhaps not as old as another which Father Scheil published from Djocha.

From these brief extracts of inscriptions belonging to the dust of ages, we get here and there a glimpse of light for the period prior to Sargon I. In some instances, perhaps, an isolated name on a fragment represents a dynasty. All of which impresses us with the fact that while we have reached far back into the misty past, the oblivion which hides the beginnings of the human race seems to grow deeper and deeper. Elam is already a recognized power in the political horizon. The inimical relations so often displayed in the succeeding millenniums have been already developed. The biblical cities, Erech, Larsa, Ur, and Nippur (which according to the Talmud is

---

[1] Read "Daudu" or "David" by the discoverer. The little inscription reads, "Esar, the mighty king, king of Adab." See Hommel in Thureau-Dangin, *Les inscriptions de Sumer et d'Akkad*.

Calneh of Genesis 10:10), and other cities, with their respective temples, storehouses, and deities, are in a great measure practically the same as we know them in later periods. The Semites are already in the land. It is scarcely possible that they entered during this known age. In short, from the archeological remains of this period we are impressed with the fact that the civilization of that age is practically the same as that met in the succeeding millenniums.

The great antiquity of Babylonian literature is also an established fact. The extant inscriptions of the early pre-Sargonic age, apart from the deeds and documents, as shown above, are largely of a historical character, such as brief records of kings' doings, in which they magnify themselves for their pious deeds in building or restoring temples and storehouses, or in which they recount their conquests of neighboring kings. In addition they inscribed brief legends consisting of their names and titles upon bricks, gate sockets and votive objects. Yet there are excellent reasons for maintaining that there existed in this age also a considerable proportion of the religious texts, such as epics, hymns, incantations, etc., some of which are recognized as having been inscribed in the Hammurabi period, although in a revised form to suit the cult or cults of that time; and which formed also to a large extent, the basis of the material that was gathered centuries later for the famous library of Ashurbanipal. In offering reasons for the early existence of

The Great Antiquity of Man 49

these texts, reference can be made to the art of the early period, in which, for instance, scenes from the national Gilgamesh epic are depicted. Incidental references to the site of Eridu at the head of the Persian Gulf would point to a great antiquity, since in comparatively early times the Persian Gulf, because of the accumulation of soil, had already receded far from the city.

The fact also that there are indications that in early times different versions of the creation or Tiâmatu epic existed in the different centers, as has been so forcibly maintained by Professor Jastrow (see p. 60), in which the patron deity of the city was made the hero, besides being accommodated otherwise to the cult in which it was made use of, is also an indication of great antiquity. This recasting of a work to suit the cult in which it was used, is now well recognized. The *Shurpu-Maklu* texts, published by Zimmern, originally were Eridu series of incantations, which had been transferred to the god Marduk of Babylon. The hymns published by Reisner, which were found in Babylon, are written in the Neo-Babylonian script, but they go back to the hymns used in the worship of Bêl at Nippur of an earlier period. Similarly, many of the texts in the library of Ashurbanipal, though reverting to originals in the temple collection in Babylon may be traced back to still earlier originals at Nippur, Eridu, Sippara and other cities. This finds support in the publication quite recently of an incantation tablet[1] which for paleographical reasons is dated at 3000 or 3500 B. C., and in which Ea alone is worshiped. Despite this early age there seem to be reasons for regarding even this tablet an edition of a still older original, and that it formed part of an incantation series. Considering also that art, writing (see below), religion—in a word the entire culture of the Semitic Babylonian—is based upon that of the earlier inhabitants of the valley, it is a reasonable conclusion that much of this early literature goes back to an exceedingly remote antiquity.

The character of the writing of this early age offers another weighty argument for a great antiquity prior to that now known; for then men wrote their thoughts in an intelligible and permanent form. The script used by the Sumerians, as is the case with every writing, goes back to original hieroglyphs or pictorial outlines of objects. The Babylonians, who represent the fusion of the Sumerians and Semites, continued to employ the script until the very close of their history. The characters in the earliest inscriptions known are so far removed from what they were originally that in scarcely more than a third of the number used can the original pictures be determined. The way these are recognized is largely by inference through the different values the characters possess. This fact determines

---

[1] Vincent Brummer, *Recueil de Travaux Relatifs.* Volume xxviii., *liv.* 3 *et* 4.

The Great Antiquity of Man 51

for us that between the introduction of this system of writing and the date of the earliest inscriptions in our possession a very long period intervened. Whether the originators of this writing—which was adapted to clay, their writing material— were the first to invent a system; whether the Sumerians who occupied the country prior to the Semites will eventually be regarded as one of the very first peoples of the earth, or whether a civilization still older than that revealed at Telloh, Nippur, Fara, and Bismya will be resurrected, further excavations will determine.

A linguistic argument may be added. Five principal Semitic languages are recognized: Babylono-Assyrian, Aramaic, Palestinian, Arabic, and the Ethiopic. All scholars agree that there was an original Semitic tongue from which these have sprung. Taking into consideration the fixed character of the Babylonian language in the earliest inscriptions; that the grammar already shows phonetic degeneration, and that there is little difference to be observed in the language nearly four millenniums later, we are prompted to inquire: How many centuries must be accounted for in the history of this tongue since its separation from the original Semitic language, when their common ancestors used a common tongue? Besides the Semitic groups, there is the Aryan, which surely had an equal antiquity, not to mention the great unclassifiable group, the so-called Turanian, to which the Sumerian belongs. And again we ask ourselves, What is the length of the period prior to that represented by the earliest known of these groups of tongues?

The work of the craftsman also offers interesting data in this connection. A great many beautiful examples of the work of the silversmith of this early age have been preserved, such as bowls, vases, and works of art. A beautiful specimen is to be found in the silver vase dedicated to the god Ningirsu by Entemena (about 4100 B. C.), which was discovered at Telloh. It stands on a bronze pedestal with four feet. A votive inscription runs about its neck. The bowl is divided into two compartments. In the upper portion, upon the flat metal, are engraved seven heifers lying down, but with the right leg extended as if in the act of rising. All face the same direction. In the lower compartment are four eagles with extended wings and tails, practically identical with the totem or coat of arms of Shirpurla. The talons of each of the four eagles are clutching two walking animals, which have their backs to each other. The animals represented are lions, goats, and stags. Although too much attention has been paid to detail, the whole is exceedingly well rendered, and indicates remarkable skill, which in no respect is less striking than that of the Egyptian contemporaries in this handicraft.

Notable examples of work in bronze are a few heads of animals which have been found. Two

Silver Vase of Entemena, with the Coat of Arms of Lagash.

54   Light on the Old Testament

goat heads, said by the Arabs who found them to have come from Abû Hatab or Fara, are especially interesting. The composition of the bronze is: 82.97 per cent. of copper, 1.33 per cent. of nickel, 0.86 per cent. of iron, 0.23 per cent. of antimony,

Bronze Head.

and 14.61 per cent. of oxygen.[1] The heads when found were heavily incrusted with patina. On

---

[1] See Helm and Hilprecht, *Verhandlungen der Berliner anthropologischen Gesellschaft*, 1901, p. 157

The Great Antiquity of Man 55

removing this, some of the original polish was still visible. The eyes are made of white and brownish shell, laid in the metal. Around the neck and on the side of the nose are similar ornamental designs also in shell. In the forehead there is a triangular design in mother-of-pearl, which is also inlaid with brown and white shell. The neck of the animal is hollow. From the top of the inside near the opening a pin is suspended. This is either for the purpose of attaching the head to a wooden body, which had been overlaid with the same material, or, more probably, for securing the head to the wall. Its design and execution is most excellent. It is a magnificent piece of work by an early Babylonian or Sumerian master. The thought uppermost in mind, in considering these antiquities, is that there was a long period of development before such a production was possible.

The work of the lapidary of this early age also deserves consideration in this connection. As works of art, according to our standard, owing to the exaggerated prominence of muscles and the heaviness of form, the seal cylinders of this age would be considered defective from an anatomical point of view; and yet the boldness in outline and the fidelity of the action displayed in them is most remarkable. They call forth admiration from all who are competent to judge. The lapidist must have possessed delicate saws, drills and other tools. The fact is that the skill manifested in their execution was never equaled in subsequent Babylonian history, and can scarcely be surpassed in the present day with all our modern improvements. A beautiful example is the seal cylinder of Ibni-sharru, the scribe of Sargon. It depicts Gilgamesh, the hero of the deluge epic, kneeling, and holding in his hand a peculiar vase. From its claws two jets of water stream forth, from which a river runs through the country. Before him is an ox, with huge horns, which throws back its head to one side in order to catch the water. The artistic ingenuity displayed in metamorphosing a bit of stone into such a work of art is remarkable; and yet it belongs to the Sargonic period.

How radically different then is our conception of these times from what it was a few years ago; especially when we carry ourselves back to the fifth millennium before Christ, and find that practically every antiquity of this early age speaks volumes for the enlightenment and the advanced civilization enjoyed by the people! We do meet with that which would be regarded as primitive, yet the culture in general with which we become acquainted, comparable in many respects with that of our own, points to a very great antiquity back of what we know as the very earliest. They make us long for more light; and we ask, To what quarter shall we look for it? Will Nippur yield documents still earlier than those discovered? Doctor Haynes informs us that he excavated to virgin soil in the

A trained Arab workman carefully separating clay tablets, *in situ*, which are very fragile from dampness.

temple mound. Will excavations in some other mound yield the desired light? Later inscriptions regard Nippur as one of the very oldest cities, but this may be due to its great prominence in later ages, in which case we look to other sites. In truth, as has been stated, earlier inscriptions have been found; and there doubtless will be others as the work of excavations continues.

III

THE BABYLONIAN CREATION STORY

In 1875, George Smith of the British Museum announced that among the treasures of that institution which had been excavated in Assyria, he had discovered the Chaldean story of the creation, and that it closely resembled the biblical account. In the following year his work, "The Chaldean Account of Genesis," appeared.[1] The tablets had been previously disinterred from the great library which had been founded by Ashurbanipal (668–626 B. C.).

The legend had been transcribed in the Assyrian characters upon several tablets, covering in all about one thousand lines. Including the fragments recently published by the Rev. Mr. L. W. King,

---

[1] Professor Delitzsch, in 1896, published all the known fragments of the legend with a critical commentary, in his work *Das babylonische Weltschöpfungsepos*. This was followed by other translations, notably by Professor Jensen, *Mythen und Epen* (1900); Professor Zimmern's appendix to Gunkel, *Schöpfung und Chaos in Urzeit und Endzeit* (1895); those of Drs. Sayce, Pinches, Jastrow, Alfred Jeremias; and especially that of the Rev. Mr. King, "The Seven Tablets of Creation" (1902), who succeeded in finding in the collections of the British Museum no less than twenty-eight additional fragments of the epic.

of the British Museum, about two-thirds of the story has been recovered.

The chief theme of the epic however, instead of being the creation of the heavens and the earth, is the glorification of the god Bêl, for whose name Marduk was later substituted.[1] Apsû and Tiâmat were two primeval water deities. They gave birth to the gods of the heavens. The latter caused the aboriginal deities much disquietude, whereupon the former decided upon their destruction. The gods of heaven appointed Marduk to fight the great Tiâmat. He slew her, and out of her carcass created the heavens and the earth. Extracts of the legend follow:

> When above heaven was not named,
> And the earth beneath was not called by name,
> The primeval Apsû was their begetter,
> Mummu and Tiâmat was the begetter of them all;
> Their waters were mingled together in one body;
> A field was not marked, a marsh was not seen,
> When the gods had not emerged,
> And they did not bear a name; and destinies had not been fixed;

---

[1] This is understood to have taken place some time after Hammurabi had caused the worship of Marduk at Babylon to supersede that of Bêl, whose sanctuary was at Nippur. It has been pointed out that there are elements in the story of two original conflicts. Professor Jastrow (see "The Composite Character of the Babylonian Creation Story," in the *Orientalische Studien*, 1906, p. 969ff.) has recently argued that there are traces of a third, which he calls the Eridu version.

The Babylonian Creation Story

Then the gods were created in the midst [of the heavens;]
Lakhmu and Lakhamu were called forth.
Time passed . . . .
Anshar and Kishar over them [were placed].

These gods are followed by others that were born to Apsû and his spouse Tiâmat. The gods of heaven, however, caused them unrest. Apsû in his complaint to Tiâmat says:

By day I cannot rest, by night I cannot lie down,
I will surely destroy their ways, I will cast them down.

They held a consultation with reference to the destruction of the gods, so that they might have rest.

Tiâmat advanced, with her brood banded together by her side. Fuming and raging, they became furious in their preparations for battle. Ummu-Khubur, who formed all things, spawned monster serpents with sharp teeth, and merciless fangs. Instead of blood she filled their bodies with poison. She made them huge in stature, and endowed them with brilliance, so that those who beheld them might be overwhelmed with fear. She set up vipers, dragons, raging hounds, and scorpion-men who bore cruel weapons. Over this band of monsters she exalted Kingu, her first-born, and put him in command of the conflict. She placed the tablet of fate in his bosom, and said that his command should be irrevocable:

"Let the opening of your mouth quench the Fire-god:
The one who is exalted in the battle, let him [display (his) might]."

These are the closing lines of the first tablet.

The second tablet relates how Ea, one of the early triad of gods (known as Anu, Bêl, and Ea), heard of the plot against all the gods of heaven. Ea told his father, Anshar, all that Tiâmat had done. Filled with rage, he bit his lip, and wailed a bitter lamentation. He addressed his valiant son Anu, and commanded him to go and stand before Tiâmat, that she might be appeased, and be merciful unto them. He made his way to her; he beheld her muttering, but he could not understand her, so he turned back. Ea, in attempting the task, became afraid; whereupon he also turned back. Two of the triad having been unsuccessful in their efforts to bring order out of chaos, Anshar finally approached Marduk, and asked him to be the champion of the gods.

The original of this particular version represented Bêl as accomplishing that important work. Doubtless in this form the myth had been edited by a priest of Bêl at Nippur.[1] In later years, after the time of Hammurabi, when Babylon had become the great political and religious center, the name of Marduk, the patron god of that city, was substituted for that of Bêl. He was placed at the head of

---

[1] As has been suggested by Professor Jastrow, it would not be surprising to find other versions, for instance, at Eridu, in which Ea was the hero.

The Babylonian Creation Story

the pantheon, and made the creator of the universe; in other words, he was given the rôle originally played by Bêl.

Marduk being appealed to, drew nigh to Anshar, his father, who joyfully beheld him. He expressed the desire to accomplish what was in his father's heart. Anshar assured him that he would trample the neck of Tiâmat under his feet. Whereupon Marduk addressed his father thus:

> Lord of gods, the destiny of the great gods
> If indeed I your avenger
> Conquer Tiâmat, and give you life,
> Call an assembly; pronounce *iba* of my fate.
> In Upshukkinnaki sit together in joy;
> Let my word like yours decree fate;
> Let everything I do be irrevocable;
> May the utterance of my lips neither be changed nor revoked.

The third tablet opens with Anshar commanding Gaga, the messenger, to summon all the gods to a feast in order that they might place their fate in the hands of Marduk, the avenger. He is commanded to repeat what Tiâmat has planned to do; and to mention the unsuccessful efforts of Anu and Ea, as well as the acceptance of the task to champion the cause of the gods by Marduk, on certain conditions which he has mentioned. The gods are therefore urged:

> Hasten then; your fate quickly decree,
> That he may go and fight your mighty foe.

Gaga in carrying the message faithfully repeated everything to the gods. They broke out in bitter lamentations, because of the acts of Tiâmat. They gathered together for an assembly in the presence of Anshar. At the banquet they sat eating and drinking until they were drunk, when they decreed the fate of Marduk, their avenger.

In the fourth tablet the gods set up for Marduk a lordly chamber, placing it before that of his fathers. They then honored him by proclaiming him chief of the gods. His commands henceforth should be supreme; they should not be transgressed. He was given power to exalt or debase.

O Marduk, thou art our avenger.
We give thee sovereignty over the entire world.

This was followed by assurances of success. And that he might know that he had the power, they laid before him a garment. At their suggestion he spoke the word, and it disappeared. He spoke again, and it returned. They did homage unto him. They bestowed upon him scepter, throne, and ring, the insignia of a ruling deity. They gave him an invincible weapon, to cut off the life of Tiâmat.

He then equipped himself with bow and quiver, which hung by his side. The spear he slung upon his back, and he grasped the club in his right hand. The lightning he set in front of him. With a flaming fire he filled his body. To enclose the inward parts of Tiâmat he made a net. In order to prevent

The Babylonian Creation Story   65

her from escaping he fixed the four winds. He created seven kinds of wind, among which was the evil wind, the tempest, the hurricane, and the sevenfold wind. Standing in his chariot, with four ferocious horses which were trained to trample under foot, and with an overpowering light about his head,

Fight of Marduk and Tiâmat.

and his thunderbolt raised, he set his face to meet the raging Tiâmat.

At the sight of Marduk, Kingu, whom Tiâmat had put in command of the monsters, became dazed and dumfounded; and his followers were troubled. But Tiâmat was not dismayed; and while raging, she heard the charges of Marduk and the challenge.

"Let thy host be equipped, let thy weapons be unsheathed.
Stand, I and thou; then let us have a battle."
When Tiâmat heard these words,
She acted like one possessed; she lost her senses.
Tiâmat shrieked wild piercing cries.
Trembling, her whole frame shook to its very foundations.
She uttered an incantation, she pronounced her spell;
And the gods of the battle put into action their weapons.
To the fight they came on; to the battle they advanced.
The lord spread out his net, and inclosed her.
The evil wind that was behind [him], he let loose in her face
As Tiâmat opened her mouth to its full extent,
He drove in the evil wind, before she could shut her lips.
The terrible winds filled her belly.
Her courage left her, and her mouth she opened wide.
He seized the spear, and burst her belly;
He severed her inward-parts; he pierced her heart.
He overpowered her, and cut off her life;
He threw down her body, and stood upon it.

After he had slain Tiâmat, her helpers turned back, and to save their lives took to flight, but he captured them in the net, and held them in bondage. The eleven monsters he placed in fetters, and trampled them under his feet. Kingu was conquered; after which he took from him the tablets of destiny, upon which he fixed his seal, and put them upon his own breast. He then turned to the conquered Tiâmat. With his merciless club he smashed her skull, and made the north wind bear away her blood to secret places. This his fathers saw, who rejoiced and were glad. As the victor gazed upon her carcass he devised a clever plan:

> He split her up like a flat(?) fish into two parts.
> He took one half and established a covering for heaven.
> He arranged a bolt; he stationed a watchman;
> And that her waters come not forth he commanded them.
> He crossed over the heavens; he inspected the regions.
> Before the abyss he built a dwelling for Nudimmud [i. e., the god Ea], etc.

The fifth tablet, which is quite fragmentary, describes the creation, and the fixing of the heavenly bodies.

> He made the stations for the great gods;
> The stars, their images, the constellations he fixed.
> He ordained the year, and into sections he divided it;
> The twelve months he fixed by three stars;
> And after the days of the year he fixed by . . . .
> He established the station of Nibir to determine their bounds,
> In order that none might err, or go astray.
> The stations of Bêl, and of Ea, he established along with him.
> He opened gates on both sides;
> He strengthened the bolt on the left, and on the right.
> In the midst of it he fixed the zenith;
> Nannar [the Moon god] he caused to shine forth; the night he entrusted [to him].
> He appointed him a luminary for the night, to determine the days;
> Monthly, without ceasing, with the disc he fashioned [it, saying]:
> At the beginning of the month, as thou riseth upon the land,
> The horns are to announce the fixing of the six days.
> On the seventh day, half the disc, etc.

68 Light on the Old Testament

The greater portion of this tablet is fragmentary. It is supposed to have referred to the creation of the earth and vegetation.

Unfortunately only the beginning of the sixth tablet has been preserved; but there is enough to

Fragment of the Sixth Tablet of the Babylonian Creation Series, Recording the Creation of Man.

show that it refers to the creation of man, in order that the gods might have worshipers.[1]

> When Marduk heard the words of the gods,
> His heart prompted him, and he devised [a cunning plan].[1]

---

[1] The restoration and translation follow King, The Seven Tablets of Creation.

The Babylonian Creation Story 69

He opened his mouth and unto Ea he spoke,
[That which] he had conceived in his heart he imparted [unto him]:
"My blood will I take and bone will I [fashion];
I will make man, that man may . . . . . .".
I will create man who shall inhabit [the earth],
That the service of the gods may be established and that [their] shrines [may be built].

The seventh tablet, known as the tablet of the fifty names of Marduk, is entirely devoted to the glorification of this deity by the other gods as well as by mankind, for his wonderful achievements. In the poem he is set forth as the creator of the heavens and earth, the giver of fulness and abundance, who bestowed mercy upon mankind, and who shepherds the gods. The epilogue is an appeal to the wise and the understanding to study the poem, to remember Marduk's deeds, to teach them, and to rejoice in him.

There are passages in the poetical portions of the Old Testament which Professor Gunkel of Berlin has brought together, in his work "*Schöpfung und Chaos,*" to show that in Israel such a conflict, prior to the creation, was known, although it is not mentioned in Genesis. Jahweh is represented as having contended with a great primeval monster, who is called in some passages Rahab, and in others Leviathan, Tihom, and the Dragon. This being seems to symbolize the chaos, or to personify the primeval ocean, which preceded the creation. In this conflict the hostile creature and its helpers are

70   Light on the Old Testament

overthrown, after which the heavens and earth are created. The most noteworthy of these passages follow:

Psalm 89: 9.   When the waves thereof arise, thou [Jahweh] stillest them.
Thou hast broken Rahab in pieces, as one that is slain;
Thou hast scattered thine enemies with the arm of thy strength.
The heavens are thine, the earth also is thine:
The world and the fulness thereof, thou has founded them.
The north and the south, thou hast created them.

The prophet in his appeal for deliverance cries:

Isaiah 51: 9   Arise, arise put on strength, O arm of Jahweh;
Arise as in the days of old, the generations of ancient times.
Art thou not he who cut Rahab in pieces, pierced the dragon?
Art thou not he who dried up the sea, the waters of the great Tihom,
Who made the depths of the sea a way for the redeemed to pass over?

The last verse manifestly is an allusion to the passage of the Red Sea, which the writer added to his cosmological references.

Job 26: 12   He stirreth up the sea with his power,
And by his understanding he smiteth through Rahab.
By his spirit the heavens are garnished;
His hand hath pierced the swift serpent.

The Babylonian Creation Story 71

Psalm 74: 13 Thou didst divide the sea by thy strength:
Thou brakest the heads of the dragons in the waters.
Thou breakest the heads of Leviathan in pieces. . .
The day is thine, the night also is thine:
Thou hast prepared the light and the sun.
Thou hast set all the borders of the earth:
Thou hast made summer and winter.

These and other passages, which are quoted in this connection by Gunkel, show that there existed in Israel the belief that, preceding the creation of the heavens and the earth, there was a great struggle between Jahweh and some primeval monster, with whom were associated other beings termed dragons.

The first chapter of Genesis contains some elements which are similar to the Babylonian legend. The latter contains references to the creation of the earth; to the heavenly bodies, as well as their purpose, namely, to rule by day and night; and finally to the creation of man. Doubtless, if the tablets were complete, the creation of the living creatures of the land and sea, besides other details mentioned in Genesis, could be found; some of these were actually given by the Greek historian Berosus (about 300 B. C.), who in his day, doubtless closely reproduced the Babylonian legend. But these resemblances are not remarkable, for we should expect them to occur in any two stories of the creation that might be written, although from entirely different quarters, and having absolutely no connection with each other. The creation story of Genesis, while it makes no reference to the conflict between Jahweh and the primeval power referred to in other parts of the Old Testament, does mention a chaotic state, an abyss of waters, prior to the creation of the heavens and the earth. The word translated "deep" (*Tihom*, Genesis 1:2), by which is meant the primeval ocean, is generally recognized to be the same as the Babylonian *Ti'âmat* or *Tiâmat*, which is equivalent to the feminine of the Hebrew *Tihom*. The absence of the definite article in Genesis, as well as elsewhere in the Old Testament, would seem to indicate that the word was also regarded as a proper name. The dividing asunder of Tiâmat's carcass, one part of which was used as a cover to keep back the upper waters, and the other half, as the version of Berosus adds, formed the earth, suggests the Hebrew *raqîa'* "firmament," which "divided the waters which were under the firmament from the waters which were above the firmament." But, as stated, Genesis makes no reference to a conflict which God, the Creator, had with *Tihom* prior to the creation of the heavens and the earth. The passages from other books of the Old Testament, however, cited by Professor Gunkel, manifestly do refer to such a conflict.

Upon the differences of the two stories we need not dwell. The crude polytheistic grotesqueness of the Babylonian, with its doctrine of emanation or evolution from chaos to order, which makes the gods

The Babylonian Creation Story 73

emerge from this chaos, or brings the firmaments out of a carcass, put it altogether into another class; and it is in no respect to be compared with the dignified and sublime conception of the beginning of things, with God as the supreme Creator, who called all things into existence. Further, its crude references to the creation are only incidentally a part of the epic. Its manifest purpose is to magnify the god Marduk, in order to give him pre-eminence above the other gods. To this end he is regarded not only as the creator of the universe, with all its phenomena and the laws which control it, but he is made the supreme one of all the gods. In short, a more appropriate title for the epic would be, The story of Marduk and the Dragon.

The question uppermost in the minds of those who take these things into consideration is, What relation has the one account to the other? Three possibilities are usually recognized: The Hebrew borrowed from the Babylonian; or the Babylonian borrowed from the Hebrew; or they have a common origin.

It is admitted that the Babylonian belongs to a period even prior to Abraham. Besides other reasons it might be mentioned that the fight was a favorite theme of Babylonian art centuries before the patriarch's day. In consequence, scholars generally conclude that the Babylonians did not borrow from the Hebrews. In support of their contention that the reverse is true, the close relation of the biblical and Babylonian deluge stories is cited, as well as the fact that Babylonian literature, to a certain degree, pervaded the West-land, especially in the period when its language was used for diplomatic and friendly intercourse between nations. This is evident from the discovery of Babylonian myths in Egypt, used as exercises to learn the Babylonian language in the Amarna period (see page 253). Further, some scholars fix its ultimate origin in Babylonia because of the idea of the watery chaos, inasmuch as that country was subject to great inundations; and because *tiâmat* is the Babylonian word for sea as well as the name of the monster.

While these arguments, if carefully analyzed, will be found to have at least some force, it is not at all impossible that at some time, perhaps long before the patriarch's day, this legend found its way from Babylonia to Palestine. It may have been transmitted by Abraham himself. That being true, such borrowing or making use of what preceded is in no respect foreign to the principle of Israel, which utilized in its own spirit for the embodiment of religious truths that which even had its origin in antiquity (see page 12); so that it might be held, with some scholars, that while there are only faint traces of that which is similar to the conflict in Genesis, the omission may be due to the fact that the story has been purified or transformed, during a long period of naturalization, when it was made to harmonize with Israel's theological conceptions.

The Babylonian Creation Story

And yet it is also quite within the range of possibility and reasonableness to conceive the idea that both stories have a common origin among the Semites, who entered Babylonia prior to their amalgamation with the Sumerians, and who may have also carried their traditions into Palestine. Contrary to the view held by some critics, that the Hebrew story belongs to the time of the exile or after, there are indications that it belongs to a great antiquity. And it is also possible that in some way, unknown to us, it had been handed down in a form more or less free from the fantastically polytheistic features of the Babylonian version.

Between two and three millenniums before Abraham, Semites entered the Tigro-Euphrates valley, after which the amalgamation of the Sumerian and Semitic cultures began, resulting in what we call Babylonian. Whence these Semites came, no one knows. Some scholars conjecture that their original home was Arabia; others, Armenia. In Abraham's age there was another Semitic invasion, as is attested by the many names of the Western Semites (see page 146). In the late Achæmenian period we find the country again filled with these people (see Chap. XV). Taking these things into consideration, it is not impossible that the idea of a conflict with this primeval power of darkness, which perhaps is echoed in the New Testament doctrine of evil angels, was brought into Shinar or Babylonia, as well as into Palestine by the Semites themselves;

in which case it would have found its way into Canaan millenniums prior to the time the story assumed the form in which it is preserved in the Old Testament.

For the present, however, in the absence of any light on the subject from archeological sources, we can only point to the relation of the one story to the other, the fact that the Babylonians possessed the tradition prior to the beginnings of Israel, and then add our hypotheses. But we insist that it must be clear that there are no grounds for the radical conjectures on the subject made by some scholars; and that while we are compelled to unlearn some things, and set aside certain traditional views, absolutely nothing has been found which compels the Christian to lessen his respect and admiration for the sublime story of the creation which has been handed down to us by the Hebrews.

IV

THE BABYLONIAN DELUGE STORY

The story of Gilgamesh (formerly known as Izdubar and also Nimrod) was a great national epic of Babylonia. It consisted of twelve tablets which contained about three thousand lines of inscription. The fragments which have been found of this work show that they represent four different copies; and that they belonged to the Library of Ashurbanipal, in Nineveh.[1] This is determined by the colophons found on several of the tablets.

At some early date, presumably before the ascendancy of Babylon (2100 B. C.), a number of myths and current traditions were brought together and woven into one long epic, which narrates the exploits of Gilgamesh. The eleventh tablet, which is a separate episode, is especially interesting to biblical students, as it contains the Babylonian story

---

[1] The late George Smith, in 1872, made the first translation of this epic. Only about one half of the story has been recovered up to the present time. In 1885 Professor Delitzsch published the text of the section dealing with the deluge. This was followed in 1890 by a critical edition of the entire text by Professor Paul Haupt. More recent translations worthy of note have been made by Dr. A. Jeremias and Professor Jensen.

of the deluge. Most nations of antiquity have preserved a flood story, but the only one which has any close resemblance to the biblical is this one, namely, the Babylonian. The following are extracts from the eleventh tablet:

> Ut-napishtim said to him, even to Gilgamesh;
> Let me reveal unto thee, O Gilgamesh, a secret story,
> And the decree of the gods let me relate to thee!
> Shurippak, a city which thou knowest,
> On the bank of the Euphrates is situated;
> That city was old when the gods within it
> To bring about a flood their hearts urged them, even the great gods.
> In it, their father Anu, their counselor, the warrior Bêl,
> Their herald, Ninib;
> Their champion, Ennugi;
> Ea, the lord of glowing wisdom, had argued with them, and
> Their purpose he repeated to a Reed-house:
> Reed-house! Reed-house! Wall! Wall!
> Reed-house, hear; and Wall, give attention!
> Man of Shurippak, son of Ubar-Tutu,
> Build a house, construct a ship!
> Leave possessions, seek life!
> Abandon property, and preserve life!
> Cause to go into the ship seed of life of every kind!
> As for the ship which thou shalt build,
> Let its dimensions be measured.
> Let its breadth and its length be proportioned to each other.
> Into the deep launch it!
> I understood, and said unto Ea my lord:
> "The command, my lord, which thou speakest thus,
> I will honor, I will fulfil it!

The Babylonian Deluge Story. The Eleventh Tablet of the Gilgamesh Epic.

But what shall I answer to the city, the people and the elders?"
Ea opened his mouth, and said:
He said to me his servant:
Man, thou shalt thus answer them:
Bêl hath rejected me and hateth me.
I will not dwell in your city,
And on the land of Bêl I will show no [more] my countenance,
I will go down to the deep; with Ea, my lord, will I live.
. . . .
On the fifth day I constructed its frame;
Its sides were 140 cubits high;
Its deck was likewise 140.
I laid down its form, I fashioned it;
I divided its hull(?) into six sections
I divided its upper deck into seven compartments;
Its main deck I divided into nine chambers.
With water-pegs on the inside I caulked it.
I selected a mast; and added all that was necessary.
Six *sars* of bitumen I smeared over the outside.
Three *sars* of bitumen I smeared over the inside.
. . . .
With all that I possessed I loaded it;
With all the gold I had I loaded it;
With all that I had of the seed of life of every kind I loaded it;
I put into the ship all my family and my dependents;
The cattle of the field, the beasts of the field, craftsmen, all of them I brought up.
Shamash had fixed a time [saying]:
"When the sender of darkness at night shall send a destructive rain,
Enter into the ship and close the door!"
That time arrived.
The sender of darkness at even sent a destructive rain.
I looked upon the appearance of the day;
I was afraid to look upon the day.

The Babylonian Deluge Story

I entered the ship, and closed the door.
To the pilot of the ship, to Buzur-Bêl, the sailor,
I entrusted the great house, together with its freight.
When the first break of dawn appeared,
There rose from the horizon a black cloud;
In which Rammân thundered.
. . . .
Like a battle against the people it came on.
A brother could not look after his brother.
The people in heaven could not be seen.
Even the gods were afraid of the flood, and
They retreated; they ascended to the heaven of Anu.
The gods cowered like dogs; in terror they lay down.
Ishtar screamed like a woman in travail;
The lady wailed with a loud voice [saying]:
"Oh, that the former day had been turned to clay,
When I in the assembly of the gods had advised this evil.
Yea, when I ordered the tempest for the destruction of my people.
I truly will give birth to my people [again], and
Like a fish brood will I fill the sea."
The gods of the Anunnaki wept with her;
The gods were downcast, they sat weeping;
Closed their lips . . . .
Six days and nights,
The wind continued; flood and tempest overwhelmed the land.
At the approach of the seventh day, the tempest, the flood and the storm which had raged like *khalti* subsided.
The sea became quiet, the tempest ceased, and the flood was over.
I looked upon the sea, [its] voice was fixed (silent);
And all mankind had returned to mud.
And as the light of day advanced, I prayed.
I opened the window, and the light fell upon my cheeks.

I collapsed, I sat weeping.
Over my cheeks (wall of my nose) flowed my tears.
I looked upon the quarters of the expanse of the sea.
After the twelfth [double-hour?] a land appeared.
On mount Nizir the ship grounded.
Mount Nizir held the ship, and did not suffer it to move.
The first day, the second day, Mount Nizir held, etc.
The third day, the fourth day, Mount Nizir held, etc.
A fifth, a sixth, Mount Nizir held, etc.
As the seventh day approached
I brought out a dove, [and] let it go.
The dove went forth, [but] turned;
A resting-place there was not, and it returned.
I brought out a swallow, [and] let it go.
The swallow went forth, [but] turned;
A resting-place there was not, and it returned.
I brought out a raven, [and] let it go:
The raven went forth; it noticed the drying up of the water, and
It ate, waded,(?) croaked, but did not return.
Then I brought out [everything] to the four winds; [and] I offered a sacrifice.
I prepared a libation upon the summit of the mountain.
Seven by seven *adagur* pots I set.
Into them I poured reeds, cedar-wood and myrtle.
The gods smelt the savor,
[Yea], the gods smelt the sweet savor;
The gods swarmed like flies over the sacrificer.
As soon as the lady of the gods drew nigh,
She lifted up the great gems, which Anu had made according to her wish.
"These gods, verily, by the precious stone of my neck I will never forget,
These days, truly I will remember, I will never forget.
Let the gods come to the offering.
Bêl [however] shall not come to the offering.

The Babylonian Deluge Story

Because, without taking counsel, he caused the deluge,
And numbered my people for destruction."
[But] as soon as Bêl appeared, he saw the ship. Bêl was wroth.
He was filled with anger [like that] of the gods,— the Igigi.
"Has any soul escaped?
Not a man was to escape from destruction."
[Then] Ninib opened his mouth and spoke,
Saying to the warrior Bêl:
"Who except Ea could have planned this thing!
For Ea knows all arts."

The so-called Babylonian Scene of the Fall of Man. An impression of a seal cylinder, with Sacred Tree, Fruit, and Serpent.

[Then] Ea opened his mouth and spoke, saying to the warrior Bêl:
"Thou sage of the gods, O warrior,
How, why, without taking counsel, didst thou cause a flood.
Upon the sinner, lay his sin!
Upon the guilty, lay his guilt!
[But] free [him]! let him not be cut off! draw . . .
Instead of thy causing a flood,
Let the lion come, and diminish mankind!
Instead of thy causing a flood,
Let the wolf come, and diminish mankind!

> Instead of thy causing a flood,
> Let famine break forth and devastate the land!
> Instead of thy causing a flood,
> Let pestilence come and slay mankind!"

. . . .

Shurippak, the scene in which the Babylonian story is pitched, has been identified as the mound known at the present time as Fara. The German government has conducted systematic excavations at this site,[1] and found antiquities of the earliest period immediately beneath the surface, showing that the city had been destroyed at a very early age, and that it had not been rebuilt.

It is apparent to all that the main features, as related in this epic, agree remarkably with those of the biblical deluge story. The most striking resemblances are: The deluge was intended as a punishment for sin; the command to build the ship according to certain dimensions, in order to preserve life; the division of the ship into three stories; the use of bitumen to make it water-tight; the preservation of the seed of all life; the way the deluge was brought to pass; the grounding of the ship on a mountain; the three sendings forth of birds; the destruction of all mankind except those in the ship;

---

[1] There is a small collection of antiquities from Fara in the Museum of the University of Pennsylvania, consisting of a number of objects in bronze, among which are two small swords; also several stone bowls, etc. These were gathered by Professor Hilprecht and Mr. Geere during the excavations at Nippur, which city is not far removed from Fara.

The Babylonian Deluge Story 85

the offering of a sacrifice on the mountain top; the smelling of the sweet savor; the assurance that another deluge would not occur because of sin;—besides other details, such as the hero of the Babylonian story being the tenth king, while Noah is the tenth patriarch.

The divergencies, are at the same time, not to be minimized, as they are almost immeasurable. Chief among them might be mentioned the exceedingly crude polytheism of the epic, which depicts the gods scheming to out-do one another; their cowering like dogs; or their crowding like flies around the sacrifice, after they smelled the savor. But taking all things into consideration, no one would presume to say that there does not exist any relation between the biblical and the Babylonian stories. And the question arises, Is the Babylonian dependent upon the biblical, or is the biblical dependent upon the Babylonian? and how is this dependence to be regarded?

In the first place, Did the Babylonians borrow their legend from the Israelites? Assuming the earliest date for the biblical, namely the Mosaic period, there is evidence to show that the Babylonians had the narrative centuries prior to this time. Babylonian civilization was millenniums old before the beginnings of Israel. This epic makes Bêl the chief god, and not Marduk, which is an indication that it belongs at least to the third millennium B. C. Then also in the fourth millennium, scenes from the

86   Light on the Old Testament

life of Gilgamesh were favorite themes for the seals of that early age (see illustration below). But more important than all else, in this connection, is the fact that a version of the deluge story has been found, which from the character of the writing, and the date which is given on it, clearly shows that it was written in the reign of Ammi-zaduga of the first dynasty of Babylon, or about 2000 B. C. These facts make it impossible to regard the story as indigenous to Israel.

Tablet and Envelope (Sargonic period), with Scene from Gilgamesh epic.

An answer which is frequently given to these inquiries is that there is a common origin for both. Doubtless this is true, and even that the story was current for a long time among both peoples prior to its being fashioned in the forms in which it has been handed down (see the discussion concerning the Creation story, page 75). But in the absence of any document to substantiate this, we confine ourselves to the relation of the one to the other.

The Babylonian Deluge Story 87

There are other reasons besides those already mentioned for believing that this story is indigenous to the land that we know as Babylonia. Its geographical setting and its local coloring point to that region. Further, the fact that there are Babylonian elements in the Creation, Eden, Babel, and other early biblical stories, seems to lead to the conclusion that Babylonia is not only the country of these scenes, and the home of Israel's founder, but that the earliest origin of some of the narratives, at least, which constitute the Hebrew literature, dealing with the period prior to the patriarch's leaving his ancestral home, *i. e.* Ur, belongs to that region.

It is not, however, necessary to hold with certain Assyriologists, that the biblical writer must have had the Babylonian version before him. In some shape or other, the tradition doubtless was transmitted to Palestine, perhaps in the days of Hammurabi, when Babylonia became the suzerain power of that land, or even later. And in that region it had an independent development, taking on, as it were, a Palestinian color. The rhythmical setting in which it appears is an indication that it was already old when put into its present form. When, therefore, the biblical writer made use of the traditions, current among his people, and used them in the spirit of his monotheism, and made them instruments whereby religious truths were set forth, showing the judgments of God upon corrupt mankind and the blessings bestowed upon the righteous, they were placed on an altogether different plane; in fact, the difference between the old and the new became immeasurable. This use of what the people actually had as their own peculiar possession, doubtless after it had passed through a period of naturalization, is but another illustration of the great principle according to which the teachers of Israel dealt with the people.

V

THE TOWER OF BABEL AND THE BABYLONIAN TEMPLE

The story of Babel in Genesis is the story of the building of a Babylonian ziggurrat, or temple-tower. Every city of prominence in ancient Babylonia had its temple, and every temple had its tower. The Ziggurrat Bâbili, or Etemenanki, is the tower of the temple at Babylon, which is the biblical Tower of Babel.

The story in Genesis is strikingly Babylonian in its coloring and details. "As they journeyed from the East," they found a valley in the land of Shinar. The earliest inhabitants of the valley, known to us, were the Shumerians or Sumerians, a people that spoke a non-Semitic language. The derivation of the name, Shinar, doubtless is from *Shungir*, usually written *Girsu*. The physiognomy of these people, determined by the remains of their art which have been recovered, some hold, clearly shows them to be a non-Semitic race. They were the originators of the peculiar cult of the valley, which belonged to the early period. They were the founders of the great cities and temples; they were the inventors of the pictorial writing, out of which the cuneiform was developed; they created a literature, and an art; they constructed palaces, and they formulated laws.

The Sumerian language is an agglutinative tongue, and, as is generally understood, is the language of the early pre-Semitic inhabitants of the southern part of the Tigro-Euphrates valley. The Semites who entered the land adopted the cuneiform writing of these people. They utilized many of the old Sumerian values as phonograms, and gave the characters additional values peculiar to their own tongue.

This language was first called Accadian. Professor Sayce, whose philological insight has advanced so materially the science of Assyriology during the last four decades, deciphered in 1870 the first Sumerian inscription. He was followed by Oppert and Lenormant, who greatly advanced the knowledge of the language. The latter published a grammar, calling the language Accadian. In 1874, Joseph Halévy, who had gained great distinction as an Orientalist, advanced the theory that this ideographic system of writing was arbitrarily arranged or invented by the Assyrian priests, and that it was for the purpose of mystifying the people in their rituals. While finding some adherents for his cryptographic hypothesis, Halévy's position was strongly combated by Lenormant, Oppert, Jensen, Haupt, Bezold, Sayce, Hommel and Zimmern. Professor Haupt, who has been styled "the father of Sumerian etymology," by his publication *Die sumerischen*

Familiengesetze, in 1879, put the study of the language upon a scientific basis. Professor Bezold actually found on an Assyrian tablet that *Eme-ku*, which in non-Semitic texts means,"the land Shumer," was explained *li-sha-an Shu-me-ri*, "language of Shumer." In 1892, Lehman published a work that gave an additional death-blow to Halévy's theory. The translations of Sumerian inscriptions by Thureau-Dangin and others, left little doubt generally that the Sumeriologists were right in their contentions for the linguistic character of the language. Eventually Delitzsch, who for a time joined the ranks of Halévy, abandoned the theory; and although some scholars still adhere to it, and continue to present philological, ethnological and archeological difficulties for the Sumeriologist, and even attempt to show that the entire cuneiform syllabary and literature is Semitic, as has recently been done by Doctor Brünnow[1], the controversy is generally regarded as practically closed.[2]

---

[1] See Jastrow, A new aspect of the Sumerian question, American Journal of Semitic Languages, Vol. XXII, No. 2.

[2] For a complete discussion of this problem, see Weissbach, *Die Sumerische Frage*. Also see Prince, Sumerian Lexicon, p. VII ff., or Rogers, History of Babylonia and Assyria, Vol. I, p. 200 ff. Besides the Sumerian grammar by Lenormant, two others have been published more recently by Professors Haupt and Hommel, while Professor Prince has begun the publication of a Sumerian dictionary, the first part of which has appeared in *Assyriologische Bibliothek*, edited by Professors Delitzsch and Haupt.

Light on the Old Testament

The earliest known inscriptions that have been discovered, show that the Semites had already encroached upon the land of the Sumerians.[1] Whether the few lines preserved in Genesis concerning the building of Babel echo the early deeds of these invaders, of course cannot be determined. Exactly whence they came is a much debated question. What their system of writing was, is not known; as mentioned above, they are found to have adopted the script of the Sumerians. It is better understood what their religion was, for their pantheon of gods must have resembled, at least in a general way, that of the Sumerians, for we find Semitic equivalents introduced for the gods of that people. For instance, the writing for *Enlil* of the Sumerians was used for the Semitic Bêl. *Ninâ* must have been equivalent to the Semitic Ishtar. The culture of the Sumerians seems to have been absorbed by the Semites, but it received a significance, of course, in accord with their own ideas. A number of cities, among them Lagash, the modern Telloh, preserved the Sumerian culture and tongue, until the end of their history. At Nippur Semitic inscriptions are found as early as Urumush and Sargon, but the language of the religious and legal

---

[1] As this volume goes to press I learn that Eduard Meyer will publish very shortly in the *Berliner Akademie*, an important monograph on Early Babylonian Art, which will contain a new theory about the earliest relations of Sumerians and Semites in Babylonia.

The Tower of Babel

literature generally continued to be Sumerian through the first dynasty of Babylon. At Sippara and Babylon the people seem to have come sooner under Semitic influence; and as a result, we have not only a mixed cultus, but also a mixed people, that we call Babylonian. While the Sumerian language was supplanted by the Semitic, the scribes and priests continued to use it up to the close of Babylonian history; especially as the liturgical language in the temple service. In the Hammurabi dynasty, as well as in the Cassite, many legal phrases in the contract literature continued to be written in Sumerian. In the neo-Babylonian period these have disappeared. Semitic Babylonian was doubtless the language in the common life of Abraham's day. We can, therefore, safely conjecture that this was the native tongue of the patriarch, if he was born in Babylonia.

Shumer, or Shinar, is an alluvial plain, where the building material was "brick instead of stone." For their building operations bricks were used almost entirely. The stone that is found by the excavators had been imported from other regions, notably from along the Euphrates to the northwest of Babylonia (see also page 17). Owing to the fact that they burned them "thoroughly," and that they were like stone, some of the bricks were used again and again by the different builders in Babylonian history. The average edifice in Babylonia seems to have been built with adobes. Mud plaster pre-

94   Light on the Old Testament

served them intact for centuries if the walls were regularly cared for. Most of the great towers of the land in the early period were also constructed with mud bricks, being faced wholly or partially with kiln-dried bricks, in order to protect them from the elements.

One of the Asphalt Springs near Hit which furnished the "slime" (Asphalt) used by the builders of Babel instead of mortar.

The word translated "slime," in the story of Babel, which they used for mortar, means "bitumen." It has been ascertained that, especially in the early period, this material was used to lay up their bricks; and so securely did it hold together that in separating them, in the present day, six to eight millen-

The Tower of Babel

niums later, the bricks themselves are often broken. In the neighborhood of Hit, some fifty miles to the northwest of Babylon, springs of bitumen are found. They are in fact springs of water, on the surface of which collects a thick scum of asphalt. Frequently the spring is seen in a state of ebullition. The bitumen gathered by the people is used for various purposes, as, for instance, they pitch with it the inside of their pottery vessels, which are intended to retain liquid; they pitch on the inside and outside of their boats; they mix it with other material for roofing, and, in general, use it for mortar.

The city that the people intended to build is known in the inscriptions as Bâbilu (Babylon). In the Old Testament the name was "called Babel; because Jahweh did there confound the language of all the earth" (Gen. 11:9). In view of the fact that the Babylonians interpreted the name as meaning "Gate of God" (*Bâb-ili*), scholars generally claim that the Hebrew etymology is incorrect; and therefore the name cannot be derived from the Hebrew root *babal*, "to confuse." Driver says: "It is simply a popular etymology, which lent itself conveniently to the purpose which the narrator had in hand."[1] Those who believe in a literal interpretation of this part of the story might claim that "Gate of God" is a popular etymology of the Sumerians and Babylonians. But the root, *babal*, "to confuse,"

---

[1] Compare his Commentary on Genesis, p. 136.

has not been found in Babylonian; and the name Babel in the earliest known reference to the city is understood by the writer of the inscription to mean "Gate of God," which is ascertained from the ideographic characters used. The expression in Genesis, therefore, until more light is thrown upon the subject, must be understood accordingly.

Already, in 1743, Carsten Niebuhr had definitely determined that the ruins of Babylon were situated near the modern Hillah. With Herodotus, however, he regarded Birs-Nimrud, on the eastern bank of the Euphrates, to be the Tower of Babel. Even at the present time, views of this mound with its peaked projection are used to show the present appearance of the ruins of the famous tower. In a building inscription of Nebuchadrezzar, translated some decades ago, the great builder said:

> At that time, Euriminanki, the ziggurrat of Borsippa, which a former king had constructed, forty-two cubits he had projected it upwards, but had not raised its head. From a distant day it had collapsed; its gutters had not been kept clear; rain and tempest had torn away its bricks; the facing bricks had opened. The mud bricks of its interior [body] were fallen together like a heap. The great god Marduk made me disposed to restore it.

This inscription seemed to offer proof for the correctness of the theory. But it is now definitely known that Birs-Nimrud—or what remains of the Ziggurrat Euriminanki, of the temple of Ezida sacred to the god Nebo, which was in Borsippa, the

The Tower of Babel

twin city of Babylon—was not the biblical tower, but that, as said before, the Ziggurrat Bâbili of the latter city, is the Tower of Babel.

With Nippur, Erech, and Eridu, Babel is mentioned in one of the Babylonian creation legends, as having been founded by the god Marduk. This, however, savors of the same influence which made Marduk the supreme god in the creation story. According to the inscriptions, Babylon did not occupy a position as prominent among the cities of Early Babylonia, prior to Hammurabi's time, as, for instance, Nippur, Erech, Ur, etc. The statement (Genesis 10:10) that "the beginning of his [Nimrod's] kingdom was Babel, and Erech, and Accad, and Calneh [Nippur]" would imply, that perhaps it was a city of great antiquity, inasmuch as the others are known to be such. But as the excavations have not revealed any light, as yet, on the "mighty hunter before Jahweh" and also because his operations were extended to cities of Assyria, among them Nineveh, which is first mentioned in the time of Hammurabi, it would seem that he was a great conqueror, such as Sargon or Hammurabi; and that he had established a kingdom, which in the beginning was composed of certain cities, but not necessarily in the earliest age.

The excavations by the Germans at Babel have not revealed antiquities of the very early period, due to the fact that they did not reach the strata which contain them, and also because some of the portions excavated had only been developed in the late centuries of the city's history, when it had grown greatly in extent. The earliest reference to Babylon in the inscriptions is in the time of Sargon I, 3800 B. C. The kings of the first dynasty of Babylon made it their capital. Babylon thereafterwards became the great religious center of the country instead of Nippur, where Bêl, the father of the gods, had received the obeisance of kings and emperors for millenniums, and as a result, Babylon was built up at the expense of Nippur. In the old epics, which glorified Bêl, the name of Marduk, the patron deity of Babylon, was substituted (see page 62). The city continued to be the great metropolis of the country, until the close of its history, after the time of Alexander the Great.

The history of Babylon's great temple, Esagila, and its tower or ziggurrat will in time be comparatively fully written. Whether any reference to its original builders will be known is questionable. Like the origin of other temples and their towers, its founding may always be shrouded in obscurity. The first reference to it is in an inscription of Sumula-ilu, the second king of the first dynasty of Babylon (about 2200 B. C.). We learn that he built a "glorious temple" for Marduk, and made a magnificent throne of gold and silver for the god, besides a statue of his consort Sarpanîtum. Zabium, his son, is credited with having built Esagila, which is the name of the temple. In the ancient language

The Tower of Babel 99

of the land, the Sumerian, it means "house with a lofty head." *E* means "house," *sag*, "head," and *ila*, "lofty." The name may refer to the ziggurrat, or tower, which was the prominent feature of the temple precincts. Zabium's reference to Esagila doubtless means that he restored the temple. Similar language has been employed by others in this connection. It is, of course, not impossible that it was at that time brought into existence, perhaps in connection with the tower which was much older. The fane of Babylon, referred to in the time of Sargon I, is called the temple *A-E*.

In different periods, Esagila had been sacked, and the statues of the gods carried to other lands, from whence they were in time returned. The Cassite kings who ruled over Babylonia carried Marduk to distant Khani. In later years Agumkakrime, the seventh king of the dynasty, brought him back and restored him, in all his splendor, to his original place in the temple. About 1300 B. C., Tukulti-Ninib destroyed the city, plundered Esagila, and carried the statue off to Assyria. In 689 B. C., Sennacherib, having suffered many annoyances on the part of the Babylonians by their repeated rebellions, his patience became exhausted, decided upon the obliteration of the city. He sacked and laid waste the temples, and carried the god away. He says he razed the temple to the ground, and threw its bricks into the canal Arachtu. He cut channels through the city, and flooded it with water, so that the destruction might be so complete that no man could find the site of the city, and the temple of the gods.

The excavations, however, reveal the fact that the destruction was not so very complete, for we know that his son and successor, Esarhaddon, after a period of ten years, began to rebuild the city and the temple. Death interfered with the latter's labors, which were carried on to completion by his son Ashurbanipal (668–626 B. C.). After the sanctuary was restored and richly embellished with gold, silver, and precious stones, Ashurbanipal surrendered the sovereignty of the temple to the god Marduk, after an absence of his statue for twenty-one years.

Hammurabi had doubtless rebuilt the temple on a scale unrivaled in his day, as had also his successors. But greater splendor in connection with any Babylonian temple was scarcely manifested than that of Esagila and its tower, in the days of Nabopolassar and his son Nebuchadrezzar (see Chapter XIV).

Xerxes, after his return from Greece, as we are told by Arrian, again destroyed the temple, thinking that it was poorly placed in the city. Although Alexander the Great collected a great army of workmen, intending to rebuild it upon its old site, the doings of Xerxes practically proved the end of Esagila, as Alexander died after he had torn down what remained of the ancient sanctuary. Antiochus I considered himself the patron of Esagila, yet as

Simpson's Picture (Reconstruction) of the Temple Esagila and its ziggurrat, the "Tower of Babel."

far as is known, the temple and its tower had not been rebuilt in the years subsequent to the reign of Alexander. It became a ruin-heap, and for nearly two millenniums its ruins, as well as others in Babylon, have furnished building-material for towns that have been built up in its vicinity, such as Seleucia, Ctesiphon, Bagdad, and Hillah. Burnt bricks, bearing the titles of the builders of ancient Babylon, are found everywhere in the buildings of these cities. Notwithstanding this ruthless plunder, most important architectural results have been obtained of other buildings by the Germans, who have spent five years in excavating the city.

To this brief sketch might be added extracts from the interesting detailed account which Herodotus gives us of the Temple Belos, *i.e.*, the Temple of Bêl-Marduk, or Esagila. He describes the tower (*i.e.*, E-temen-an-ki, the Ziggurrat Bâbili, or the Tower of Babel), as consisting of eight stages. In numbering them, he included the platform upon which the whole structure rested. In reality there were seven stages in the late period. The top, he tells us, was reached by gradually rising ascents along the sides of the platforms; so that by walking around and around, the summit was reached. Near the middle of the ascent the priests and worshipers found a resting-place. Upon the top of the uppermost platform, a room or shrine was built. In it there was a couch and golden table. It is thought they believed that the god Marduk dwelt there.

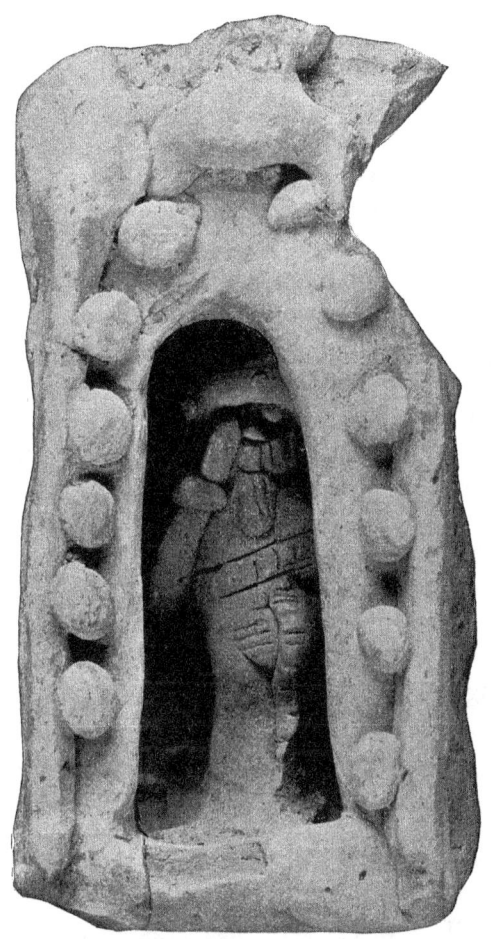

Terra-cotta Household Shrine of Bêl, found at Nippur.
(*Natural size.*)

Below, *i.e.*, in the court about the tower, there was another shrine, in which the statue of the god made of gold was found. Herodotus named the god Zeus, meaning Marduk, and represented him as sitting in a chair of gold. His table and footstool were also of the same material.

Such in brief is an outline of what is now known of the history of the "Tower of Babel." As the excavations are continued, and the inscriptions are forced to reveal their secrets, more and more completely will its history be unfolded.

The excavations conducted by the University of Pennsylvania at Nippur within the temple area, throw considerable light upon Babylonian temples and ziggurrats. As is well known, the sanctuary of Bêl, to whom most of the early rulers did obeisance, and from whom they acknowledged they had received their authority and power, was perhaps the most important in the valley. The mound covering this ancient sanctuary rises to the height of ninety feet above the plain. The highest point, as was readily recognized when the excavations were begun, covered the ziggurrat, or storied-tower of the temple. A section of this mound, perhaps one-quarter of the temple area, was excavated by Haynes through all the different strata down to virgin soil. For convenience' sake let us begin with a stratum in the center of the mound; then consider briefly those which lie above it; afterwards those which lie below.

The Tower of Babel 105

In this middle stratum we have evidence of immense operations by the famous temple-builder Ur-Engur, who lived about 2700 B. C. A great many

Stamped brick of Ur-Engur, 2700 B. C.

of his bricks, which are about twelve inches square and about four inches in thickness, have this inscription: "Ur-Engur, king of Ur, king of Accad, and Shumer, the man who built the house of Bêl."

In the accompanying illustration, the ziggurrat as he restored it is seen. It was the most prominent feature of the temple architecture. It occupied about one-third of the inner court. In this early age, it probably had three stages, which rose in diminishing sizes, one superimposed upon the other. Dr. Haynes reported that the lowest was twenty feet high, the second thirteen, while the upper was so much destroyed that exact measurements could not be taken; but it was approximately about ten feet high. On the top of the whole mass a shrine doubtless stood, such as Herodotus tells us was on the tower at Babylon. The platforms were in the shape of right-angle parallelograms, the lower being 169 feet long by 106 feet wide, with the corners pointing approximately to the four cardinal points. With the exception of the facing wall, this large structure was built of sun-dried bricks, and as far as is known had no chamber or cavity, but was solid. To carry off water from the platforms, conduits of burnt brick were built in the middle of three of the sides of the ziggurrat. These Haynes found only in the lower stage. Doubtless the upper stages had also been provided with them. These prevented the water from washing over the encasing walls, and in this way the structure was preserved. Gutters covered with bitumen surrounded the ziggurrat on all sides at the base, except in the front, to carry away the water. The ascent of some ziggurrats, especially of the late

Mound Covering the Nippur Tower as it appeared in 1893.

The Tower of Ekur, the Temple of Bêl, built by Ur-Engur (2700 B. C.) showing three stages.

period, were in all probability in the form of winding balustrades. The ziggurrat at Nippur had an immense causeway built out from the lower terrace on the front, at right angles to the face of the tower, leading into the open space of the court. It was built of two nearly parallel walls of burnt bricks. Crude bricks were filled in between these walls to form the ascent, which originally doubtless had steps, now no longer discernible. The means of ascent to the top of the platforms of the ziggurrat was only found to extend as high as the first stage. It was thought that the causeway which ascends only to the first stage was continued straight up to the top,[1] but Architect Fisher holds the view that there was a stairway from the first platform to the second, and the third, which was built parallel with the sides of the platforms.

Close by, on the northeast side of the ziggurrat, a wall was cleared on three sides of a structure belonging to the late period, more than 150 feet long, and over 100 feet wide. Two entrances were found facing the ziggurrat, the principal one, which was near the south corner, being ten and a half feet wide.[2] In excavating the ziggurrat and the later fortress, which was built on top of it, débris was piled high upon this part of the mound, as was

---

[1] This account of the ziggurrat is based on the reports and photographs by Haynes, of his work. See Hilprecht, The Babylonian Exp. of the University of Pennsylvania, Vol. I, part 2.

[2] See Hilprecht, Explorations in Bible Lands, p. 471f.

The Tower of Babel 109

quite natural, inasmuch as no facilities for removing the dirt to the plains beyond the mounds had been provided. This structure has been regarded as being the "house of Bêl," or the temple proper.[1] A future expedition will doubtless undertake the exploration of this part of the mound, when it can be determined what it represents. Owing to the fact that it belongs to the late period, it has not been included in the accompanying plan, page 114.

A portion of the walls serving as an enclosure of the precincts was excavated. In the southeastern wall of the court a large gate was found. The gate is quite similar to those found in Assyrian temples of the late period, but considerably smaller. The passage, though it is only six feet wide, is augmented by a series of stepped recesses on either side, which make it stand fourteen feet wide. These give it an imposing appearance. The depth of the gate was fifty-two feet, which included the thickness of both walls and the space between them. In the middle, on either side of the narrow passage-way, were the guard chambers. No gate-socket was found *in situ*, but one belonging to the great builder mentioned, namely Ur-Engur (2700 B. C.), was found almost directly over the old position of the gate, in an upper stratum, which contained antiquities of the age of Ashurbanipal (650 B. C.). This showed that as the accumulations of débris caused

---

[1] *Ibid*, p 472.

the surface of the temple area to rise, the gate and door-socket was elevated with it, and the entrance, two millenniums later, remained practically at the same place. It illustrates also the custom commonly found in the Orient, where door-sills and gate-sockets are reset at higher levels from time to time as the accumulations make it necessary (see page 33). In the plan, found on page 114, this gate, although belonging to the period long before Sargon, 3800 B. C., is incorporated, as it very likely was restored on a similar plan in later periods. It is an indication of the grandeur of the plan upon which the temple was laid out in the early age. Immediately in the rear of the ziggurrat there were slight indications of another gate.

Dr. Peters, in 1890, discovered to the southeast of this enclosure the remains of a small building which had two rooms. Its bricks were stamped one to three times upon the edges with a brief legend of Bur-Sin, king of Ur (about 2500 B. C.). It reads, "Bur-Sin the mighty king." He discovered two door-sockets *in situ* at the entrance of the two rooms, which record the fact that the structure was a temple or shrine called *Ki-shag-gul-la* Bur-Sin, "House of the delight of Bur-Sin," which the king dedicated to the god Bêl.

At the end of the wall to the west of the gate above described, a wall ran to the south. This was traced a short distance. A wall corresponding to the other was found extending also to the south of

Topographical map of the northeastern section of Nippur, showing in the lower part the outer and inner court of the Temple.

112   Light on the Old Testament

the wall on the east side of the gate. The extension of these two walls made it appear as if there was also an outer court. On the last expedition, a topographical map of a portion of Nippur was found. It includes, besides walls, gates, canals, buildings, and roads, a plan of the temple. It clearly shows that it had two courts. An available photograph of this map, which was taken before it was thoroughly cleaned, appears to show that there is written upon the inner court the words *E-kur*, which is the name of the temple. The temple had, therefore, an outer as well as an inner court. If this outer court was square, or approximately so, it included the shrine of Bur-Sin. Further excavations in this part of the temple area, although a considerable portion of the mound has been washed away, may reveal similar shrines having been built by other rulers.

Between the double walls which divided the courts, vaults were found. One of these was excavated on the third campaign. It was thirty-six feet long by eleven and a half feet wide, and eight and a half feet deep. There was a ledge, one and a half feet wide, running around the four walls two and a half feet from the floor. This was capped by a layer of burnt bricks. It is not improbable that in these vaults the temple literature was also kept, consisting of hymns, prayers, incantations, and all ritualistic writings used in connection with the Bêl cult. Here also the stone votive vases may have been stored.

The Tower of Babel

Between the temple proper and the vaults, Dr. Haynes, on the last campaign, found a large stone vase about three feet high, which had been presented to the temple by Gudea, the priest-king of Shirpurla (Telloh). The inscription reads: "To Bêl, the lord of the gods, for the temple at Nippur, Gudea the patesi of Shirpula presented the long boat of Ekur for his life."

On the basis of the actual excavations and the plan of the temple which is found on the topographical map in clay, and also taking into consideration the restorations which have already been proposed, the plan on the following page by Mr. Clarence S. Fisher is offered as a ground plan of the Temple of Bêl about the time of Ur-Engur.

Stone vase presented to Bêl by Gudea

This, in brief, is a picture of the temple and its tower as it existed in the first half of the third millennium before Christ. In the course of time, from some unknown cause, perhaps through neglect, or in consequence of an invasion, the pavement of Ur-Engur was lost sight of. A ground floor then existed in the area, at least in some portions of it,

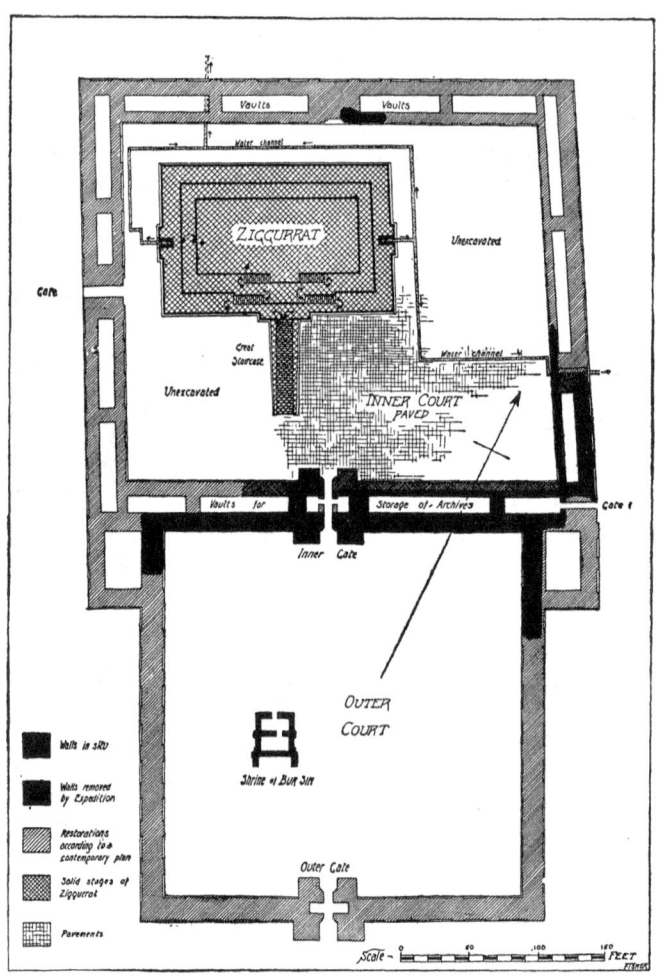

Plan of Ekur, the Temple of Bêl. Inner court 308 x 250 feet. Outer court about 260 feet square.

The Tower of Babel 115

until the time of Ur-Ninib (about 2550 B. C.). Dr. Haynes reported that one hundred and thirty-five of the one hundred and forty-three bricks which he took from the section excavated, were inscribed for this king. The inscription reads: "Ur-Ninib, the all-sublime shepherd of Nippur, the pastor of Ur, he who delivers the command of Eridu, the gracious lord of Erech, the king of Isin, the king of Shumer and Accad, the sublimely chosen one of the goddess Ninâ."

Ur-Ninib's pavement lies, on an average, about three feet above that of Ur-Engur. The débris between has revealed many important fragments of inscribed vases. They contain some of the oldest inscriptions known. Professor Peters excavated a goodly number of these on the second expedition, and Doctor Haynes the others on the third. As has been shown by Professor Hilprecht, these fragments belong, not to the period between Ur-Engur and Ur-Ninib, but to the age prior to Sargon I. The only possible explanation is that these vases, dedicated to the god Bêl by kings and patesis, had been in the possession of the temple, perhaps used in its service for many centuries, and at the time of some great disaster which befell the city, doubtless at the time of a foreign invasion, but not that of Kudur-Nankhundi, as has been claimed, because he lived after Ur-Ninib, these ancient votive objects were ruthlessly smashed in pieces. Naturally in the débris of that age the fragments would be found. They contain brief fragmentary legends (see page 37). In this stratum Dr. Haynes found also a torso of a statue in dolerite nearly life size, in many respects similar to the statues of Gudea found at Telloh (see page 158). He also found a straight nose in basalt, belonging to a statue fully life size; also a small white marble head, and other antiquities. As only a portion of this stratum of the temple area has thus far been excavated, very important discoveries can be looked for when the work in this mound is resumed.

Ur-Ninib's pavement must have been used, or in other words kept cleared, for many centuries, otherwise the accumulations between it and the next one above would be greater. One and a half feet above, the pavement of Kadashman-Turgu, who lived about 1250 B. C., is found in some parts of the mound. This Cassite monarch extended the sides of the ziggurrat, raised its terraces, restored its conduits, and replaced its gutters.

About two feet above this is the pavement of the Assyrian king Ashurbanipal (668-626 B. C.). This great monarch, out of reverence for the Nippur gods, or for political purposes, devoted considerable time to the embellishment of this ancient sanctuary. As far as is known he is the last restorer of Ekur. The inscription on his bricks, which is written in Sumerian, reads: "To Bêl, lord of lands, his lord, Ashurbanipal, his good shepherd, the mighty king, the king of the four quarters of the earth, Ekur,

The Tower of Babel 117

his house he built with burned bricks." In the stratum above the work of Ashurbanipal is found the large fortress built upon the old temple and its tower. This eventually fell into ruins. Finally, the late inhabitants of Nippur buried their dead in the mound covering the remains of the sanctuary where the ancients had worshiped their gods.

Only the builders or restorers of the temple and its towers who laid pavements within the sacred precincts have been mentioned. A number of the other builders, after Ur-Engur's time, are represented by stamped bricks. These built or rebuilt shrines, walls, etc.

Returning to the stratum representing the work of Ur-Engur and going downward, there is found, from six to eight feet below, another pavement which was laid with the bricks of Sargon I and Narâm-Sin, his son, about 3800 B. C. Sargon's bricks are stamped with his legend: "Shargâni-shar-âli, king of Accad, the builder of the temple of Bêl." Narâm-Sin's inscription reads: "Narâm-Sin, builder of the temple of Bêl." It is quite interesting to note that a large number of terra-cotta stamps, used by the brickmakers in making these impressions upon the soft clay for Sargon and Narâm-Sin, have been found. Some are very much worn from long usage. These bricks measure about twenty inches square, by about four inches in thickness. All have been carefully made in molds.

In the strata beneath the pavement of Narâm-

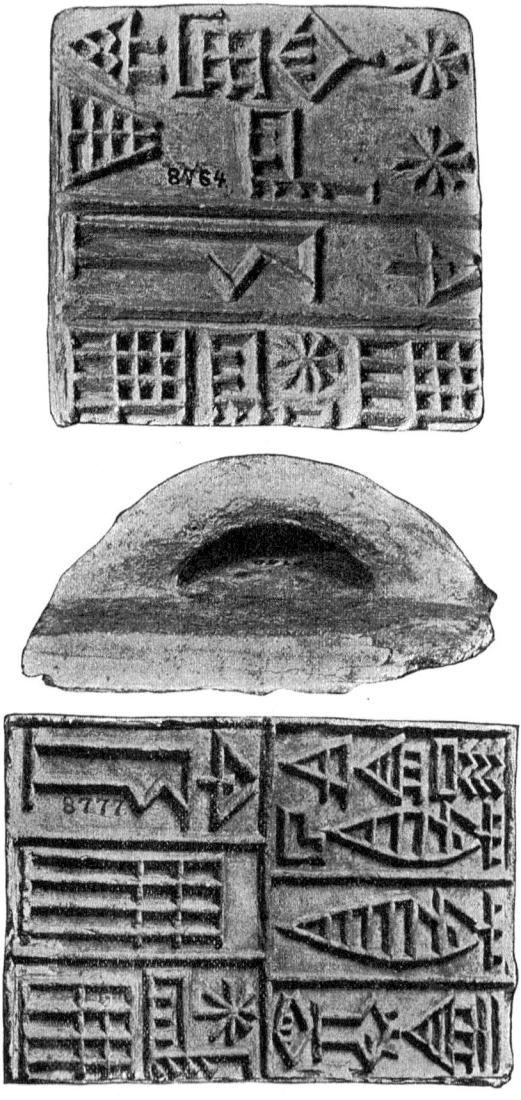

Terra-cotta stamps used by brick-makers. Upper: "Narâm-Sın."
Lower: Shargâni-shar-âli (Sargon).

The Tower of Babel

Sin, to the depth of over twenty-five feet, were found thousands of urns and pottery vessels containing remains of bones and wood partially consumed by fire. In some were found cups and dishes; in others, objects in copper, such as nails and battle-axes; or objects in stone, such as beads, seal cylinders, and different kinds of jewelry. Few of these jars and urns were found intact, having been crushed by the settling of the ground. Beds of gray and white ashes, mixed with fragments of pottery, were found at practically every level in these strata. Here and there were discovered terra-cotta drains composed of perforated rings. Three and a half feet below Narâm-Sin's pavement, on the third campaign, the excavators came upon a curb, which was about twelve feet from the ziggurrat. It stood some twenty inches high, and evidently served as an enclosure for something in that early age. Within what would be the supposed enclosure, Dr. Haynes found what he regarded as an altar. It was built of sun-dried bricks, thirteen feet long by eight feet wide. It had a ridge of bitumen running about its edge seven inches high. The top of this construction was covered with a layer of several inches of white ashes. Near it was found a bin, also containing several bushels of ashes. It was quite natural for the excavator to regard this as "an ancient place where sacrificial victims were burned."

The results obtained by the Germans under Moritz, Koldewey, and Meyer, in 1887, at El-Hibba and Surghul, which are about six miles distant from each other, were similar to those obtained by Dr. Haynes. Around an immense circular tower of two stories were found drains, ashes, bones, vases, and other buried remains. Koldewey concluded that both sites represent fire necropoles, which antedate the earliest civilization known. In other words, the tower was the center of a great cemetery, where the people buried the incinerated remains of their dead in jars and urns, and where the rich built houses, in which the defunct were supposed to live. It has been pointed out that in pre-Sargonic times the conditions at Nippur were the same.

To Professor Hommel belongs the credit for conceiving the idea that the Babylonian stage towers were originally sepulchral monuments. Taking this into consideration with Strabo's reference to the "sepulcher of Bêl" in Babylon, and Diodorus' "tomb of Ninos," in Nineveh, and also a name of the ziggurrat of Nippur found on a cylinder of Ashurbanipal, in which it is called *E-gigunu* "house of the tomb," the idea was then suggested[1] that the ziggurrat in the early pre-Sargonic or Sumerian age was a tomb of the patron deity, and like a huge mausoleum was surrounded by smaller ones of the rich, and graves of the common people. Future investigations will doubtless give us more light upon this interesting question.

---

[1] See Hilprecht, Explorations in Bible Land, p. 462 ff.

The Tower of Babel

Some scholars hold that the ziggurrat is symbolical of the heavenly seat of the gods. The deities being astral, the whole constellation represents the god. The ziggurrat they claim is the god's heavenly shrine. The figures cut in relief on the upper part of boundary stones which represent the deities seem to express this theory.[1] In some instances the shrine, god, and weapon are given. In others, the shrine and the weapon, or even one symbol. A shrine on one of the stones appears to be a good representation of a ziggurrat. This has led some scholars to conclude that the ziggurrat is an earthly symbol of the god's heavenly seat.[2]

In the story of Babel there is an expression which may have some bearing upon the significance of the tower. That the builders intended to raise its head into the very ether of heaven has been the usual explanation of the familiar passage. For centuries the illustrations of the tower not only make it reach, but pass through the clouds; or as a recent commentator says: "The expression is probably meant here, not hyperbolically, but literally, "heaven" being regarded as an actual vault, which might be reached, at least by a bold effort."[3]

---

[1] On this subject see Dr. W. J. Hinke's forthcoming work, "A New Boundary Stone of Nebuchadrezzar I."

[2] Winckler, *Himmelsbild und Weltenbild der Babylonier. Der alte Orient* III 2 and 3.

[3] Driver, Commentary on Genesis, p. 135.

The expression in Genesis, "That its head shall be in the heavens," must be understood differently. Concerning Ekur and the temple of Bêl at Nippur, it is written: "O great mountain of Bêl, Imkharsag,

Building inscription of Nabopolassar, giving an account of his restoration of the Tower of Babel, in which he says he raised " its head into the heavens."

whose summit rivals the heavens." But it was really less than fifty feet high. An expression like that of Genesis is found, almost word for word, in connection with ziggurrats in a number of building

The Tower of Babel

inscriptions dating as early as the time of Abraham. For instance, Nabopolassar, the father of Nebuchadrezzar, in an account of his restoration of the Tower of Babel, says: "The god Marduk caused me to lay its foundations in the breast of the earth, and to raise its head into the heavens."

The Babylonians, in their cosmological conceptions, divided the world into three parts, corresponding to the regions dominated over by the triad of gods, Anu, Bêl, and Ea. The region of Anu, the god of heaven, is that of the heavenly ocean (An), or that which is above the starry vault. The region of Ea was that of the terrestrial ocean (Ki), or the subterranean waters. Bêl's region (Lil) was between the two, and corresponded to the *raqîa‛* of Genesis, translated "firmament," which was "in the midst of the waters," which was to divide the waters from the waters. "And God made the *raqîa‛* and divided the waters which were under the *raqîa‛* from the waters which were above the *raqîa‛*" (Gen. 1:6, 7). The *raqîa‛*, therefore, was between, or joined heaven and earth. The name of the tower of Babel *E-temen-an-ki*, "house (E) of the foundation (*temen*) of heaven (*an*) and earth (*ki*)," seems to couple in some way the two regions. *E-ur-imin-an-ki*, "the house of the seven stages of heaven and earth," the name of the tower of Borsippa, and *E-gubba-an-ki* in Dilbat, likewise convey this idea. One of the names for the ziggurrat at Larsa and Sippara, as well as at Nippur, was *E-dur-an-ki* "house (*E*) of the link (*dur*) of heaven (*an*) and earth (*ki*)." It is quite probable that the expression referred to in Genesis, as well as those referred to in the building inscriptions, have some connection with these names of ziggurrats.

The theory has been proposed, in connection with the name *Dur-an-ki*, that the ziggurrat of Bêl at Nippur "is the local representation of the great mythological mountain of the world," the region over which Bêl ruled; and that it is symbolically the "link of heaven and earth" which connects the two extreme parts of his empire. The theory is based on the fact that Bêl ruled over the region between *An* and *Ki*. But to say that ziggurrats are symbolical of the region over which Bêl ruled, and also to assume that the epithet *Dur-an-ki*, with this particular meaning, was afterwards applied to other ziggurrats which were dedicated to other gods, would be to connect the name of Bêl with all ziggurrats. The former cannot be proved; and as the name is a general one, it does not seem possible to give Bêl such prominence in connection with other ziggurrats,—for example, those of Sippara and Larsa, which were dedicated to Shamash. Sufficient for the present is it to know that the expression in Genesis was used in connection with these towers, according to the inscriptions; and that names of ziggurrats also contain similar ideas.

VI

THE FOURTEENTH CHAPTER OF GENESIS

Ever since Professor Nöldeke, who, as early as 1869, declared that criticism had forever disproved the claim that Genesis 14 was historical, the chapter has proved a storm center in biblical criticism. It relates how, in the days of Amraphel, four kings of the East, after the five kings of the Vale of Siddim had rebelled against Elam, invaded the land and fought them. Abraham, hearing of their victory, and that his brother's son Lot had been taken captive, gathered his trained servants, and also his allies, and pursued the kings, Chedorlaomer, Tidal, Amraphel, and Arioch, as far as Dan, where, through some strategy at night, he routed them and pursued them unto Hobah, near Damascus. On returning, he restored Lot and the possessions of the king of Sodom, and paid tithes to Melchizedek, king of Salem.

The theory of the late origin of all the Hebrew Scriptures prompted the critics to declare this narrative to be a pure invention of a later Hebrew writer; in fact, a fanciful midrash, or a post-exilic forgery. The patriarchs were relegated to the region of myth and legend. Abraham was made a fictitious father of the Hebrews. He was created in the late days of Judaism by an idealizer of ancestry, in order to project backwards the beginning of the Hebrew race. Some saw in Abraham the name of a clan; others declared him to be a product of the Israelitish tendency to personify ideas; while others considered him to be a god, presumably the moon-god. Genesis 14, some claim is a narrative of some predatory raid against Canaan by a party of Bedween Arabs, to which legend the names of Lot and Abraham were tacked on; the whole story being afterwards elaborated by some later writer into the shape in which it now presents itself. Or, again, the whole story is a fiction based upon the Assyrian conquest of Palestine in the later days. These critics usually begin the history of the Hebrews with the Exodus of Israel from Egypt, or with the entrance into Western Canaan.

Even the political situation was declared to be inconsistent with fact. A military expedition of such proportions at that early date was regarded as incredible. Even the names of the kings are etymological plays upon subsequent events. In short, they said, monumental evidence to show that the narrative is historical is totally wanting.

In the light of what has been discovered, Professor Nöldeke and his line of followers naturally have changed a few of their views. Certain scholars now seem to think that, as some of these theories

The Fourteenth Chapter of Genesis

are no longer held, by reason of what is now known, there is no longer any occasion to refer to them. But inasmuch as a large number are still maintained, some of which are exceedingly far-reaching, and are based on highly insufficient grounds or, in fact, no data whatever, the general public has a right to know what has become of the others which were advanced by scholars of repute, as well as to consider the theories which are still promulgated.

Weighing carefully the position taken by the critics in the light of what has been revealed through the decipherment of the cuneiform inscriptions, we find that the very foundations upon which their theories rest, with reference to the points that could be tested, totally disappear. The truth is that wherever any light has been thrown upon the subject through the excavations, their hypotheses have invariably been found wanting. Moreover, what remains of their theories is based upon purely speculative grounds.

In the first place, instead of the names of the four kings being "etymological inventions" of imaginary characters, we now know that they are real; and the persons that bore them are historical. It is now generally admitted that Amraphel, king of Shinar, and the great Hammurabi are to be identified as one and the same person. In a text from Sippara, his name is written Ammurabi. In a letter written by Asharidu to Asnapper (Ashurbanipal), his name is written Ammurapi. The first element in the names of two other rulers of the first dynasty, *i. e.*, Ammi-zaduga and Ammi-ditana, in all probability is the same; namely, *Hammu*. Although explained by the Babylonian writer as having the same meaning

Biblical Amraphel in bas-relief.

as *Ḫammu* (namely, "*kimtu*") in these names, the element in the latter names is always written without *ḫ*. For the addition of the letter *l* in Amraphel in the Hebrew orthography, no satisfactory

The Fourteenth Chapter of Genesis 129

explanation has as yet been offered. Some call attention to the fact that in the contract literature of this period there is a name $Hammurabi\text{-}il(u)$ "Hammurabi is a god." The change of b to p offers no philological difficulty. These scholars have suggested that this name is "letter for letter the Amraphel of Genesis." This view, however, is not generally accepted by Assyriologists.

While great uncertainties exist in all chronological calculations for the years before Christ, the date of Amraphel, according to the Hebrew chronology, synchronizes in a general way with that of Hammurabi, according to the inscriptions. By the Hebrew chronology is not meant Ussher's, with which all English Bible students are familiar. The author of that system, thinking that the sojourn of Israel in Egypt could not have lasted four hundred and thirty years, used in this connection the number of years given by the Septuagint version; namely, two hundred and fifteen years. Using the Hebrew text throughout, Abram's entrance into Canaan should be fixed at about 2136 B. C. instead of 1921 B. C.

A number of Assyriologists fix the date for Hammurabi at 2250, while others make it 2100 B. C. At the present time there is no way of fully determining this point. There are dynastic lists of kings for the second millennium, but they are more or less incomplete and uncertain. The statement by

130   Light on the Old Testament

Nabonidus[1] that Hammurabi lived seven hundred years before Burna-Buriash, who reigned about

Clay cone of Hammurabi, referring to his buildings.

1400 B. C., would make his date about 2100 B. C.

[1] Rawlinson, Inscriptions of Western Asia, I, 69 b 4–8.

The Fourteenth Chapter of Genesis

This statement is remarkable, for it makes his date in the Babylonian practically the same as in the Hebrew chronology. This fact is strikingly important. Why? Think of a late Hebrew writer inventing the story of Abraham, in which he makes use of the names of historical personages, as some critics now declare, and has so arranged his chronological statements in making Abraham their contemporary that their dates synchronize. This Hebrew fiction-writer, or collector of legends, it surely must be acknowledged, was a phenomenal chronologer.

Hammurabi had his capital at Babylon. The limits of Shinar, over which he ruled in the early part of his reign, are not known. If it is correct to regard the name as the Hebrew equivalent of Shumer, which was the name of Southern Babylonia, then we must recognize the fact that Arioch calls himself, not only King of Larsa (Ellasar), but uses as well the general title, "King of Shumer and Accad" (page 136). Doubtless in the early part of his reign his kingdom was limited to the environs of Babylon. After the control of Elam was shaken off, and Rim-Sin (Arioch) was conquered, Shumer in its entirety came under his sway, after which time he adopted this general title.

Chedorlaomer, king of Elam, has not as yet been identified. His name, however, is composed of two elements which are well known; namely, *Kudur*, meaning, in the language of Elam, "servant," and the god *Lagamar*, which is one of the prominent Elamitic deities. The name, in other words, is similar in formation to the Elamitic names, Kudur-Mabug and Kudur-Nankhundi.

Doctor Theophilus G. Pinches offers a translation[1] of fragments of a tablet, which some hold may refer to the king mentioned in the Old Testament. On one of these he informs us that after referring to Babylon, and to the property of that city, small and great, it is said that the gods [apparently]

> in their faithful counsel to Kudur-Lakhgumal, king of the land of Elam . . . . said, "Descend." The thing which unto them was good [he performed, and] he exercised sovereignty in Babylon, the city of Kar-Duniash.

If correctly translated by Doctor Pinches, it would imply that an Elamitic ruler, named Kudur-Lakhgumal had conquered Babylon. Dûr-ṣîr-ilâni son of Eri-Ekua (also written Eri-Eaku), together with "Tudkhula, attacked and spoiled Babylon." For paleographical reasons, Doctor Pinches regards these inscriptions as belonging to the age following the Persian period, and holds that the peculiar association of these three names is simply a striking coincidence. If these three names are correctly translated it would almost seem that they represent the biblical Chedorlaomer, Arioch, and Tidal, and that we doubtless have an effort on the part of a late

---

[1] The Old Testament, in the Light of the Historical Records of Assyria and Babylonia, p. 222 ff.

scribe to put in writing some early legendary material. Other scholars, who have seen the inscriptions, seem to be disposed to question the reading of the names.

As early as the days of Rawlinson and George Smith, Rim-Sin, king of Larsa, the son of Kudur-Mabug of Elam, has been regarded as identical with the biblical Arioch, king of Ellasar. This identification, however, has been questioned by some scholars, who say that it cannot be proved.

The first element in the name of this ruler is usually written with the sign commonly read *ardu*, "servant." The variant reading, *Ri-im*, determines its value in this name. A bilingual text gives for the same sign the value *E-ri*, which may be Sumerian or Elamitic, or it is a dialectical value for the character. *Aku* is a well known equivalent for the moon-god Sin. In the light of these facts, and because of other considerations, it follows that Rim-Sin in all probability is a Semitized form of the name *Eri-Aku* (Arioch), and that they are identical.

The difference between the name of the city Larsa and Ellasar must, of course, be taken into consideration. But corruption in the text, due to frequent transmission, could easily be accepted as a reasonable explanation in order to account for this change.

Kudur-Mabug, the son of Shimti-Shilkhak, was the father of Arioch. Exactly what relation Chedor-

134   Light on the Old Testament

laomer was to Kudur-Mabug cannot be determined. He was doubtless his father or his brother. Kudur-

Bronze Canephorus dedicated to Nanâ by Kudur-Mabug, the father of Arioch of Ellasar, mentioned in Genesis xiv.

Mabug does not have the title "King of Elam," but only Prince of Emutbal, *i. e.*, the western part

The Fourteenth Chapter of Genesis   135

of Elam. Chedorlaomer was in all probability king of Elam, while his son or brother was prince of Emutbal, and his grandson or nephew was king of Larsa.

Prior to Hammurabi's thirty-first year, when he threw off the yoke of Elam, Arioch the Elamite reigned over a considerable portion of southern Babylonia. Up to the present time only three rulers of Larsa are known. Nûr-Rammân, the builder of two sanctuaries in that city, was succeeded by Sin-idinnam (not the governor under Hammurabi by the same name), who restored and embellished the fane of Shamash, also in that city, besides constructing canals and other works. He calls himself "the Preserver of Ur, King of Larsa and King of Shumer and Accad," which title embraced practically lower Babylonia. The third known ruler of Larsa is Arioch. Exactly how Elam came to dominate over this region is not known, as the inscriptions of these rulers throw no light upon the subject. Perhaps it was brought about by the invasion of Kudur-Nankhundi, who invaded Babylonia, according to Ashurbanipal, about 2285 B. C. Or, it may date from the fall of Nisin. The seventeenth year of Sin-muballit, the father of Hammurabi, was called "the year in which the city of Nisin was taken." The dating of contracts bearing Rim-Sin's name shows that that event marked an epoch for dating tablets; for example: "The fifth year of the taking of Nisin." They are found dated as high as the thirtieth, which corresponds to the twenty-sixth year of Hammurabi, if that event took place in the seventeenth year of his father's reign. Arioch ruled, besides Larsa where he had the seat of his government, over Ur, Eridu, Lagash, and Nippur; in other words, as mentioned above, southern Babylonia. Taking these things into consideration, and especially in view of the fact that he used the title "King of Shumer and Accad," which really embraced the city of Babylon, there can be little doubt but that Hammurabi, although ruler of Babylon, inherited a throne which was subject to Elam, and that he was a dependent upon this son of that land in the early years of his reign. This means that the army of Shinar, and its king, could be controlled by that nation. We have here a reason why Shinar and Elam were associated together in the campaigns against the kings of the West-land. Further, as mentioned above, Arioch king of Larsa was the son of the Elamite Kudur-Mabug, which fact offers a very satisfactory reason why the armies of Larsa and Elam should be allies in this campaign. In short, we have reasons why three of the four kings should be allied in reconquering these rebellious subjects of the king of Elam. This is a remarkable confirmation of the historical value of the chapter. When history records such a confederation of powers, it is highly important to ascertain the cause of such a union. And that we are able in these days to give the reasons for the

The Fourteenth Chapter of Genesis

coalition of three of the four nations, in this earliest of Hebrew records that we can hope to corroborate by the help of the monuments, seems wonderful.

In a number of inscriptions, Kudur-Mabug also calls himself *Adda Martu*, which means "Prince of the land of Amurru (Palestine and Syria)." In other words, the inscriptions prior to the overthrow of Elam and Larsa record the supremacy of Elam over this region. This is in strict accordance with Genesis, for we are told, "twelve years they (the five kings) served Chedorlaomer (the king of Elam), and in the thirteenth year they rebelled." This is another remarkable confirmation of the accuracy of the historical details of this chapter.

After Hammurabi conquered Elam and Arioch, he adopted this title. We learn that the second in succession after Hammurabi, namely, Ammi-ditana, continued to regard himself as prince of this country. This fact doubtless explains why Shinar heads the list in the first verse of the chapter. The episode is dated in the days of Amraphel, whereas the country, when the invasion took place, was subject to Elam. It is because the record was written after Hammurabi had become the suzerain of the land.

The critics also urged as an argument against the credibility of the campaign, the difficulty in believing that a military expedition at this early date could be sent from that region. We have seen that the inscriptions of Elam of this time claim for the king, supremacy of Syria and Palestine. That

138 Light on the Old Testament

fact conclusively meets their argument. But further, in an inscription of Lugal-zaggisi, about 4000 B. C., we learn that this ruler accomplished, about two thousand years before Abraham was born, what these critics said was not to be considered as possible as early as the patriarch's days. In other words, he conquered the land from the Persian Gulf unto the Mediterranean. On the following page a portion of his inscription which is in the Museum of the University of Pennsylvania (see page 44) reads:

> When Bêl, lord of lands to Lugal-zaggisi the kingship of the world had given, before the world had made him to prosper, lands under his power had given; from the rising of the sun to the going down of the sun he subdued; then from the sea, the lower, the Tigris and Euphrates, to the sea, the upper, his path he made straight; from the rising of the sun to the going down of sun. Bêl, the ruler over everything (?) delivered unto him, [and] the lands dwell in peace.

The bearing of all these results upon the question has forced the critics to propound a new hypothesis, which in substance, as regards its relation to the historicity of the patriarchal period, is equally obstinately negative in character. In the exile the Hebrew writer became acquainted with these names of ancient Babylonian and Elamitic history, besides other authentic data, and then invented the story, in which the fictitious Abraham was brought into conflict with them and made the hero. In the light of ancient discoveries, were this correct, we should be forced to exclaim, What accurate knowledge of early Babylonian, Elamitic, and Palestine affairs

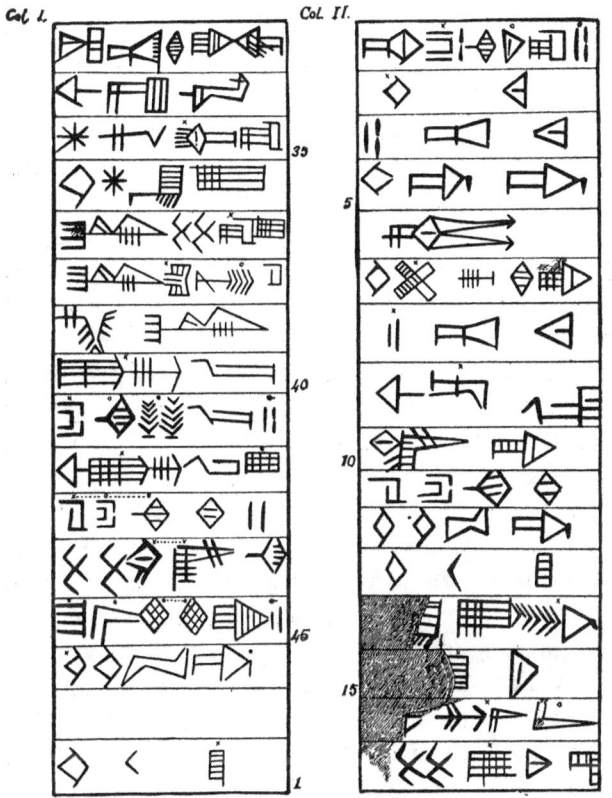

A portion of the inscription on the votive vases of Lugal-zaggisi. See opposite page for the translation beginning at line 4.

was possessed by this historian! In short, the work of this Hebrew investigator of questions in historical geography and in the political affairs of several ancient nations, which, as mentioned before, shows such a surprisingly accurate knowledge of chronological and other data, would certainly be unique. Historians should insist that this unknown savant be canonized or immortalized.

The chapter on the other hand, as has been pointed out, offers every indication that the data bearing upon Palestine belong, not to the late days of Hebrew history, but to very ancient times. With possibly only one exception, the names of peoples and places, as far as they have been identified, indicate that they belong to a pre-biblical period. When the document which had been handed down was used, the writer found it necessary to introduce, by way of explanation, the names familiar in his own day; as, for instance, "Bela (the same is Zoar)," "En-mishpat (the same is Kadesh)." Would these critics suggest that the writer introduced these explanatory notes in order that his romance might have the appearance of an ancient document? These glosses, and in fact everything, seem to point to early Palestine origin for the record. But with this phase of the subject, upon which considerable can be said, we are not at the present concerned.

In order to demonstrate what a change archeology has wrought in a few years, and also to show how some critics have readjusted themselves, offering that which is still far-reaching as regards the historical worth of the chapter, let me quote the following

The Fourteenth Chapter of Genesis

by Professor George Adam Smith. In his "Modern Criticism and the Preaching of the Old Testament" (p. 101), he says: "We must admit that while archæology has richly illustrated the possibility of the main outlines of the Book of Genesis from Abraham to Joseph, it has not one whit of proof to offer for the personal existence or characters of the patriarchs themselves. . . . But amidst all that crowded life we peer in vain for any trace of the fathers of the Hebrews; we listen in vain for any mention of their names. This is the whole change archæology has wrought: it has given us a background and an atmosphere for the stories of Genesis; it is unable to recall or certify their heroes."

What a change recent researches have brought about! With what silence the former conclusions, which were proclaimed with the utmost assurance, are now treated! Instead of the historical background being altogether different from that represented in Genesis, it is now admitted to be in strict accordance with it. And on the other hand, while so much light has been thrown upon this chapter, in which the very "atmosphere" is acknowledged as having been restored, absolutely nothing has been revealed whereby its accuracy can be impugned,—let me repeat, *absolutely nothing*. Doubt, however, continues to be thrown upon the historicity of the patriarchs themselves; and they are relegated to the region of myth and legend; not because a single datum has been found to substantiate, inferentially or otherwise, such a view, but because some have "peered in vain for any trace" of them in the records of the past; or they have their fanciful theories to propound.

As stated before, when contact with a foreign power is mentioned in the Old Testament, and we are able to examine the annals of that power, reference to such contact is in nearly every case found. While Elamitic and Babylonian inscriptions may be discovered which will mention this well-known invasion, the truth is, even the most sanguine archeologist could not expect from such sources any mention whatever of the patriarch himself.[1] Abraham was a small shaykh, a tolerated inhabitant; perhaps one of the many who in his day occupied that region. He grazed his flocks in one locality until the pasture was insufficient for his herds, after which he found it necessary to move on. When he desired to secure Lot from the invaders, he could

---

[1] Some years ago Professor Hommel, through an oversight, made the statement that the name *Abi-ramu* (Abram) was found on a contract tablet of the Hammurabi dynasty. (See also Pinches, Old Testament in Light, etc., p. 148.) This has quite frequently been used by others; but the name is to be read Abi-erakh. See Ranke, *Die Personennamen in den Urkunden der Hammurabidynastie*, p. 48. *Abi-ramu* (Abram) is found to be the name of an official during the reign of Esarhaddon, and recently has been found on an Egyptian monument belonging to Shishak, as reported in the Palestine Exploration Quarterly Statement, Jan. 1905, p. 7.

only muster three hundred and eighteen men, which included those of his allies, Aner, Eshcol and Mamre. And although the four kings were routed by some kind of strategy, even if annals were written, as in later times, any reference to a disaster would be entirely unlooked-for; besides, Abraham was very likely unknown to them by name.

The increase of knowledge gained through the inscriptions of this period has in every instance dissolved conclusions arrived at by those critics who maintain that the patriarchs are not to be regarded as historical. And in view of these things is it not reasonable to expect the specialist who desires to theorize to confine his suppositions and conjectures, until he has some kind of facts upon which to base them, to scientific journals, or, in other words, that he should not popularize them, and bring them within the range of the understanding of the Sunday-school scholar.

In the Arab camp at Nippur, illustrating woman grinding corn, the ancient mill for grinding flour.

VII

BABYLONIAN LIFE IN THE DAYS OF ABRAHAM

Not many decades ago, Abraham was supposed to belong well-nigh to the dawn of civilization. That there was a nation with a highly-developed culture millenniums before his day was not generally appreciated, notwithstanding the fact that we learn in Genesis that he came in contact, for instance, with the Hittite, a representative of a mighty nation to the north of Palestine, the Amorite, and other peoples of Canaan, besides a pharaoh of Egypt. The excavator, archeologist, and decipherer have given a clearer conception of those days, and have already restored the history of a period about as long prior to Abraham as we are after; or, in other words, they now place the patriarch midway in the written history of man.

The dynasty that governed Babylon during Abraham's life is known as the first dynasty of Babylon. The names of the rulers are: Sumu-abi, Sumu-la-ilu, Zabium, Abil-Sin, Sin-muballit, Hammurabi, Samsu-iluna, Abi-eshukh, Ammi-ditana, Ammi-zaduga, and Samsu-ditana. With the exception of one or two scholars, who believe that all the rulers were of Babylonian origin, scholars unite in saying that they are not indigenous to the land, except perhaps Sin-muballit and Abil-Sin. Even these were doubtless foreigners, who had assumed Babylonian names, a practise commonly known to have existed. The nomenclature of the contract literature of this dynasty, having hundreds of foreign names, shows unmistakably that a large foreign Semitic population was settled in Babylonia at this time, especially in the vicinity of Sippar. Earlier literature does not show this influence, while in the Cassite period, several centuries later than the time of which we speak, it has totally disappeared.

The exact source of this foreign influence is also a controverted point. Some scholars declare that the origin of the dynasty is Arabian, while others regard the rulers to be Canaanites. This much seems to be certain: They can be called Western Semites or Amorites. The country *Amurru, i. e.*, the Westland, embraced the entire country west of the Euphrates up to the shores of the Mediterranean. Perhaps it even included the northern part of Arabia; this would account for the foreign element in Babylonia at this time, which shows Arabic influences.

Our knowledge of the Semitic tongues of Arabia, Canaan, and other parts of this district of this early time, is too meager to come to any further conclusions on the subject. The earliest date tenta-

Babylonia in Days of Abraham 147

tively fixed for the Minæan (Arabic) inscriptions is 1400 B. C. The earliest extra-biblical inscriptions of Canaanite origin are the glosses written in Hebrew on the Tel el-Amarna cuneiform tablets, which belong to the same period; in other words, about seven centuries after the time of Hammurabi. What language was spoken in Canaan in his day is not known. The Western-Semitic names in question may be found later on to represent the Palestine language of that time. It may have been a kind of a mixture of Arabic, or of some other Semitic language, which developed into what we know as Hebrew. But the writer is inclined to think that the language of Canaan, as represented in the later times by the Hebrew, Phœnician, and the Moabitic dialects, goes back to a time in Palestine so remote as to be lost in the mists of antiquity. If, for instance, the Babylonian is already a fixed tongue at 4000 B. C., and has changed grammatically very little in the four thousand years of its known history; and, also, if the oldest portion of Hebrew, generally fixed not later than 1500 B. C., is very little different from the latest Hebrew, showing that it was already a fixed language at that early date, it seems that we have excellent reasons for concluding that the language of Canaan was practically the same in the days of the first dynasty of Babylon as it was a few centuries later. If, therefore, the foreign elements referred to cannot be regarded as belonging to the Canaanite language, or the Hebrew with which we are familiar, then the influence must come from elsewhere. Presumably, however, this much is certain: the language is one of the Western-Semitic tongues.

While a number of kings reigned in this dynasty prior to Hammurabi (the Amraphel of Genesis 14), the country over which they ruled seems to be limited to the district about Babylon. The land was divided into petty principalities, each having its independent system of government. An Elamite, whose name was Rim-Sin or Arioch, exercised control over the southern part of the valley, with his government at Larsa. But in Hammurabi's thirty-first year, when he conquered this land as well as Emutbal, a part of Elam, the entire country came under his sway (see preceding chapter).

The usual order had been that, when a king conquered one of the surrounding rulers, tribute was exacted, and the conquered one was held in subjection by force. Such a union was dissolved as soon as the one conquered was strong enough to throw off the yoke, or the conquering city had in turn been conquered by another. Hammurabi, however, introduced a new policy. He not only controlled effectively the country which he had acquired through conquest, but he amalgamated the heterogeneous and discordant elements into a united kingdom. He unified them by reorganizing their administrations, and appointed over them those who were familiar with his own form of government.

Babylonia in Days of Abraham 149

His officers assumed control of the various centers, which were developed along prescribed lines until all were welded into one united whole, with the central government at Babylon. For nearly two millenniums, including the centuries of the foreign rule of the Cassites, Assyrians, Persians, and others, the hegemony of Babylon which was established by his efforts was not disturbed.

Hammurabi's administrative ability is well illustrated by a large number of his official letters, which have been published by Mr. L. W. King, of the British Museum. They were all written by the same scribe, and addressed to his governor Sin-idinnam, at Larsa. The latter had jurisdiction over several other cities, among them being Ur and Erech. The fact that he was stationed at Larsa would imply that the letters which are not dated belong to the period subsequent to the defeat of Elam, *i. e.*, after the thirty-first year of his reign; for Arioch, the Elamite prince, had his capital at that city.

The letters originally had been encased, the envelopes containing the address, something like "To Sin-idinnam." The cases doubtless contained, in addition to the address, the impressions of Hammurabi's seal. On the receipt of a letter the case was peeled off. Here and there small portions of the envelopes have adhered to the letters. Being a king's epistle to a subject, the opening formula is brief: "Unto Sin-idinnam say:—thus saith

Hammurabi." What he desired to communicate immediately followed.

Through this correspondence we get a remarkable insight into the internal affairs of his administration. From it we learn that one of the characteristic features of his reign was that he gave personal attention to minor details, as well as to the general oversight of the affairs of his kingdom. In one letter, an order is given that certain Elamite goddesses, which had been taken in conquest, should be brought to Babylon. In another letter, he orders that they should be returned to their shrines. Special attention is devoted to the construction, repairing, and dredging of canals, in order to develop the natural resources of the land. The work seems to have been conducted by the government. The residents along the canals were required to keep them in repair, but the general oversight of this work was in the hands of the king. He is found superintending the collection of revenues, exercising control over the priesthood, and requiring the strict observance of omens in order that disasters might be avoided.

Again, we find the king giving orders for the restoration of property, which had been illegally claimed or retained, or for the investigation of personal claims. In some instances he sent instructions as to how cases were to be tried. Several letters are practically warrants for the arrest of certain individuals, who were to be brought to Babylon. Some are summonses for officials to render their accounts, that they might be audited. Orders are given for the despatching of troops, and ships, or for the sheep-shearers to come to the capital in order to take part in the annual festival. Directions are given for the cutting of certain kinds of trees, or for the transportation of slaves and workmen, or of products, to Babylon. He arranged for the inspection of royal flocks and herds. In other words, the king seems to have given attention to the smallest detail of his administration. While the governor is requested to investigate certain affairs, and render decisions, everything he does is subject to the king's approval. Babylon seems to have been the seat of the supreme court, with Hammurabi acting as the chief justice. He even tried ordinary cases himself. In one instance he rendered a decision favorable to a citizen against one of his governors. Money-lenders he punished for extortion, or for failing to cancel mortgages after they had been satisfied. In order to prevent collusion on the part of witnesses, in cases that he tried, he ordered his governor to send them separately to Babylon.

A very interesting letter shows how the calendar was regulated. Throughout their history the Babylonians observed the lunar months, the names of which the Jews substituted for their own after the captivity. In consequence, it became necessary about every third year to insert an intercalary month. This was usually done in the middle, or at the end, of the year. Hammurabi in a letter to his governor Sin-idinnam, after he mentioned the fact that the year had a deficiency, ordered that the month upon which they were entering should be called "Second Elul," instead of Tishri, the month that followed Elul. But he added: "Instead of the tribute arriving in Babylon on the twenty-fifth day of the month Tishri, let it arrive in Babylon on the twenty-fifth day of Second Elul." In other words, he pushed on the calendar, but was unwilling to wait a month for his revenues.

A king's piety seems to have been determined by what he accomplished in the way of restoring and embellishing temples, building shrines, or making endowments to the sanctuary. One of the ways the people recognized these works, as well as commemorated other great deeds of the king in the way of conquest or in serving the people, was by naming the year of the king's reign after the event. This manner of dating offers considerable information for the reconstruction of history. The first year usually mentions the beginning of the reign; *viz.*, "The year in which Hammurabi became king." Unfortunately the chronicles, or rather the lists of titles given to the separate years which record these dates of the first dynasty, are fragmentary; but the following selection from Hammurabi's reign will serve to illustrate their character, and what they teach us. "The year [third] in which the throne of Nannar [was made]." "The year [fourth] in which the wall of Malga was destroyed." "The year

Babylonia in Days of Abraham 153

[ninth] in which the canal Hammurabi [was dug]." "The year [twelfth] in which the throne of Sarpanîtum [was made]." "The year [fourteenth] in which the wall of Sippara was built." "The year [thirtieth] in which the army of Elam [was defeated]." "The year [thirty-first] in which the land of Emutbal [was conquered]." "The year [thirty-second] in which the army of . . . . ." "The year [thirty-eighth] in which the city Umliash [was destroyed] by flood." The closing line of this list, which gives the years for his reign reads: "The forty-three years of Hammurabi the king."

All documents in the early period of Babylonian history are dated according to these titles of the years. This system was exceedingly cumbersome in comparison with the method adopted in the later centuries in Babylonia, when the number of the years of the reign of the king was used. It must have been necessary for business men as well as others who kept records to have their individual lists of the names of years, as it would be difficult to remember them for any length of time. Further, in some sections of the land another set of titles was employed, commemorating events which were of greater importance to the people of that portion of the country. In the Assyrian inscriptions of the late period, as is well known, a system somewhat similar was used. Each year was known by the name of an official. For example, the first year, the king's name was used; the following, the next highest official; like, *Limmu Bêl-illatua*, *i.e.*, "The eponym of Bêl-illatua." But in Babylonia, during the centuries which followed the Hammurabi dynasty, all dating was according to the year of the king's reign.

In the prologue and epilogue of his code, which is discussed in the following chapter, Hammurabi mentions numerous temples and shrines that he enlarged and restored or adorned; also that he enriched certain cities; that he brought prosperity to others by giving them abundance of water; in general, that he was a most benevolent monarch. He calls himself a "father of his people." As a lawgiver and as an administrator of laws he appears in a most favorable light, and seems to have earned the flattering and honorific titles he credits himself with, in his code. His letters to his governor justify him in thus regarding himself. In short, Oriental despotism, which characterized the rule of so many ancients, is not apparent; but, on the other hand, we find a benevolent ruler who, by his energetic efforts in improving the social and material conditions of the people, must have won their favor.

Quite a number of letters written by private individuals living in this age, have also been found. They are, as a rule, more difficult to understand than official letters, as they presuppose private relations of which we can have no knowledge. In one, a man who is held in prison sent the letter with the jailer or gateman to the man who imprisoned

Babylonia in Days of Abraham   155

him, complaining of his treatment. He calls the jail a starvation house. He says he is ill, and asks for food and clothing. He pleads that he is not a robber, nor a burglar, but he is imprisoned because the *Sutu* fell upon him, and took the oil which he, his master, sent him with across the river.

In another letter, a son wrote to his father that he was located at Dûr-Sin, where there was no meat fit to eat. He sent his father two-thirds of a shekel of silver, that he might send some nice fish and other viands. A votary from a royal family, who was in connection with some temple, wrote to her father, reminding him of his promise to send a sheep and five minas of silver, which he failed to keep.

The following [1] may be regarded as a love letter of Abraham's time, although the exact relations of the correspondents cannot be determined. Bibea, the one addressed, is a lady.

"To Bibea say, thus saith Gimil-Marduk: May the gods Shamash and Marduk permit thee to live forever for my sake. I write to inquire concerning thy health. Tell me how thou art. I went to Babylon, but did not see thee. I was greatly disappointed. Send the reason for thy leaving, that I may be happy. Do come in the month Marchesvan. Keep well always for my sake."

There are indications that a regular post, or

---

[1] Published by Father Scheil, *Une Saison de fouilles à Sippar*, p. 131.

system of despatching letters and packages, was in existence at this time. Besides letters, other evidences of such a post have been found; notably a large number of lumps of clay, which are labels or tags, belonging to this and other periods. On some the marks of the cord which passed through the bit of clay are clearly visible. Others contained the names of the individuals for whom the parcels were intended, besides the seal impressions of the sender. Several found at Telloh contain impressions of the seal of Sargon, king of Agade (about 3800 B. C.), which belonged to parcels he sent to his son Narâm-Sin, who was then acting as viceroy in that city. In all probability there was a regular post in existence between the different cities of Sargon's empire.

The following translation of a little Sumerian record belonging to the latter half of the third millennium B. C. shows how messengers were provided with the necessities of life on their journeys. It records what was furnished them for their journey between the city in which it was written and In-nanna-erin. The amounts were paid from the treasury of the temple storehouse. The record is for one month. Whether the tablet indicates the number of trips made each month, or whether the carriers were despatched only when something was to be delivered, cannot be determined.

3 *qa* of date wine for Shunagargid, the messenger.
5 *qa* of date wine for Awil-Nannar, the courier, who came

Clay labels or tags having holes through which a cord passed. Some contain the seal impressions of the sender, while others contain records; *e.g.*, "one sheep, the shepherd Uzi-ilu."

from the city Innanna-erin. 5 *qa* of date wine [for one day's stay] in the City, and 1 *gur* of wine, made from the *SA* herb, for the journey for Susha-laba,the courier,who goes to the city Innanna-erin. 10 *qa* of date wine for two days' [stay in the city] for Nabium (?), the courier, who comes from Innanna-erin. 5 *qa* of date wine [for one day's stay] in the city, and 1 *gur* of wine from the *SA* herb for the journey for Dingir-masu(?), the courier, who goes to Innanna-erin. 3 *qa* of date wine for Ubar, the messenger, who comes from Innanna-erin. 20 *qa* of date wine for four days' [stay in the city] for Awil-Ea, the courier. 60 *qa* of oil for the herdsman of the City Gishgal(?) [all of] which are to be taken out of the temple [storehouse, in the] month Ezen-Dumuzi (*i. e.*, the Hebrew month Tishri).

Babylonia being an alluvial plain, somewhat removed from stone, developed architecturally almost entirely with clay as a building material. As a result the remains of the builders' work are largely in terra-cotta or sun-dried clay. Occasionally some great ruler imported stone from central Arabia, or the mountains along the Euphrates to the northwest, for statues, door-sockets, vases, votive objects, etc., but generally the antiquities discovered, which belong to the every-day life of the people, are in clay.

There have been found, however, a number of stone statues of the third millennium which are remarkable creations for this stoneless land. At Telloh, eight headless statues over and under life size were found in the central court of Gudea's palace. Several heads of other statues were also

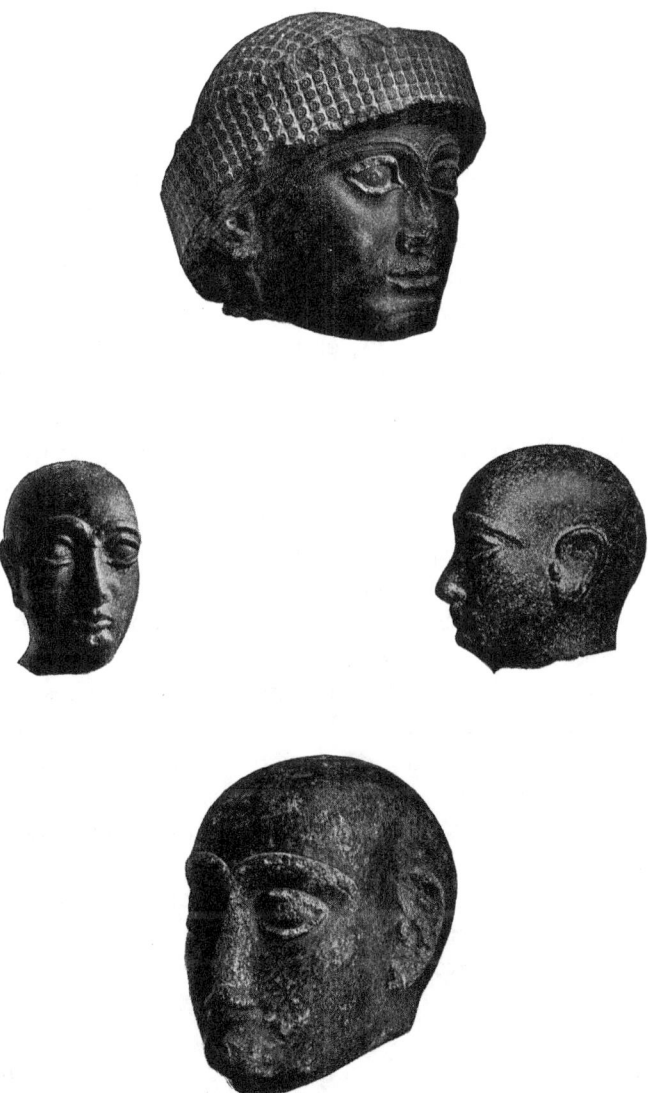
Heads of dolerite statues found at Telloh.

recovered, broken off doubtless at the time of some invasion. At Nippur were found a torso and a head, besides other fragments, belonging to similar statues. They are made of a hard igneous rock, dolerite. Gudea imported this stone for his statues from Magan, *i.e.*, Northeast Arabia, which borders on Babylonia.

The anatomy of the figures is surprisingly well rendered. The cheeks, chin, and mouth have been carefully studied. The nose is somewhat arched. The eyelids are good, although too wide open. The hair is represented by lines arranged in herringbone fashion. The muscles of the arm swell because of the folded or clasped hands. The finger-nails are delicately carved. The drapery is in awkward folds over the left shoulder, leaving the right arm bare. Two of the statues found at Telloh represent Gudea (about 3000 B. C.) as an architect or builder. In one of these he has a plan of his palace resting on his lap. It shows the large gates and towers. The scale according to which the plan is drawn accompanies it. The skirt of the statue is covered with inscriptions in the Sumerian language. There is a lack of animation in the face, and a heaviness and a squattiness of the form, which is not at all pleasing, especially when compared with the work of the Memphite sculptor of a still earlier age; yet the knowledge of anatomy displayed, and the minutiæ of detail as worked out, besides taking into consideration the skill of the workman who cut

Statue of Gudea. The building plan of his palace rests on his lap. It is accompanied with the scale according to which it was drawn.

his statues out of the hardest kind of stone, rightly deserve our admiration. Allowances must be made for school conventions, but these statues offer valuable material for the physiological study of the Sumerian people, the early inhabitants of the valley.

A great many vases, of different sizes and shapes, cut out of hard as well as soft stone, have been found belonging to the third, the fourth, and the fifth millenniums before Christ. Some show on the inside the marks of the tools which were used in making them. All such marks are obliterated on the outside, as the vases had been polished. The regularity of these tool marks and the symmetry of the vases clearly indicate that a lathe was employed in their manufacture. The neatness and fineness of execution and the beautiful designs make some of them superior to the products of later times. The same is true of the skill of the gem-cutter (see page 55).

The work of the smith is represented by many antiquities in silver and bronze. Objects in gold, such as the images of gods which were placed in the temples, have not been discovered. In a number of instances, gold objects used as jewelry have been found in the coffins which were excavated. In bronze, there have been found votive images, various utensils, jewelry, weapons, and tools of many kinds. Gudea informs us that he imported copper from Nejd, and gold from Medina and Melukhkha in the Sinaitic peninsula.

Statues in dolerite from Telloh, illustrating the female dress of the third millennium before Christ.

Of special interest are the bronze canephori or basket-carriers, which have been found at Telloh. They were usually dedicated to the gods for the preservation of the donor's life. De Sarzec found small cavities constructed in the platforms of buildings in which these and similar votive objects, used doubtless as talismans, had been walled up. As in Greece, with a single exception they are female figures. It is well known that the office of a canephorus carried with it great distinction among the classic Greeks. Only the daughters of the first Athenian families were honored with this exceptional distinction.

In one of the images found at Telloh, the limbs are not worked out, but the lower part forms a cone. On this there is an inscription of Dungi, king of Ur, about 2750 B. C. Another has a skirt, but it is not inscribed. The third is that of a male figure, carrying a basket exactly as the females. It bears a votive inscription to the goddess Nanâ by Rim-Sin (the biblical Arioch), king of Larsa. Several female basket-carriers have been found which contain votive inscriptions of Kudur-Mabug, father of Arioch. The Berlin Museum has secured an exceptionally well-preserved specimen (see illustration, page 134). It is dedicated to the goddess Nanâ, "who is adorned with splendor and overflowing with grace."

Little is known concerning the musical attainments of this age. At Telloh, belonging to an earlier

Babylonia in Days of Abraham 165

time, a fragment of an interesting bas-relief was found in the ruins of Gudea's palace. It has two compartments. In the upper, one of the four figures is represented with a kind of cymbal, or paten,

Bas-relief in stone, depicting musicians. (Third millennium B. C.)

and an object which was used for striking it. Another carries something like a flute. In the lower part of the relief, there is a seated figure playing a harp, which has eleven strings. The foot of the harp is adorned with the figure of a bull. Before the harper stands a singer, or a worshiper, in a reverential attitude, perhaps before a deity.[1]

In the first dynasty of Babylon, there was a large number of scribes. Nearly all the legal documents of this period that have been translated are found to have been written by different scribes. A number of women are known to have belonged to this profession, as seems to be the case also in the Assyrian period.[2] There are indications that lead us to suppose that the scribe shaved his head and beard, that he wore his toga thrown over his left shoulder, and kept his right arm bare.

The scribe wrote the legal documents, and doubtless most of the letters of private individuals. In writing a contract, the entire document was his work, even to the making of the seal impressions upon the tablet, in proximity to which he wrote the name of the owner. The individual, therefore, whose seal was used handed it to the scribe for him to make the impression. This is clearly shown by the regularity with which they were made, and their position on the tablet.

---

[1] For the later Assyrian period of the first millennium B. C., considerable is known of musicians and their instruments.

[2] The Rev. C. H. W. Johns of Cambridge, England, in his valuable treatise, Babylonian and Assyrian Laws, Contracts, and Letters, p. 151, calls attention to an Assyrian document which mentions six female *aba*, which word he translates "scribe" or "secretary." In the Neo-Babylonian period, women scribes are not mentioned.

The writing materials in all ages of Babylonian and Assyrian history were clay, stone, and metal. If papyrus was ever used, no trace of it has been preserved. The number of noteworthy objects which have been found in metal is comparatively small, as, for example, the canephorus in bronze, described on page 164, or the silver vase of Entemena (see page 52) found by De Sarzec at Telloh. Inscribed objects which were dedicated to the gods, such as vases, slabs, etc., were usually in stone. This and other materials were employed for seal-cylinders, door-sockets, boundary-stones, etc.

In all ages, so far as is known, clay was the standard writing material for literary, historical, legal, and personal matters. A clay was used which was free from grit, or which was washed well, in order to clear it of as much of the sand as possible. The scribes apparently selected a clay containing considerable marl or chalk.[1] They doubtless had observed that clay with a good percentage of chalk does not shrink much and crack upon drying out. This is due to the fact that the chalk is not hydrous, and will not take up water. After the clay had been washed and thoroughly kneaded, it had remarkable adhesive power; so that tablets which were simply sun-dried, although buried in the damp earth for chiliads, have remained intact. Naturally, the

---

[1] See the writer's, Business Documents of Murashû Sons, B. E. Vol. X, p. I.

greatest care must be observed when unbaked tablets are excavated, for they fall to pieces if roughly handled. After they are thoroughly dried out, the old adhesiveness is again restored. Some sun-dried clay tablets are so hard that even experts are at times misled into regarding them as kiln-dried.

The clay in a plastic condition is shaped into the size desired. As the style of paper in the present age is in a measure an indication of the general character of the document, so the size and shape of the inscribed clay tablet is indicative, in a general way, of the contents. Historical literature of the Assyrian period, as well as inscriptions which record the erection or restoration of buildings, is found as a rule on cylinders of various sizes and shapes. Some are quadrangular, pentagonal, hexagonal, etc. Some are cone-shaped, or are in the form of a bombshell. Literary writings of the Assyrian people were generally inscribed on good-sized tablets. Legal documents, although differing in form in the various periods, are also readily recognized by their shape. In the Hammurabi and Cassite dynasties, the scribe usually held the tablet so that the lines passed across the narrow part, while in the Neo-Babylonian they ran across the tablet lengthwise. Letters are usually written across the narrow side. Inscribed votive cones, plans of cities, and estates, and topographical maps, are also found in clay, and have been found in various sizes and shapes.

The stylus used by the scribe was a very simple

Babylonia in Days of Abraham 169

affair. Any stick of metal or hard wood which had a square corner could be used. By holding it beneath the palm of the hand between the thumb and the index finger, and by pressing the angular corner into the soft clay, the impression will be that of a wedge. Using the Latin word *cuneus* for wedge,

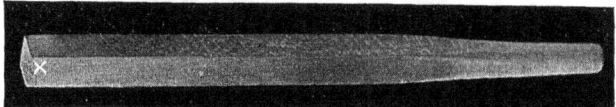

Square end stylus.

Beveled end stylus.

the writing has been called the cuneiform. All characters are made up of single wedges at different angles, and the *winkelhaken* ("angular hook"), which is made by laying the stylus over on its side with the handle towards the right, using the angle x. When the square end stylus is used the writing appears thus:

From the time of the first dynasty, a very marked peculiarity of many of the styli was that the top was made to slope to one side (see illustration). In consequence, the top of the perpendicular wedge was higher on the left side than on the right, and the angle of the *winkelhaken* was less than a right angle. thus: ⌑ when the beveled end stylus was used.

An original tablet.

Written with beveled end stylus.

The latter varies according to the slope of the top of the stylus. The greater it is, the smaller is the angle of the "hook."[1] This slope was made to vary according to the desire of the scribe, which enabled

---

[1] On this subject, see further remarks by the writer in Documents from the Temple Archives, B. E. Vol. XIV, p. 19 f.

him, in this way, to emphasize the individuality of his writing.

The stylus in Assyrian was called *qanû* ("reed"), or *qan-duppi* ("tablet reed" or "stylus"). This would imply that the scribes usually used reed-wood to make their styli. Attention has been called[1] to impressions on some tablets which show the roundness of the reed out of which the stylus was made. The wood of reeds, which grow in abundance in marshy places, is quite hard, and does not readily absorb water; in consequence, it is quite suitable to write upon the soft clay.

Judging from the thousands of seals, signets, and seal-cylinders which have been found, and the thousands of tablets which contain seal impressions, the information given us by the classical writers that practically every man of any standing in a community had his seal, is intelligible. They were usually cut out of hard stone, such as lapis-lazuli, carnelian, green jasper, agate, onyx, crystal, slate, shell, etc. Some are in metal, and judging from the exquisitely fine work, as indicated on some tablets, especially in the Cassite period when a characteristic feature was a decorative border at the top and bottom of the seals (see illustrations page 173), it is thought[2] that some had been capped with gold.

---

[1] See Dr. Messerschmidt's interesting article in *Orientalistische Litteraturzeitung*, Vol. 9, No. 5.

[2] See Dr. W. H. Ward's remark in my Documents from the Temple Archives of Nippur, p. 15.

Seals and Seal-cylinders from the Museum of the University of Pennsylvania. (Nearly natural size.)

Babylonia in Days of Abraham 173

The cylinders usually have a hole passing through them, presumably for the purpose of inserting some kind of an instrument that enabled them to roll the cylinder over the clay, or to insert a string in order to attach them to their person. Seal rings and

Case tablets of the Cassite Period, containing seal impressions.

signets were used, especially in the Neo-Babylonian and Persian periods. In a number of instances the impressions of both a cylinder and a signet of an individual are found upon documents.

The use of the seal did not differ from its ordinary

usage in modern times. It was equivalent to the individual's signature. The entire document, as mentioned (page 166), was written by the scribe; but the use of the seal made it binding by the contracting parties. Usually only the obligor or debtor or the one who gave the document as a receipt left his seal impression; in some cases there are found the seal impressions of the witnesses and the judge before whom the business was transacted. On not a single document of the sons of Murashû does the seal impression of the individual appear in whose interest the tablet was made, or who was the creditor. He held the tablet as a receipt, or as a record of the debtor's obligations. In the Cassite archives, the man who delivered at the residence of the officers their salary, which was paid in kind, left his seal impression upon the records of that payment. This was held by the bursar of the Temple storehouse.

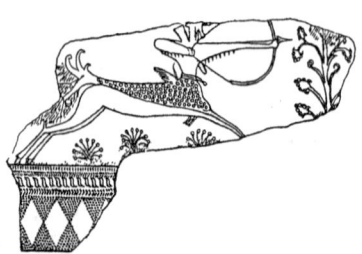

The earliest known form of the centaur, reproduced from seal impressions on a tablet, time of the Cassites.

In most periods, notably later than the Hammurabi dynasty, the individual who did not possess a seal made thumb-nail marks in the soft clay, alongside of which the scribe usually wrote *ṣupurshu*, "his thumb-nail mark," or added his name, *ṣupur*

Babylonia in Days of Abraham

Bêl-erba, "thumb nail of Bêl-erba." In some cases the words *kima kunukkishu*, "instead of his seal," were added. These were regarded as equivalent to his seal. In the tablets of the Cassite period, I found another substitute for the seal, which the ancients called *sisiktu*.[1] The word means "cloth." A tablet in the Berlin Museum, which was also recently published, clearly shows cloth marks[2] near the marks of the *sisiktu*. A tablet of the University of Pennsylvania collection, which is roughly made,

Thumb-nail marks instead of seal impression, Achæmenian Period.

may have cloth marks; but on the four tablets of the latter collection on which the marks of the *sisiktu* were made, there is a clearly-defined little hole. This shows that the *sisiktu*, which perhaps referred to some part of the garment, had in connection with it that which could be used to make this little hole. In a building inscription of Nebuchadrezzar the king is referred to as standing before

---

[1] See Documents from the Temple Archives of Nippur, B. E. Vol. XIV, p. 13.
[2] Ungnad, *Orientalistische Litteraturzeitung*, Vol. IX, No. 3.

176   Light on the Old Testament

the image of his god, whose *sisiktu* he takes hold of. It is thought that this refers to his garment. Perhaps it was his girdle, to which something was appended. On one of the Cassite records from the temple storehouse, an individual left his thumb-

Tablets showing holes made by the *sisiktu*.

nail marks as well as that of the *sisiktu*, which were used instead of his seal.

Letters, contracts, and certain kinds of records were frequently encased; that is, the tablet was wrapped in a thin layer of clay, which formed an envelope. In connection with the study of the administrative temple records of the Cassite dynasty,

Babylonia in Days of Abraham 177

the writer made some experiments which enabled him to arrive at the following conclusions: It was not necessary to allow the tablet to dry out before it was enveloped, in order to prevent the case from clinging to it; and the statement that the tablet was powdered with clay to prevent the case from permanently sticking to it can not be based upon experiments made in encasing tablets, for it would have been found that material thus used tends to

Tablet and envelope. The inscription of the tablet is repeated on the envelope.

close up the impressions of the stylus. Immediately after the document was written, or perhaps after the clay had set somewhat, so that it could not lose its shape when being encased, the thin layer was folded about it. By dipping it into water, the scribe could readily remove all traces of cracks with his fingers. Occasionally the case clings here and there to the tablet, but as a rule it can be peeled off without much difficulty. If it were a letter, the name of the individual for whom it was intended was written upon the envelope, the sender at the same time making impressions of his seal upon it. If it were a contract or record, the entire contents, as a rule, were repeated on the outside. Occasionally the tablet proper does not contain the name of witnesses, or the name of the king, in whose reign the tablet is dated. These were written on the envelope. On the other hand, if it is a record of a debt, the envelope may not contain the statement that the obligor received what is mentioned on it. The full statement was written upon the tablet proper. The seal impressions which are found on the case made it clear that the man whose name was written in connection with his seal was the debtor.

The reason why tablets were encased was practically the same that we have for using envelopes. Primarily it was for prudential purposes. It was an easy matter to change amounts recorded on clay tablets, even if the documents were baked. By cutting a perpendicular wedge before the sign which equals 10 (the *winkelhaken*, pages 169, 170), the amount would be 70.[1] But if the tablet was encased and the impression of the obligor's seal was made on the envelope, it would be impossible for the creditor, who held the tablet, to alter the amount unless he peeled off the envelope,—in which

---

[1] The Babylonians used the sexigesimal system of numbers. The perpendicular wedge equals one and also sixty. Placing the perpendicular wedge after the *winkelhaken, i. e.*, 10)=11, but by putting it before it=70.

case he could not replace it, inasmuch as it contained the seal impressions of the debtor.

The envelopes of contracts, as stated above, were usually inscribed, with some variations, the same as the tablet itself. This made it possible to consult the terms of the document without disturbing the tablet proper. If a charge that alterations of the inscription on the case were made, it was, of course, an easy matter to have the tablet proper examined, if need be, in the presence of the judge, when the terms of the contract could be verified. In short, it is impossible to conceive of a better sealed contract than a clay tablet with an envelope, which contains the seal impressions of the witnesses, scribe, and contracting parties.

In the Temple Archives of the Cassite period, a familiar phrase is, "the debt he shall pay, whereupon the seal he shall break." In other words, after the obligation had been met, the case containing the man's seal was broken off; but the inside tablet was preserved in the archives as a record of the transactions.[1]

Letters were frequently encased, especially in the Hammurabi period. On the envelope, the name of the individual for whom the letter was intended was written, *e. g.*, *Ana Warad-Bêl*, "To Warad-Bêl."

---

[1] For a further discussion on Case Tablets by the writer, see Documents from the Temple Archives of Nippur. B. E. Vol. XIV, p. 10 ff.

180 Light on the Old Testament

The sender then made seal impressions on all sides of the epistle.

Some tablets are ruled. This could have been done in most cases by means of a cord, as has been suggested, but in the lists and contracts of certain periods the edge of the stylus was doubtless used to make these lines. They were easily produced by laying the stylus flatly upon the clay surface, using the edge or corner of the stylus to make the lines. In the early periods, the circle (see page 86) had the value one and the semi-elliptical impression, ten. In making the numerals, the scribe very likely used the upper end of the stylus, which was round. The circle was made by pressing the stylus perpendicularly into the soft clay. In making the semi-elliptical impression the stylus was made to lean, as was done in writing the ordinary characters.

Some tablets are less concave on the reverse, and comparatively flat on the obverse. This is due to the fact that the tablets are thicker in the center than at the edge. In writing the tablet, the scribe frequently laid it upon a table or stand. In writing the obverse, the tablet would settle, and the reverse would become flattened out. When the other side was written, the obverse would become more or less flat, in which condition it remained. Temple records, historical cylinders, and important inscriptions of a mythological or religious character were, as a rule, baked. Contracts and documents of certain periods were also baked. Of the tablets

THE TEMPLE SCHOOL OF NIPPUR.
Series of rooms or buildings found about twenty feet below the surface of Tablet Hill.

found at Nippur, however, the unbaked outnumber the baked ten to one. This is an indication that most of the tablets did not see the kiln.

The fact that scribes were so numerous implies that there were schools in which they had been trained. In 1892 an expedition, which had been sent out by the Turkish government to excavate at Sippara, located within the temple precincts a building in which were found many tablets containing material that had formed the equipment of such a school. Among them are syllabaries or sign dictionaries, grammatical exercises, lists of names and the elements contained in them, mathematical tablets, such as lists of fractions, measures, weights, etc. In other words, the excavator found the remains of a school which was in direct connection with the famous temple of the Sun-god. Father Scheil has published a selection of these tablets in his *Une Saison de Fouilles à Sippar* (1903), in which volume also he gives a plan of the school and a full account of its arrangement and the pedagogical methods employed.

Similar material has been discovered at other sites, notably at Nippur, where exercises of students and practise tablets have been found in considerable numbers. The accompanying plan,[1] which was made by Mr. C. S. Fisher, one of the architects of the last expedition sent out by the University of

---

[1] See Fisher, Excavations at Nippur, Part I.

Babylonia in Days of Abraham 183

Pennsylvania, shows the remaining walls of buildings in a mound known as Tablet Hill. It lies south of Temple Hill. In the eastern and western sections of this great mound, far removed from each other,

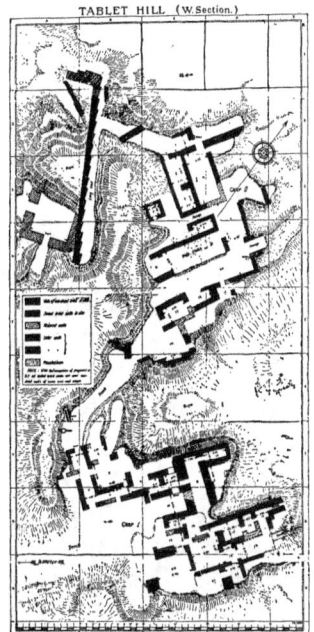 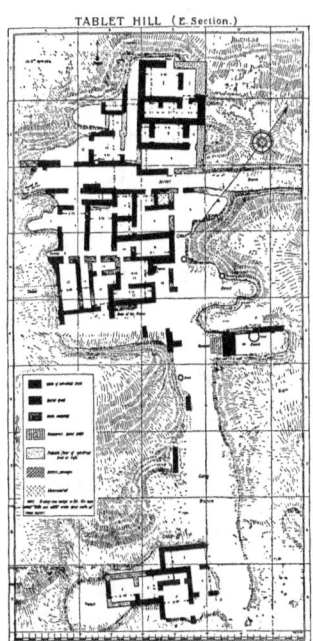

Plan of buildings in Tablet Hill.

series of rooms or buildings were uncovered at a depth of from twenty to twenty-four feet below the surface. They are of special interest in this connection, as the antiquities found in them seem to indicate that the buildings belong to the Hammurabi period. In three of the rooms in the eastern section, and in two of the rooms of the western, large quantities of tablets and fragments of tablets were found. It yet remains to be determined whether the buildings or rooms of the one section have anything to do with the other. Haynes cut a trench between the two sections, but could not establish any connection between them. Unfortunately for the solution of this question, records of the provenience of most of the inscribed material were not kept. Also exactly what relation, if any, these tablets and the rooms in which they were found have to the temple proper, remains to be determined. Another problem involved is the relationship which the two or three rooms of the one section and the three of the other, in which tablets were found, bear to the entire complex of more than sixty rooms and buildings which were uncovered. But with the knowledge we possess that the temple was the all-important institution of the city, and that in all probability all city offices came under its control, it is plausible to assume that these buildings, although at some distance from the sacred precinct, stood in close connection with that institution. Moreover, from the character of the tablets discovered it would seem that Haynes had found the remains of an equipment which had belonged to a school, in many respects similar to that found by Scheil at Sippara. Of special interest are a number of large cones, from six to ten inches

Babylonia in Days of Abraham 185

high, quadrangular, pentagonal, and hexagonal in shape. Some of these have a hole running length-

Reference cylinders from the Temple School of Nippur.

wise through them, in all probability for the purpose of mounting them on revolving stands for reference. These generally seem to contain lexicographical material. In fact, great quantities of fragments of tablets of the same character were found in these rooms, which give us a right to conjecture that they belong to the Library of the Temple School. Considering the importance of the Bêl temple, we have reason to suppose that the collections in connection with that institution included practically all the Babylonian works in law, science, and literature. The latter was largely religious, and doubtless was made to conform to the Bêl cult.

In an upper stratum of this same mound in which the buildings above described were uncovered, although not necessarily at the same spot, many important tablets besides much lexicographical material, not contracts, were found during the excavations conducted by Doctor Peters in the first and second years. As it has been suggested,[1] it is not improbable that at the time of some great invasion the more ancient building or buildings were thrown into ruins; that they were later partially restored; and that the tablets found in the upper stratum of this mound belonged perhaps to the same building, but of a later period. The exact character of these, as well as their relation to the finds belonging to the earlier age, above described, if any, can only be determined after they have been translated. Suffice it to say, that the general appearance holds out the hope of their containing important

---

[1] Hilprecht, Explorations in Bible Lands, p. 516.

Babylonia in Days of Abraham 187

material. Yes, it is not impossible that among these tablets and fragments will be found, when translated, copies of some of the literary productions that belonged to the ancient Bêl cult, which for millenniums had formed the ritual texts of the temple. From our knowledge of the Babylonian religion, gathered from the hundreds of texts which have been published by Scheil, Zimmern, King, Reisner, Boissier, Craig, and others, it is reasonably certain that each religious center had its collection of texts, such as hymns, incantations, omens, and ritual texts in general, which were used in connection with the cult, as well as all that the Babylonians knew about law and science. Further, it is reasonable also to assume that such texts formed part of the equipment used for instruction in their schools.

All kinds of pupil exercises have been found, from tablets containing a repetition of single wedges, to exercises in multiplication and grammar, and in the copying of various kinds of lists. Some contain the repetition over and over of the same character. Others contain lists of various kinds, doubtless copies from sample tablets, or which were written after dictation. In many instances it is as easy to recognize these tablets as it would be to determine at the present time what a paper meant which contained the exercises of a schoolboy. It would seem from the quantities of this material, a great deal of which is clumsily made, that in some instances the excavators had struck the waste-heaps of the school, or, as we might say, their waste-paper baskets. As a rule, exercise tablets of this character were probably broken up, and the material used again and again.

At Nippur and elsewhere have been found a great many tablets about three inches in diameter, inscribed on one side only, which is nearly flat, while the other side is rounded. They usually contain four lines of inscriptions written between five ruled lines. The second line and the fourth, as a rule, contain repetitions of the first and the second. Some are carefully written as if a teacher had made them, to be copied by the scholar, while others are not so carefully made, indicating probably that they are exercise tablets.

Besides these are found numerous tablets containing multiplication tables, many of which seem to have been carefully made by scribes, and doubtless were used as texts for study; while others may have been used for reference in business transactions. This may be inferred from the fact that they have been found at different parts of the city by the different expeditions sent out to Nippur. Some of these tablets contain the multiple of numbers as high as 1350.[1] The accompanying illustration is an 18 x 1 table. It was found on one of the earlier expeditions to Nippur. It reads: 18 a–du 1   18 (*i.e.*, 18 x 1 = 18); $a = du$ 2   36, (*i.e.*, x 2 = 36), etc., until

---

[1] See Hilprecht, Explorations in Bible Lands, p. 531.

Babylonia in Days of Abraham 189

in the twentieth line: *a–du* 20 360, (*i. e.*, x 20 = 360). This is followed by: x 30 = 540; x 40 = 720; x 50 = 1080. It will be noticed that the result of the last calculation is a mistake. It is that of 18 x 60 instead of 18 x 50. The text-book, or reference-table is therefore faulty.[1]

OBVERSE   REVERSE
Multiplication Table. 18 x 1 = 18, etc.

It is quite natural to suppose also that scribes possessed such productions as hymns, incantations, and other kinds of literature in their own collec-

---

[1] From Professor Hilprecht I learn that in his forthcoming work, Mathematical, Metrological and Chronological Tablets from the Temple Library, he will show that the Babylonians knew the binomial theorem, how to extract cube roots, and important equations in higher mathematics.

190 Light on the Old Testament

tions. Syllabaries, or lists of signs with their values, because of the great number in use, must also have been in the possession of most scribes for reference. In our day there have been collected, by one scholar,[1] over twelve thousand different values for the known cuneiform signs and combinations of signs which had been used by the Babylonians and Sumerians; and another list,[2] which is now being compiled from syllabaries and other sources, which have been brought to light since the first was made, will contain about ten thousand. These facts make it reasonable to suppose that scribes had their own lists for reference, especially as writing material cost them nothing. Further,.it is reasonable to expect to find wherever scribes lived practically all the kinds of literature, except official documents, which are found in temple or school libraries.

Pottery objects of various shapes and sizes have been found belonging to this and other periods. For the burning of pottery, small tripods or stilts were used, in order to prevent the objects from touching anything. Especially the glazed pottery shows the marks of these stilts, the same as all glazed ware of the present time. In the potteries of to-day, devices exactly similar are used.

The excavations along the inner side of the city wall at Nippur revealed a great many rooms and

---

[1] Brünnow, Classified List of Cuneiform Signs.
[2] Meissner, *Seltene Assyrische Ideogramme*.

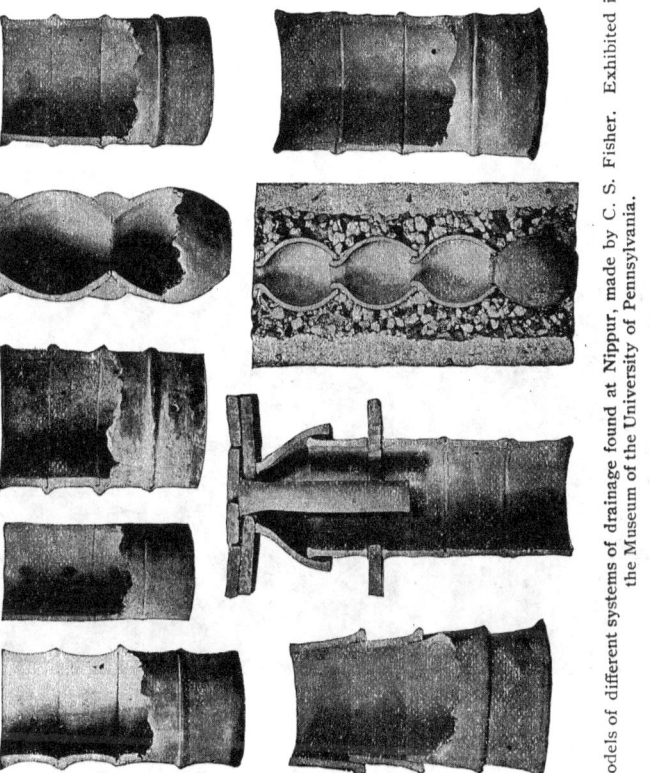

Models of different systems of drainage found at Nippur, made by C. S. Fisher. Exhibited in the Museum of the University of Pennsylvania.

192   Light on the Old Testament

booths which were used by merchants living in the third pre-Christian millennium. A large baking-furnace of this period was found, built against a wall which had been constructed by Ur-Engur, 2700 B. C.[1] It was likely used for the purpose of burning pottery. The top of it was about thirteen feet by

Babylonian Furnace of the time of Abraham.

seven. Its height was nearly four feet. It consisted of a series of elliptical arches, beneath one end of which the fire was kindled. The flames and smoke ascended between these arches, which were separated

---

[1] See Hilprecht, Exploration in Bible Lands, p. 489 f., and Fisher, Excavations at Nippur, Part I, Pl. 3.

Babylonia in Days of Abraham 193

by spaces. Tiles were placed upon the top of the vertical flues thus formed. They served the purpose of covering the chambers, thus forcing the smoke and flames to the rear of the furnace, where the flue was located. At the same time, these tiles formed the top of the stove. At the back of the oven, a flue was constructed the entire length of the stove, whence the smoke escaped. Stoves similar in type are used at the present time in the cities of that district. One writer is of the opinion that a room was built around the oven in which the pottery was arranged; while another thinks that the pottery was placed beneath the arches, as is done in modern kilns, not unlike this archaic furnace of Abraham's time.

Small terra-cotta statues of the gods have been found in large numbers, belonging to all periods of Babylonian history. At Nippur, these frequently represent Bêl and his consort Bêltis. Molds used in their manufacture have also been found, showing that they were extensively used by the people. These images served evidently the same purpose as the *teraphim*, familar to Old Testament students, which seem to have been household gods, or talismans. They were used by the people, doubtless, in a manner similar to the Penates of the Romans.

A great many small clay objects, made in a naïve manner, representing horses, goats, sheep, elephants, and other animals, have been found. Frequently the horses have riders. These evidently

Small terra-cotta images, or household gods, of Bêl and Bêltis, found at Nippur.

were children's toys. At Nippur, no less than four baby rattles have been found. They are shaped like a chicken, doll, drum, and a head. There is a little stone in the hollow body of each, in order to make a noise when the object is shaken. The exact age of these, however, cannot be determined.

Terra-cotta baby rattles from Nippur.

The patriarch's home was in Ur, where he is supposed to have spent his early days. In former years Urfa, not far from Harran, was identified as the ancestral city of the patriarch, but it is now fifty years since Rawlinson identified the mounds known as Mugayyar, in the southern part of the valley, as the home of Abraham. Ur is a very ancient city. Lugal-zaggisi, Lugal-kigubnidudu, and his son Lugal-kisalsi (about 4000 B. C.), known from Nippur inscriptions, call themselves kings of Ur. How much earlier the history of Ur will in time be known, remains to be seen. Following this period, many of the kings of Babylonia call themselves kings of Ur; in fact, two dynasties of Ur are recognized.

The city is situated on the west bank of the Euphrates, about one-hundred and forty miles southeast of Babylon. The narrow strip of land between the Euphrates and the Arabian desert as far as the Persian Gulf, including the marshy land surrounding the outlet of the rivers, was called Kaldu, especially in the second and first millenniums B. C. From the Greek Χαλδαῖοι we get the word Chaldeans. The original pronunciation of the Babylonian Kaldu was likely Kashdu, from which the Hebrew Kashdim is derived.[1] The biblical Merodach-baladan of the time of Hezekiah, who established himself on the throne at Babylon, was a Chaldean. It is thought by some scholars that Nabopolassar, the father of Nebuchadrezzar, was also from that land.

No extensive excavations have been conducted up to the present time at the group of mounds which represent the city, but through the explora-

---

[1] See Hommel, Ancient Hebrew Tradition, p. 210 f.

Babylonia in Days of Abraham

tions of Taylor and Loftus, and inscriptions found elsewhere, considerable is known about the city. The principal temple of Ur was called *E-gishshir-gal*. Others are *E-mu-ri-a-na-ba-ak* and *E-shu-gan-du-du*, which, however, some think may be the same as the first mentioned. In returning from Nippur on his second campaign, Doctor Peters found a door-

The Temple of the moon-god Sin at Ur of the Chaldees.

socket at Ur, lying on the surface. It is in diorite, and bears an inscription of Gimil-Sin, king of Ur. The inscription reads:

> To the god Nannar, the first born of Bêl, his beloved king Gimil-Sin, the beloved of Nannar, a king whom Bêl had appointed in his heart to be shepherd of the world, and of the four corners of the earth, the mighty king, king of Ur, king of the four corners of the earth, *E-mu-ri-a-na-ba-ak*, his beloved house he has built.

198   Light on the Old Testament

The socket, because of its connection with Ur of the Chaldees, and the fact that it is so well preserved, is one of the treasures of the Archæological Museum of the University of Pennsylvania.

Door-socket of Gimil-Sin, found at Ur of the Chaldees.

The results of the excavations of the Bêl temple at Nippur (see page 114) enable us to picture in mind the temple of Ur when Abram lived there. The style of dress, as shown on the statues discovered at Telloh, of men and women (see page 163), is doubtless an indication of that which was worn by Abram and Sarah. In fact, every antiquity dis-

Babylonia in Days of Abraham 199

covered belonging to that period is illustrative of the life in the patriarch's home.

When Abram lived in Ur, the city was under the suzerainty of Elam. About 2285 B. C., Kudur-Nankhundi with his hordes had invaded the land, and put most of the cities under his subjection. The lower part of the valley continued to be a dominion of Elam until the thirty-first year of

Impression of a seal cylinder. Ur-Engur standing before the moon-god Sin.

Amraphel, when that ruler was able to throw off the yoke, and conquer the country.

From Ur, Abram with his father proceeded to Harran, which was about 560 miles to the northwest of the city. It is situated along the banks of the Belias, a tributary of the Euphrates. The name Harran, means "road" (*harrânu*) in Assyrian, doubtless having derived its name from being on the high-road between Syria and the Mesopotamia valley. Harran was affiliated with Ur, in so far that the tutelary deities of both cities were the same. If Terah, whom we imagine was a devotee of the god Sin, from the passage in Joshua (24:2), and because his house had been in Ur, it is not at all improbable that, feeling at home in Harran after leaving Ur, he refused to proceed further. This suggestion has been offered as a reason why Abram tarried with Terah in that city before he completed his journey to Canaan.

In the past it has been customary to draw freely from what is known as the contract literature to portray the every-day life that pulsated in the streets of ancient Babylonian cities. The discovery of the Code of Hammurabi, however, gives us in a systematic form much important information concerning the family, state, and other subjects that enables us to get even a clearer idea than heretofore of life in the age of Abraham.

VIII

CODE OF HAMMURABI

At the close of the year 1901 and the beginning of 1902, M. de Morgan, the French archeologist, who had been excavating for the past years, for his government, at the acropolis of Susa, (or "Shushan the palace," as it is referred to in the book of Esther), discovered the now famous Code of Hammurabi. It is the longest cuneiform inscription known, and perhaps the most important monument of antiquity thus far discovered in the history of excavations. It was found in three large fragments, which were readily joined together. It is cut out of a block of diorite, and stands seven feet, four inches high. At the base it is about twenty-two inches wide, and at the top just above the bas-relief it is about sixteen inches. On the uppermost part of this enormous block of stone, Hammurabi had himself depicted in bas-relief, standing before the sun-god, Shamash, who is seated on a throne. The god wears a swathed head-gear, which is adorned with horns and a flounced garment. In his hand is a staff or scepter and a ring, emblematic perhaps of authority and eternity. Rays emanate from behind his shoulder.

In reverent obedience, Hammurabi stands before

the god with his right hand near his face, perhaps to emphasize the fact that he is listening. His left hand is resting against his body at the waist, an attitude quite similar to his position in a relief upon a brick in the British Museum. He wears upon his head a cap with fillet, well known from the early Sumerian heads of statues found at Telloh and Nippur (see page 159). He is clothed in a long tunic, which lies in folds; it is hemmed in at the waist. Like the gods, he wears what we know as the artificially-plaited Assyrian beard.

Beneath the bas-relief are sixteen parallel columns running belt-wise, beneath which five additional lines had been erased, and the stone polished. On the reverse there are twenty-eight parallel columns, containing in all about four thousand lines of a closely-written cuneiform inscription. It is possible that some king may have desired to alter certain laws; but more probable that the invader, who had carried away the stele, desired to inscribe upon it an account of its recovery from the Babylonians.

It is quite probable that the stone discovered is one of many copies set up in different centers of Hammurabi's great empire. A fragment of another stele, containing a portion of the epilogue, was also found by de Morgan at Susa. The closing lines of the complete stele seem to show that it had been set up in Ebarra, the temple of Shamash, in Sippara. Another expression in the inscription seems to

The Code of Hammurabi.

indicate that a similar stele stood near the statue of the god Marduk in his temple Esagila in Babylon. This, doubtless, was the original, as Babylon was the capital, and the others which were deposited in the different cities were copies.

Several fragments of tablets, now in the British Museum, which had been written for Ashurbanipal (668–626 B. C.), and which were called "The judgment of the righteousness which Hammurabi the great king set up," indicate that his scribes had copied somewhere these laws. In Babylonia also a series was known by: *Nînu-ilum-ṣîrum,* "when the lofty Anu," which are the opening words of the code. Fragments of these having been published by Professor Peiser before the discovery of the stele, Professor Delitzsch inferred the existence of the code, and even styled it the "Code of Hammurabi." By the assistance of these copies, attempts have been made to restore some of the erased portions of the code.

This stele was carried to Elam by some conqueror of Babylonia. In the vicinity of the place of discovery another stele, which recorded a victory by Narâm-Sin, was found. A part of its inscription was also erased, and recut by Sutruk-Nankhundi (about 1200 B. C.), who says that he secured this stele at Sippara, and dedicated it to his god Shushinak at Susa. De Morgan also found a large number of Babylonian boundary-stones belonging to the Cassite period. These facts point to an in-

Code of Hammurabi 205

vasion by the Elamites at the close of the Cassite dynasty, and make it probable that Sutruk-Nankhundi had also carried away the stele of Hammurabi.

The inscription is divided into a prologue, code, and an epilogue. In the prologue, Hammurabi gives his titles, mentions the gods he worshiped, enumerates the cities over which he ruled, and in general magnifies himself by referring to the beneficent deeds which he conferred upon his people and country. Including the number of laws erased, which are estimated at about thirty-five, the code has about two hundred and eighty-two paragraphs of laws.

Contrary to the conclusions arrived at by other scholars, Professor Lyon of Harvard has shown that Hammurabi has arranged his laws in a definite and logical system. He says:[1] "In the skilful arrangement of its material, the code has never been excelled, and it has probably never been approached."

On some subjects but one law is given, while upon others as many as thirty. The following brief outline will afford an idea of the subject-matter treated: Witchcraft, witnesses, judges; concerning offenses involving the purity of justice, as tampering with witnesses, jury, or judge; crimes of various

---

[1] The Structure of the Hammurabi Code, Journal of the American Oriental Society, Vol. XXV, p. 254.

sorts, as theft, receiving stolen goods, kidnaping, fugitive slaves, burglary; duties of public officers in their administration; laws relating to landlords, tenants, creditors, debtors; canal and water rights, licenses, messengers, herdsmen, gardeners, slander, family relationship, marriage, divorce, desertion, breach of promise, adultery, unchastity, concubinage; rights of women, purchase money of brides, inheritance, adoption, responsibility for all kinds of assaults; fees of surgeons, branding of slaves, fees and responsibilities of builders and boatmen, hiring of boats; agricultural life, the purchase and punishment of slaves who repudiate their master, etc.

In the epilogue, Hammurabi recounts his noble deeds, and credits himself with faithfulness in administration and loyalty to the interest of the people. He charges that every ruler shall observe the laws and commandments after him. He pronounces a blessing upon those who will faithfully administer the laws; and in long-drawn-out curses, he calls upon the gods of Babylonia to destroy those who neglect and annul them, or who alter the inscription.

There is no definite information as regards the origin of the code, but many things point to the fact that earlier collections of laws were utilized by the codifier. The legal phraseology employed, the existence of the early Sumerian family laws, the fact that some of the same laws were quoted in the contract tablets of an earlier period, all point to the existence of a code or codes prior to Hammurabi.

Code of Hammurabi

The fact should be taken into consideration that the greatest confusion must have existed in Babylonia prior to the conquest of Hammurabi because of the many petty independent states. Also Elam, having dominated a portion of the land for a long period with Rim-Sin (Arioch), the king's son, stationed at Larsa, must have influenced greatly the courts of justice and their decisions in that section of the country. The codification of laws under such conditions, or the promulgation of old but accepted judicial decisions,—sentences of judgment, as Hammurabi himself regarded them,—was surely a task of no mean proportions.

The study of the code reveals the same peculiar mixtures of laws suitable for different states of society as is found in the Old Testament. In short, the code doubtless amalgamated the diverse elements of the small states, which had been handed down by the former inhabitants of the valley, the Sumerian as well as the Semitic. In the establishment of his mighty empire, which held together for centuries, this unification of laws, dispensed in regular courts of justice, doubtless was one of the most important factors in overcoming the great confusion that must have existed.

The code recognizes three grades in society. First, the *amêlu*, which included the aristocrat, the gentleman, the free citizen, the professional man, the officer, the tradesman. Secondly, the *mushkênu*, who was, as the term implies, the poor man, or pleb, the man of a lower rank; the freedman who had been a slave was also included. His temple offerings could be less. His fines were lower, but at the same time, in case of injury, the damages he received were also less than those of the gentry. Thirdly, the *ardu*, or the slave. There seem to have been a great many slaves in Babylonia at that time. Besides recognizing these three grades, the code legislated also for certain classes of men and women, professions, trades, and occupations.

It has been the custom with most peoples in a large part of the ancient as well as the modern Orient, including the Hebrews, to base a betrothal upon an agreement of the man or his parents to pay a sum of money to the father of the girl. In Babylonia this was called *terḫatu*, "bride money." This, together with the gift of the husband and her dowry, formed the marriage-portion which was given to the bride. It would hardly be right to call the money which was paid the price of the bride, as the transaction was primarily for prudential purposes. It gave her protection against ill treatment and infidelity on the part of her husband, as well as divorce. She perhaps could not get this protection in a better way. For while her husband may have made use of her money, if she returned to her father's house she took it with her, unless she was the offending party. This made the position of woman higher than it would have been otherwise. If she died childless, her dowry was returned to her family.

If she had children, the marriage portion was divided among them. In case the father of the girl rejected her suitor, double the amount of his *terḫatu* was returned. If the suitor broke his engagement, the girl's father retained the *terḫatu*. If he had been slandered by a rival, the latter could not marry the woman. It seems that the betrothal took place when the parties were young; and the engagements were usually made by the parents. If the father died before all the sons were married, prior to the distribution of the estate, the *terḫatu* for those not having wives was first deducted.

In the marriage contracts, which were necessary to make the marriage legal, it is not unusual to find conditions,—such as the bride being required to wait upon her mother-in-law, or even upon another wife; or certain conditions relative to the disposition of property given by her father; or in case the man broke his agreement and took a second wife, that she could secure a divorce.

Concubinage was indulged in, especially where the first wife was childless, and she had not given her husband a slave-maid, in order that he might have children. The concubine could not place herself on an equality with the wife, although she was a free woman, and lived in the same house. If she became insolent she could be reduced to slavery, but could not be sold if she had borne children. After the man's death, she had the usufruct of house and garden to raise her children. When they came into possession of their inheritance, she received a child's portion, after which she could again marry. If the man recognized the concubine's children as his own, at his death his estate was equally shared by the children of both, with preference, however, of choice to the wife's children. If he had not recognized them as his own, they received nothing, but gained their freedom.

The wife received, at her husband's death, her marriage portion and anything deeded to her by her husband during life. If he had not made her a gift, she received a son's share. At her death, what she possessed was divided among her children. After her husband's death, the children could not force her to leave her home; but, if she desired to marry again, she could take along her marriage-portion. At her death, this was shared by the children from both marriages. A widow with young children could only marry with the consent of the judge. An inventory was made of the former husband's property, which was then entrusted to the couple for the children. Not a utensil could be sold. The buyer of an article lost it, and the price paid for it.

According to the Sumerian laws, which are frequently found quoted in the contracts of this age, a man could divorce his wife by paying her one half mina. These laws doubtless belonged to an earlier age. The code provided that if a man divorced a wife, whether a concubine or votary, if she had borne him children, her marriage-portion was to be given to her, besides the necessaries of life, to bring up her children. After they were grown up, they were compelled to give the mother a son's share. She was then free to marry again. In case she had not borne children, she received back her dowry including the bride-price. In case there was no bride-price, she received one mina of silver if the man belonged to the gentry; but if a commoner, one-third of a mina. A woman who had lived properly could divorce her husband who had been faithless, in which case she returned to her father's house with her dowry. In the case of a worthless woman, the code provides for her divorce without any provision. The husband could marry again, and degrade her as a slave. If she had been unfaithful, she could be drowned. Disease offered no grounds for divorce. The man, however, could marry a second wife, but was compelled to maintain, in his home, his invalid wife as long as she lived. If she preferred to return to her father's house, her dowry was returned to her.

The code legislated concerning desertion. If a man was taken captive in war, having provided for his wife's maintenance during his absence, and she entered another man's house, she was condemned to death as an adulteress. If he had not provided for her, and she had borne the other man children, on the return of her husband she was compelled to return to him, but the children remained with their father. If the desertion was voluntary, and he had not provided for his wife, on his return he could not reclaim her.

The father, while he had no control over the life and death of his child, could treat him as a chattel, and pledge for a debt. In four years the child became free. For disobedience, in the old Sumerian law, a father could brand a son and sell him as a slave; or, according to the code, his hands could be cut off. If the father desired to favor one of his children, this could only be done while he was living, and by contract. After the father's death, the law of inheritance fixed the child's share. To cut off a child from sonship, it was necessary to make charges of wrong-doing before a judge. Only after the second offense, and for a serious misdemeanor, could he be disinherited. If an adopted child of a votary or palace favorite repudiated his foster parents, his tongue should be cut out; and if he ran away, his eyes were to be put out, for his ingratitude.

A number of the laws refer to the adoption of children. A great many adoption contracts belonging to this time are known. If a child that had been adopted discovered its parents, and desired to return to them, this could be done, provided a handicraft had not been taught, nor he had been considered a son, or had not been adopted by one belonging to the court. If a man desired to disinherit a foster-child, he could do so by paying it one-third of a child's share. A great many contracts show that children were adopted by aged people, that they might care for them in their old age.

A great many laws in the code bear upon slavery; considered in connection with the many contracts and documents dealing with slaves, these give very satisfactory knowledge concerning this class of social beings. The slave was treated like a piece of property. He could be sold or pledged. If he received injury at the hands of another, compensation for the same was paid to the owner. For insolence he could be branded, or tattooed; but his master could not put him to death. If agreeable to his master, he could engage in business and acquire wealth. With this he could buy his freedom. He could marry, and live in a house of his own, by his master's consent. If he married a slave girl, the law permitted the owner to regard his children and property as his own. If he married a free woman, the master had no claim upon the children or property. At the slave's death, the property was divided between the wife and himself. Her children were free. A slave could become a concubine. At the death of her master, she gained her freedom. The law of adoption enabled him to adopt their children, when they could become his heirs. In case he had no other children, these would have first choice in the distribution of his property. As Sarah gave Hagar to Abraham, the Babylonian wife could give a slave girl to her husband for wife.

The woman, however, retained the right to punish her in case of insolence. If she had not borne children, she could sell her as a slave. If she had borne children, the wife could not send her away, but could put a slave mark upon her, and reckon her with the slaves. The story of Hagar was in strict accord with Babylonian custom, except the sending of her away.

Provision was made also with reference to disease when a slave was sold. In case the buyer detected any weakness or disease within a month after the purchase, the owner could be compelled to redeem the slave. In the case of a runaway slave, the captor was compelled to return him to his master, when he received two shekels. The death penalty was the punishment for the captor who retained or harbored the slave. A great many of the slaves were the captives of military expeditions, and, for a certain period, certain obligations were due the state on the part of those who received them. Freemen could also be enslaved to settle unsatisfied obligations.

The code makes us familiar with a class of votaries. They were, however, altogether different from the prostitutes dedicated to the goddess Ishtar at Erech. Some seem to have been women of means, and were highly respected. Their vow included virginity. They lived in a convent, or bride-chamber. On taking the vow, they usually received a dowry, as the bride of the god. It was possible for them to leave the convent and marry, but they must remain virgins. If her husband insisted upon having children, she was required to give him a maid, in which case he could not take a concubine. If she refused, he could take one; but she could not rank on the same equality with the votary. In case the concubine bore children, and placed herself on an equality with the votary, the latter could brand her, and reckon her as a slave. If she had not borne children, she could be sold for insolence. If the votary broke her vow, and bore children, she had no legal right to their possession. They could be adopted by others.

Votaries seemed to have engaged in business relations with others. They were, however, not permitted, on pain of death by burning, to keep a beer shop or even enter one. At a father's death, the votary was entitled to one-third of a son's share. Her estate could be managed by her brothers, but in case dissatisfaction arose she could appoint a steward to look after her affairs. In the event of her death, her property reverted to her brothers. If the father had made a deed of gift, she could dispose of it as she desired. There was a class of votaries dedicated to the god Marduk, at Babylon, who enjoyed the privilege of disposing of their property at death as they saw fit.

It seems the wine shops were usually kept by women, for whom the code had especial legislation. The measure for drink was to be the same as for corn. In case she overcharged her customers, they could throw her into the water. If she did not inform the authorities in case she overheard treasonable conspiracy in her shop, the penalty was death.

For surgery and the practise of medicine, there was special legislation. If the physician cured a broken limb, or healed a diseased bowel, his fee from the gentry was fixed at five shekels; from the commoner, three; and from the master of the slave treated, two. As in later periods, magic and medicine were doubtless intimately connected with each other. Decoctions of various kinds were employed in connection with the repertory of incantations and exorcism. Whether the aid of one who possessed priestly functions to conduct this part was necessary, is not known.

In order to discourage the surgeon from making rash operations, and overcharging his patients, severe penalties were fixed in case of unsuccessful operations; and for successful ones the fees were regulated. For an operation upon the upper class, the surgeon received ten shekels; the lower class, five; and a slave, two. If the patient died, the surgeon's hands were cut off. In the case of a slave, he had to replace him with one of equal value. If the eye of a slave was lost, the owner received half the price of the slave.

The veterinary surgeon was already recognized as being in a distinct class. If his operations were successful, his fee was one-sixth of a shekel. If the animal died, he was compelled to pay one-sixth of the value.

Similar legislation was enacted for builders. For a completed house, he was paid at the rate of two shekels per *sar* of house. The punishment for his bad workmanship, in case the house fell down, was the death penalty if the owner was killed. If a son of the owner was killed, one of his own sons was put to death. A slave had to be replaced by another, and the loss of goods he had to make good. Further, he was compelled to rebuild the house at his own expense.

The boat-builder was paid at the rate of two shekels, per *gur* in the boat. His work was guaranteed for one year. In case it did not prove trustworthy, and the boat suffered injury, he was compelled to repair it, or replace it. If a man hired a boat, and it was lost or injured, he had to make good the loss. If the owner hired a boatman, his wages were fixed at six *gur* per year. If the boat suffered injury through his carelessness, he made good the loss. If the ship grounded, and he refloated it, he had to pay the owner one-half its price. If a boat was sunk at anchor by another, the owner made an affidavit regarding his loss, which was refunded by the one who had done the damage.

The office of judge seems to have occupied a position relatively the same as in these days. His pronounced decision, however, was to be irrevocable. In case he altered it, he was to pay twelvefold the penalty of the judgment, and be publicly expelled from his seat. Thereafter he could not even sit with the judges at a trial.

A defendant in a serious case was granted six months if necessary to produce his witnesses. Tampering with witnesses was penalized heavily. If the witnesses testified falsely, and the judgment involved the death penalty, he was killed. The oath figured prominently in the code, and in the contracts that have been deciphered. Considerable importance in this age was attached to it in the purgation of charges, and claims for injury. It seems to have been administered at particular places, *e.g.*, at the *Shasharû* of Shamash in Sippara, or before the sculptured dragon on the door of the temple of Marduk at Babylon. The gods invoked in the oath were the patron deities of the city; at Sippara, for example, Shamash, Ai, and Marduk were invoked; at Nippur, Bêl, Ninib, and Nusku. In many of the documents, the name of the king was invoked with the gods. It usually follows the names of the gods.

The decision was generally drawn up by the scribe, who gave the names of the witnesses and the judge. These documents usually contain the seal impressions of some of the witnesses and the judge. If the decision in a criminal case was unfavorable to the prosecutor, and it involved the death penalty, he himself was killed. For a false accusation of slander, he was branded, and generally he was required to pay the penalty that would have been exacted from

Code of Hammurabi

the accused if he had been successful in gaining the suit.

The death penalty seems to have been inflicted for a great many offenses; at least the code requires it as the punishment. But whether the judges generally inflicted the extreme penalty, cannot be ascertained. Considering that the judges had legislative power, the code could not be regarded as much more severe than some codes of the Christian era. It was inflicted for witchcraft, bearing false witness in a capital trial, housebreaking, highway robbery, adultery, neglect of duties on the part of certain officers, criminal negligence on the part of a builder, permitting conspiracy in a beer shop, for theft at a fire, for desertion on the part of a woman, for kidnaping a child, and harboring a runaway slave. In many cases the kind of death is not stated; but in others it is. Drowning is mentioned for a woman caught in adultery, unless her husband appeals to the king in her behalf; impalement for a woman who had her husband killed for the sake of another; burning for incest with his mother or stepmother after the father's death.

Corporal mutilation or punishment was freely indulged in. The *lex talionis*, eye for eye, tooth for tooth, the cutting off the hand for striking a father, or for unlawful surgery; the branding of the slave on the forehead of an individual for slandering a votary, are mentioned in the code. On the death of a child, the wet-nurse's breasts were cut off if it was learned that she had suckled another child at the same time. For grossly assaulting a superior, scourging was the penalty. Sixty lashes with an ox-hide whip were publicly administered. If the offender was a slave, he had his ear cut off. For an assault upon an equal the penalty was one mina of silver; if upon a plebeian, one half-mina. If a man struck a free woman who was pregnant, resulting in a miscarriage, he was compelled to pay ten shekels; if he assaulted a daughter of a plebeian, five shekels; and if a man's maid, two. If the woman died, and she was a free woman, his own daughter was killed; but if a plebeian, one half-mina of silver; and if a maid, one-third. If the slave brander removed the marks of a slave without the owner's consent, his hands were cut off. If a man had deceived the brander concerning the slave, he was put to death; the brander, on swearing that he did not do it knowingly, was permitted to go free.

A man could give his wife, son, daughter, or slave to work off a debt; but in the fourth year, he or she could gain freedom. A creditor could sell a slave he held as a pledge, providing, if it was a female, that she had not borne children for her master; in which case it devolved upon him to redeem her. If while in service a free-born hostage died from ill treatment, the creditor's son was put to death. If a man contracted a debt before marriage, the creditor could not take his wife for it. The same applied to the woman's debts before marriage. After their

Code of Hammurabi 221

marriage, together they were responsible for debts contracted.

In the code the duties of those having the use of government lands is clearly defined. There are a great many laws relating to farming, the hire of laborers, oxen, cows, wagons, and the regulation of hire and wages, the grazing of flocks, the renting and cultivation of fields, and of damages through carelessness.

The every-day life of the Babylonian in Abraham's day can be understood in no better way at the present time, than by a careful study of the Hammurabi Code,[1] as well as the legal documents of that period.[2]

To the biblical student the study of the code is especially interesting as it throws light upon customs among the patriarchs, for example on Abraham seeking a wife for his son (Gen. 24:4), the possession of Machpelah Cave being placed on a legal

---

[1] For the text, transliteration, translation in English, glossary and sign list of the Hammurabi Code, see Professor R. F. Harper's excellent publication, The Code of Hammurabi.

[2] In his "Babylonian and Assyrian Laws, Contracts and Letters," the Rev. C. H. W. Johns of Cambridge discusses at length the contracts and letters of this period which have been published by Strassmaier, Meissner, Pinches, King and others. as well as give a complete translation of the Code of Hammurabi. Recently two volumes by Drs. Frederick and Ranke on the Contract literature of this age appeared. The latter is in the series, Babylonian Expedition of the University of Pennsylvania, Vol. VI., Part 1. It will be followed by Part 2, by Dr. Arno Poeble.

basis (Gen. 23:14-20), or Rachel giving her handmaid Bilhah to Jacob for wife (Gen. 30:1-4) as well as the story of Hagar (Gen. 16:1,2).

An immense literature on the code has sprung into existence since its discovery. It was first translated and published by Father Scheil. Translations by Doctors Winckler, Johns, Pinches, and R. F. Harper followed. As there remains much that is obscure in the code, for years to come it will form the basis of studies on the part of scholars.

IX

MOSES AND HAMMURABI

Some scholars have indulged in extravagant statements with reference to the possibility of a code of laws having been promulgated as early as Moses. Such questions will no longer be raised, but another, now uppermost in the minds of some scholars, is, whether the Mosaic code is dependent upon the Hammurabi. It seems reasonable to assume that the Israelitish Code is based on precedent, the same as the Babylonian, but exactly what indebtedness there is due to the Babylonian, if any, or to general Semitic law, will be a question long debated by investigators. Inasmuch, however, as Abraham's ancestral home was in Babylonia, and as Hammurabi was suzerain over *Amurru* (which included Palestine), it would be quite natural to suppose that the latter established his laws in that land as well as in Babylonia; in which case, later Palestinian laws would probably show such influence. But nothing is known at the present which proves that this was done.

Laws in the two codes have been pointed out as being strictly parallel. Others treat of the same subjects, having penalties which are quite similar. Besides, the study of one code throws light upon the other. In consideration of these facts it is natural and reasonable to suppose that Israel's code owes some indebtedness to the Babylonian. If such should eventually be proved to be true it would in no wise detract from the Israelitish code. But contrary to what has been declared, this does not seem to be the case. The spirit underlying the Oriental *lex talionis*, which has existed in that region for millenniums, and prevails even at the present day, is in both codes. Also certain laws arising from common customs, peculiar to that entire district, might be pointed out. But beyond these the similarities can reasonably be explained as coincidences which are due to the existence of similar conditions. For the sake of comparison, some of those which are strikingly similar or are parallel in the Hammurabi and Mosaic laws follow:

Law number 7 reads: "If a man has received, without witness or contract, from the son of another, or a servant of another, silver or gold, male or female slaves, ox, sheep, or ass, or anything else, or has received [the same] in trust, that man shall be put to death for theft." This enactment refers to any one who buys or receives on deposit anything without a witness or a contract, regularly drawn up, who is liable to have his act regarded as a theft, punishable by death. The Mosaic law (Lev. 6: 2–7) legislates against similar offenses, but because the individual is guilty, he shall make restitution of that which he has fraudulently obtained. If he

Moses and Hammurabi

have sworn falsely, he shall even restore it in the principal, and shall add the fifth part thereto, besides making a trespass offering, when "it shall be forgiven him."

Law number 8 reads: "If a man has stolen ox, or sheep, or ass, or pig, or goat, if from a god (temple), or a palace, he shall pay thirtyfold." The Mosaic law (Exod. 22:1) reads: "If a man shall steal an ox, or a sheep, and kill it, or sell it; he shall pay five oxen for an ox, and four sheep for a sheep." Theft, in the Hammurabi Code, is more severely dealt with than in the Mosaic. In many cases it is punishable by death. Inability to pay a severe penalty might also mean death.

Law number 14 reads: "If a man has stolen a child of another, he shall be put to death." The Mosaic law is the same (Exod. 21:16). "He that stealeth a man, and selleth him, or if he be found in his hand, he shall surely be put to death."

Law number 21 reads: "If a man has broken into a house, he shall be killed before that breach, and they shall thrust him into it." Exodus 22:2-4 reads: "If the thief be found breaking in, and be smitten so that he dieth, there shall be no bloodguiltiness for him. If the sun be risen upon him, there shall be bloodguiltiness for him; he shall make restitution: if he have nothing, then he shall be sold for his theft." The Mosaic law regards breaking into a house as an unpardonable sin. If in the act he escapes with his life, and he has not

The zebu, called the ox by the ancient Babylonians.

wherewith to make restitution, he shall be sold as a slave.

Law number 57 requires a shepherd who has not made an agreement with the owner of a field to pasture his sheep on his crop, to pay to the owner of the field, after he has harvested his crop, over and above his crop, twenty *gur* of grain for each *gan* of land. The Mosaic law (Exod. 22:5) requires the shepherd who has unlawfully pastured his flock to make restitution out of the best of his own.

Law number 117: "If a man owes a debt, and he has given his wife, his son, or his daughter [as hostage] for the money, or has bound them over to render service, for three years they shall serve in the house of the creditor; but in the fourth year he shall set them free." The Mosaic code (Exod. 21:2) says: "If thou buy a Hebrew servant, six years he shall serve: and in the seventh he shall go out free for nothing." Also (Exod. 21:7): "If a man sell his daughter to be a bondwoman, she shall not go out as the men-servants do."

Law number 125 requires a man who has received something on deposit, which has been lost or stolen, to make good all that has been given to him. The owner of the house shall look after that which has been lost, and recover it from the thief. (See Exod. 22:7-9). The Mosaic law (Exod. 22:12) requires that in case an animal which has been placed in the care of a neighbor for safe-keeping is stolen, he shall make restitution.

Law number 129 enacts that those caught in adultery be bound and cast into the water. If the husband desired to save his wife, or the king his servant, he could do so. The Mosaic code (Lev. 20:10), reads: "And the man that committeth adultery with another man's wife, even he that committeth adultery with his neighbor's wife, the adulterer and the adulteress shall surely be put to death."

Law number 155 enacts that a man who has been caught in adultery with his daughter-in-law, shall be strangled, and cast into the water. Leviticus 20:12 reads: "If a man lie with his daughter-in-law, both of them shall surely be put to death: they have wrought confusion; their blood shall be upon them."

Law number 157: "If a man, after his father's death, has lain in the bosom of his mother, they shall be burnt, both of them together." The Mosaic provision (Lev. 20:11), reads: "And the man that lieth with his father's wife hath uncovered his father's nakedness: both of them shall surely be put to death; their blood shall be upon them."

Law number 195: "If a son strike his father, they shall cut off his fingers." Exodus 21:15, reads: "And he that smiteth his father, or his mother, shall surely be put to death."

Law number 196 reads: "If a man has destroyed the eye of another, they shall destroy his eye. Law number 197: "If one has broken the limb of another, they shall break his limb." Law number 200:

Moses and Hammurabi 229

"If a man has knocked out the tooth of a man who is his equal, they shall knock out his tooth." This ancient system of the *talio*, as mentioned above, is paralleled in Exodus 21:24, 25; Leviticus 24:20; Deuteronomy 19:21; Matthew 5:38, etc.

Law number 199: "If he knocked out the eye of a man's servant, or broke the leg of a man's servant, he shall pay one-half his value." The Mosaic code (Exod. 21:26, 27) requires that a man who destroyed the eye of his servant shall let him or her go free for the eye's sake. The same in the case of a tooth.

Law number 206: "If a man has struck another in a quarrel, and wounded him, that man shall swear, 'I struck him without intent,' and shall be responsible for the physician." Exodus 21:18, 19 reads: "And if men contend, and one smite the other with a stone, or with his fist, and he die not, but keep his bed; if he rise again, and walk abroad upon his staff, then shall he that smote him be quit: only he shall pay for the loss of his time, and shall cause him to be thoroughly healed." Compare also Exodus 21:12, 13.

Law number 209: "If a man has struck the daughter of a man, and has caused a miscarriage, he shall pay ten shekels for her miscarriage." Law number 210: "If that woman die, they shall kill his daughter." Exodus 21:22–25 reads: "And if men strive together, and hurt a woman with child, so that her fruit depart, and yet no harm follow; he shall be surely fined, according as the woman's husband shall lay upon him; and he shall pay as the judges determine. But if any harm follow, then thou shalt give life for life."

Law number 245: "If a man has hired an ox, and has caused his death through carelessness, or abuse, he shall restore ox for ox, to the owner of the ox." The Mosaic law (Exod. 22:14, 15) provides: "And if a man borrow aught of his neighbor, and it be hurt, or die, the owner thereof not being with it, he shall surely make restitution. If the owner thereof be with it, he shall not make it good: if it be a hired thing, it came for its hire."

Law number 250: "If the bull has gone wild, and in his path has gored a man and caused his death, that case shall have no penalty." Exodus 21:28 reads: "And if an ox gore a man or a woman to death, the ox shall be surely stoned, and his flesh shall not be eaten; but the owner of the ox shall be quit."

Law number 251: "If a man's ox was wont to gore, and its habit as a gorer they made known to him, and he has not blunted its horns, or penned up the ox, and then the ox has gored the son of a man, and has caused his death, the owner shall pay half a mina of silver." Law number 252: "If it be a slave that has been killed, he shall pay one-third of a mina of silver." Exodus 21:29 reads: "But if the ox was wont to gore in time past, and it hath been testified to its owner, and he hath not kept it in, but it hath killed a man or a woman; the ox shall

Moses and Hammurabi 231

be stoned, and its owner also shall be put to death." Exodus 21:32: "If the ox gore a man-servant or a maid-servant, there shall be given unto their master thirty shekels of silver, and the ox shall be stoned."

There are other laws among the two hundred and eighty-two of the Babylonian code which are paralleled by laws of the Mosaic period, but these appear to be the most striking and noteworthy.

Not a few scholars, in discussing the question of the dependence of the Israelitic code upon the Babylonian, seem to think that the Hebrew code is indebted to the older. Some see similarity in the phraseology, besides in the thought embodied in the code. Others maintain that the origin of both is to be found in Arabia, either because they hold that the original home of the Semites is to be found in that land, or because of the influence of Jethro the Kenite father-in-law of Moses (see Exodus 18:14–27); and the fact that it is probable that the kings of the Hammurabi dynasty were Arabian.

If the laws which have been pointed out as being similar are carefully considered from a common-sense point of view in connection with the entire code, the only conclusion that can be reached is that the similarity of those laws must be ascribed to similar conditions which would give rise to them no matter how far the one people was removed from the influence of the other, except as indicated before, those laws which were influenced by the barbarous law of retaliation or Oriental law in general. To give a single illustration: when an African or a North American Indian owns a vicious animal and knows its habits, and does not restrain it from doing violence, the only penalty thought of is that he shall be accounted responsible for any damages done. Where slavery exists, or where one may become enslaved for a debt, similar laws may be expected. The same is true of the laws of chastity and of the family, or the relations of one member of a family to another. Such to a great extent are not confined to civilized peoples. Moreover, similar customs will give rise to similar laws, as human nature is the same everywhere.

The phraseological and philological arguments that have been advanced seem to have less in them. Also, we have no evidence from the Old Testament that Jethro taught Moses a single precept. His advice as regards the administering of law cannot be construed as such. That Arabia is the original seat of the Semites, or that it is the home of the kings of the first dynasty of Babylon, are theories held by some, for which there is no proof. In short, dependence upon the Babylonian code, or even a common origin for both, cannot be proved at the present, and from the light at hand it does not seem plausible.

Between the Mosaic and the Hammurabi codes there is an exceedingly wide gulf. If for no other reason, the responsibility of the individual for his own deeds, whereby the son is not punished for his father's deeds, or the father for the son's, gives superiority to the Hebrew code. There are some humanitarian considerations in the Babylonian, as for instance the provisions for an invalid wife, or an enraged father who wishes to disinherit a son; but if the codes, even from this point of view, were compared, it will be found that the Mosaic is not wanting.

The Hebrew also in almost every respect religiously and ethically is far superior to the Babylonian. The gods are prominently mentioned in the prologue and epilogue of the latter, but play no rôle in the code itself. Pure and simple external conformity to the law is all that is required. Inasmuch as Hammurabi is known to have been religiously inclined, it may be unfair to judge the code from this point of view; as it deals with civil law, and he may have intentionally omitted the religious element. There is not, however, even a semblance of a law in the Babylonian against covetousness and selfishness.

The fundamental principle of the Israelitish command: "Be ye holy, for I am holy," on the other hand has an inward emphasis which makes its impress upon all actions. "Thou shalt love thy neighbor as thyself," as well as purification and devotion to God, is the keynote of the Mosaic law. It was God's commandment that the Israelite was required to obey. Cursed was he that fulfilled not the words of the law to do them. This especially was the spirit of the prophets. This is totally foreign to the Babylonian code.

X

THE NAME JAHWEH IN CUNEIFORM LITERATURE

A question which has aroused considerable interest, by reason of its discussion in the *Bibel und Babel* literature, is whether it shall be acknowledged that certain scholars are right when they insist that the two names *Ja-a'-ve-ilu* and *Ja-ve-ilu* contain the name Jahweh, and that these names, which are nearly a thousand years older than corresponding names in the Old Testament, attest the worship of a single god *Jahu* (meaning Jahweh); or as stated by another scholar: "both composita contain the name of the god *Yaveh, Yahu.*" Others are inclined to regard the view as "not improbable," and further state that names meaning "*Jahu* is God," do not play such an important part in the question as one would like to assign to them; but, on the contrary, their early existence, even from the biblical point of view is expected.

If this hypothesis obtained, a number of important problems would be solved, and we should be compelled to readjust our understanding of a number of passages in the Old Testament. But while it has been made by noted scientists with the greatest assurance, it will not be out of place to weigh carefully their conclusions, especially as a general acceptance has not been accorded them.

The two names that play the important rôle in the question are on tablets in the British Museum, belonging to the contract literature of the so-called Hammurabi dynasty. Professor Sayce, of Oxford, was the first to call attention to them. They are: *Ja-w(p)i-ilu* and *Ja-aḫ(?)-w(p)i-ilu*. It should be said that there is considerable uncertainty as regards the character *aḫ*, or what is known as the "breathing" in the second name. However, granting that it is read correctly and treating it in connection with the first name, it would probably be read: *Ja'wi-ilu* or *Ja'pi-ilu*. Besides the interpretation mentioned, namely, "Jahweh is God," various other interpretations have been offered, as for example: *Jaḫpe-el*, "God covers," or "God protects;" *Jahweh-el*, "God exists," *Jahve-ilu*, "God gives," etc.

The interpretation, "Jahweh is God," means that the unabbreviated form of Jahweh is used in this name. In fact, there is not a single instance in the Hebrew literature, early or late, where the name of Jahweh is found in its full form, when compounded with other elements in personal names. Why should we not expect to find the same contracted form, namely, *Jehô* or *Jô*, when it is the first element, as is the case in every instance in the hundreds of names, of those preserved in the Old Testament

Jahweh in Cuneiform Literature   237

which contain the divine elements? In Assyrian, the scribe wrote *Jau*, doubtless reproducing what he heard; for example, he wrote *Ja-u-ḫa-zi*, for Joahaz or Ahaz. In Neo-Babylonia, the scribe in writing these names wrote *Jāḫû*, (or *Jāḫô*), which is a very close reproduction of the Hebrew (see below). If, then, in the Hebrew, the Assyrian, and the Neo-Babylonian literature, we always find the name of Jahweh in the contracted form when compounded with other elements, can much reliance be placed in the above understanding of this isolated name, which is very probably to be interpreted quite differently? A more reasonable disposition of the element is to regard it as a verbal form, and to consider the name in connection with the many other West Semitic names having a similar formation, which are found in the tablets of the same period, as, *Jadaḫ-ilu*, "God knows;" *Jarbi-ilu*, "God heals," *Jaqar-ilu*, "God is precious;" *Jaḫzar-ilu*, "God helps," *Jamlik-ilu*, "God reigns," etc. *Jawi-ilu* or *Ja'wi-ilu* would mean: "God exists;" or "God lives," or "God has spoken." Or, if the second of the two names is to be read *Jaḫpi-ilu*, it could be translated, "God protects," etc.

The name *Ia-u-um-ilu*[1] is also offered to prove the existence of the name of Jahweh in the Baby-

---

[1] For the lay reader it might be mentioned that the name can be understood as standing for *Iau-ilu*, as the first element contains the mimmation that was characteristic of the early period.

238   Light on the Old Testament

lonian literature of the early period; although it is regarded as of secondary importance by some of the writers, as they say it presupposes the fuller form, *Ja'we-ilu*. Inasmuch as the Assyrians reproduced the divine element in its contracted form as *Jau*, and the name in question is similar in form to Joel, which many scholars interpret as having the same meaning, it is really of greater importance than the so-called "fuller form." It should be said here that while the later Hebrew perhaps considered this the proper interpretation of the name Joel, some of the best authorities think that its original significance was otherwise.

Without taking into consideration the many theories concerning the origin of the divine name which have been propounded, the introduction of Jahweh as the divine name for Israel, according to the Old Testament, was in the time of Moses. In this discussion we are concerned only with those occurrences in extra-biblical literature that would seem to imply the existence of the name in the time prior to Moses. Eliminating the two so-called "fuller forms," the only name[1] that can possibly have the abbreviated form of Jahweh as an element is the one in question (namely, *Ia-u-um-ilu*), and

---

[1] The reading of the name *Jama-arakh*, cited in The Expository Times, Vol. XV., 1904 p. 560, can scarcely be taken into consideration, owing to its being so poorly preserved. Dr. Ranke, Personal Names p. 113 reads: *Ja-ma* (?)-*e* (?)-*ra-akh* "Jama (?) is the moon (?)"

Jahweh in Cuneiform Literature 239

the only name of the Old Testament is Moses' mother, Jochebed.

It must be conceded that the single name *Iau(m)-ilu*, *i.e.*, "Iau is god," is difficult to explain if it is not conceded that the name Jahweh existed as early as the Hammurabi period. As mentioned above, it is exactly the form in which the abbreviated element of Hebrew names appears in the cuneiform inscription. Similar names, even though it can be proved that Joel is to be explained otherwise, and that there is no other name parallel in meaning in the Hebrew literature, were common in that age, for example: *Bêl-ilu*, "Bêl is god," *Marduk-ilu*, "Marduk is god," *Shamash-ilu*, "Shamash is god," etc.

In this connection I desire to call attention to several names which I recently found on tablets from Nippur belonging to the second or third century after Moses. They are[1] *Ja-u-ba-ni*, *Ja-u-a*, *Ja-a-u*, *Ja-ai-u*, and the feminine name *Ja-a-u-tum*. *Jau-bâni* means "Jau is creator," and taken in consideration with many similar names, which are compounded with *bâni*, as Ilu-bâni, Shamash-bâni *Jau* must be regarded as a god. As was mentioned above, in the later period, the name of Jahweh as the first element of Hebrew names in the Assyrian inscriptions is written exactly the same, namely

---

[1] See Documents from the Temple Archives of Nippur, B.E. Vol. XV.

Jau. Further, it will be noticed that *Ja-u-a* is exactly the writing of the biblical name Jehu, which is found upon the black obelisk of Shalmaneser (see page 320 f).

Names compounded with the contracted form of the tetragrammaton grew in popularity in the later centuries of Hebrew history. The number of those with El decreased, while those with Jahweh steadily increased, until the latest period of the Old Testament literature. The kings of Israel and Judah having come into contact with Assyrian and Babylonian rulers, we should naturally expect to find among the archives of the latter reference to the former, some of which had names compounded with Jahweh. As Israel and Judah were carried into captivity, we should also naturally expect to find in the land of their servility some reference to the people themselves in the business affairs of the people. In what is known as the contract literature of Assyria and Neo-Babylonia, Hebrew names are frequently met, especially in the periods corresponding to the times when the Hebrews were held in bondage, and afterwards. The latter fact is due to many having remained for generations in those lands. It is singular, however, that the number of Hebrew names compounded with Jahweh, in the known Assyrian literature, is exceedingly small. They are confined, with one or two exceptions, to a few names of kings. This may be due to the fact that excavations have not as yet been conducted

Jahweh in Cuneiform Literature

in those parts which were populated especially by the Hebrews; or because names compounded with Jahweh were not as popular in the northern as in the southern kingdom. In the Neo-Babylonian contract literature, especially in the period of Nehemiah and Ezra, Hebrew names abound in the tablets discovered at Nippur (see last chapter). At the present we are concerned especially with the form in which names compounded with Jahweh appear.

In Assyria, as stated before, when it is the first element, it is written *Jau*, e.g., *Ja-u-ḫa-zi* (Joahaz or Ahaz) *Ja-u-bi-'-di;* and when it is the final element it is written *Jau* or *Jâu*, e.g , *Ḫa-zi-qi-Ja-u*,[1] *Ḫa-za-qi-Ja-a-u Ḫa-za-qi-a-u* (Hezekiah); *Iz-ri-Ja-u, Az-ri-Ja-a-u, Az-ri-a-u* (Azariah); *Na-ad-bi-Ja-a-u*; and to this brief list must be added the name found two years ago on a tablet discovered in Palestine at Gezer, namely, *Na-tan-Ja-u* (Nethaniah).

Many interesting Hebrew names have been found in the contract literature of the Neo-Babylonian period, belonging especially to the time after the children of Judah had been carried into captivity. In studying the Murashû business documents, dated about the time of Ezra and Nehemiah (see Chap. XV), the writer had the delightful experience of recognizing the first known Hebrew names in the Babylonian literature, with Jahweh as the first element. The element is here written *Jāḫû;* for example,

---

[1] These names we usually transliterate *Ha-zi-qi-ia-u*.

Ja-ḫu-u-na-ta-nu (Jonathan), *Ja-a-ḫu-u-la-ki-im*, *Ja-a-ḫu-lu-nu*. The *u*, as the writer has pointed out elsewhere,[1] is to be read *o*, there being no other way to represent that vowel in the cuneiform script.

Hebrew names in the Neo-Babylonian literature with Jahweh as the final element are numerous, especially in the Murashû archives. It is written *Ja-a-ma*, which would be equivalent in pronunciation to *Jâwa* in Hebrew. This was recognized some years ago as the divine element by Doctors Sayce, Pinches, Hommel, and others. As the identification was questioned by a few scholars, in publishing many additional examples of names from the Murashû texts the writer set forth his views, being convinced of the correctness of the theory. This elicited opposition; and a theory which was published some years ago when only a few examples of names ending in *Jâma* were known, was revived. It was claimed[2] that "*iâma* at the end of West-Semitic names like *Aḫi-ia-a-ma*, is nothing but the Hebrew *jam*, which in all probability is a 'Weiterbildung' of *jah* or *ja*' by adding an emphatic *m* or *ma*. For, compare Hebrew *Abijjam* (Kings) alongside of *Abijjah* (Chronicles), a name borne by the same person." When this theory was originally propounded,[3] some ten years ago, other examples

---

[1] Business Documents of the Murashû Sons, Bab. Exp. U. of Pa. Vol. X, p. 19.

[2] Hilprecht, Editorial Preface, *ibidem*, p. xv.

[3] Jastrow, Journal of Biblical Literature, p. 114 ff.

Jahweh in Cuneiform Literature 243

were offered to substantiate it, but these have been wisely omitted. It might be added that the author has since abandoned it, owing to the large number of examples found in the Murashû texts, but as it has been revived by the other scholar to combat the writer's position, and especially as *Abijjam* is the only example in the Hebrew literature which can be quoted to illustrate the theory, the following is offered.

Theophorous names in Hebrew are usually compounded with either *El* or *Jahweh*. The formations commonly found are: deity + verb or substantive, *e.g.*, *El-nathan* (Elnathan) *Jăhô-nathan* (Jonathan); or, verb or substantive + deity, *e.g.*, *Nathan-El* (Nathaniel) or *Nathan-Jāhû* (Nathaniah). Among the Hebrew personal names found on the cuneiform tablets of the late period, both formations compounded with *El* are well represented. Of the formations with *Jahweh*, those having the deity as the first element, as mentioned above, are also recognized, as, for example, *Jāḫû-natanu*. If, therefore, three of the four theophorous formations are represented by many examples, why should we not expect to find the other very common Hebrew formation also represented? I say common or popular formation because Hebrew persons, bearing names compounded with Jahweh, and mentioned only in the Book of Chronicles according to Gray[1] number, when it is the first element, twenty-seven; but when it is the

---

[1] *Hebrew Proper Names*, p. 162.

final element, one hundred and seventy; while those compounded with *El* as the first and final element together number fifty.

The names having the element *Jâma* which I have been able to gather from the Murashû and other published texts of the Neo-Babylonian period follow:

A-bi-Ja-a-ma	Abaiah
Akhi-Ja-a-ma[1]	Ahijah
A-qa-bi-Ja-a-ma	Akabiah
Az-zi-Ja-a-ma	Azziah
Ba-li-Ja-a-ma	Bealiah
Ba-na-Ja-a-ma	Benaiah
Ba-rik-ki-Ja-a-ma	Bereikiah
Ga-da-al-Ja-a-ma	Gedaliah
Ga-mar-Ja-a-ma	Gemariah
Kha-na-nu-Ja-a-ma	Hananiah
Khu-ul-Ja-a-ma	Huliah
Ja-a-da-akh-Ja-a-ma	Jedaiah
Ja-she-'-Ja-a-ma	Jeshaiah or Isaiah
Ig-da-al-Ja-a-ma	Igdaliah
Ish-ri-bi-Ja-a-ma	Compare Sherebiah
Ma-tan-ni-Ja-a-ma	Mattaniah
Ma-la-ki-Ja-a-ma	Malchiah
Na-ta-nu-Ja-a-ma	Nethaniah
Ni-ri-Ja-a-ma	Neriah
Pa-da-a-Ja-a-ma	Pedaiah
Pi-il-lu-Ja-a-ma	Pelaiah
Ti-ri-Ja-a-ma	Tiria
Tu-ub-Ja-a-ma	Tobiyah
Shu-bu-nu-Ja-a-ma	Shebaniah
Za-bad-Ja-a-ma	Zabadiah

[1] Compare also the interesting name *Akhi-Ja-mi*, from a letter found at Ta'annek which has been recently published by Hronzy, *Denkschriften der Kaiserlichen Akademie, Band L.*

Jahweh in Cuneiform Literature 245

The examples show that no less than twenty-five names are found which have as the first element a word that has its exact equivalent or parallel in the Bible, which is followed by *Jâma* or *Jâwa*. Moreover, all occur in the Old Testament in connection with Hebrew persons or families.[1] Exact parallels for twenty-three of the twenty-five names are found in Hebrew, if *Jâma* (= *Jâwa*) is regarded as equivalent to the abbreviated form of *Jahweh* of the Hebrew text. The remaining two, *Aqabi-Jâma* and *Ishriba-Jâma*, are not found in the Old Testament, but the former Aqabiah is found in Talmudic literature, and the latter is found in the Old Testament, in the present instead of the imperfect, *viz.*, Sherebiah (Neh. 8:7). If, therefore, the names having *Jâma* (= *Jâwa*), all of which are West Semitic, do not represent Hebrew names, having the apocopated form of Jahweh, then there are no Hebrew names, except perhaps the questionable variant *Abijjam* of *Abijjah*, with which to compare these twenty-five; every one of which has a biblical word as the first element. And on the other hand, if they cannot be so regarded, then three of the four common Hebrew theophorous formations are frequently found in the cuneiform literature of this period; but we look in vain for the fourth, whose frequency of occurrence, in Chronicles alone, in comparison with other formations, is nearly seven to one. *Jâma,*

---

[1] Gray, Hebrew Proper Names, p. 158.

therefore, unquestionably represents the Hebrew form of the divine name Jahweh at the end of personal names in the cuneiform inscriptions.

In the Hebrew, the element appears at the beginning *Jăhô*, or shortened into *Jô;* and at the end *Jāhû*, or shortened into *Jâh*. The Assyrian scribe, as already referred to, wrote *Jau* when the divine element was the first as well as the second. The Babylonian wrote: *Jāḫû* (= *Jāḫô*) as the first element, and *Jâma* (= *Jâwa*) as the final. Can the Assyrian and Babylonian be reconciled with the Hebrew, and do these writings throw any light upon the actual pronunciation of the names? The Babylonian *Jāḫô* can be regarded as a satisfactory reproduction of *Jăhô*. The Assyrian *Jau* can also be read *Jao*, because in their orthography they did not distinguish between the *u* and *o* vowels. There is no philological difficulty in regarding the Assyrian equivalent to the Hebrew *Jăhô* because of the syncopation of the Hebrew letter *He*, which is in accordance with a common phonetic law. The abbreviated form *Jô*, and the transliteration of the Septuagint which makes it the same, viz., 'Ιω, would indicate that *h* was scarcely heard.

The final element is not so easily disposed of. The Assyrian *Jau* may be a satisfactory reproduction of *Jāhû*, but what shall be done with the Babylonian *Jâwa*. The form *Jāhû* in Hebrew must be explained as coming from *Jahw*, which according to phonetic laws passes regularly into *Jāhû*. The Massorites

Jahweh in Cuneiform Literature 247

vocalized the characters and read *Jāhû*. The *u* of the Assyrian *Jau* may have been sounded like the semi-vowel *w*; to cite a single example, compare the Hebrew writing of Nineveh, *i.e. Nînewe*, with *Ninua* of the cuneiform inscriptions; in which case the Babylonian *Jâw(a)* (written *Jâma*) would be equivalent. This would require the assumption that the final vowel in the Hebrew was apocopated, and the form remained unaltered, *e.g., Jahw*. If this were true, the final vowel of *Jâw(a)* in Babylonian was not pronounced, which is well known to have been frequently the case. If this explanation is correct, then the name *Aḫi-Ja-mi*, found on the Ta'annek tablet, which is mentioned on page 244, is especially interesting.

The writing *Jâwa* is strikingly similar to the traditional pronunciation of the Samaritans as preserved by Theodoret, *i.e.* 'Ιαβε or 'Ιαβαι, for the divine name, as well as *Yahwa* or *Yahwe*, written in Arabic characters in a letter to de Sacy, to which Professor Montgomery recently called attention.[1] This makes another explanation quite reasonable, namely, that *Jâwa* represents the exact and full pronunciation of the divine name as it was heard by the Babylonians. This has been previously suggested by others, but no attempt was made to explain why the full form was used and not the shortened. The theory I suggest is that the Babylonian scribe, rec-

---

[1] Journal of Biblical Literature, Vol. XXV., 1906, p. 50.

ognizing the element as being the Hebrew God Jahweh, arbitrarily decided to write it, when it was final in these West-Semitic names, always in accordance with the way they heard the full name pronounced. The fact is, in the Murashû archives, names compounded with *Jâwa* occur more frequently than the Babylonian names that are compounded with some of their own prominent deities as: *Addu, Bau, Ea,* etc. The names of their gods are usually written with an ideogram. In their guilds or schools, the scribe was taught to write Babylonian names, not phonetically as they were pronounced in everyday life, but according to fixed rules. The name of the Babylonian ruler, so often mentioned in the Old Testament, was not pronounced *Na-bi-um-ku-du-ur-ri-u-ṣu-ur*, nor *Nabû-kudurri-uṣur*, as it was written; but something like Nebuchadrezzar. It was necessary for the scribe to learn to analyze all Babylonian names, according to their elements. It is, therefore, quite reasonable to suppose that the scribe learned in the schools to write this element *Ja-a-ma* (=*Jâwa*), not as he heard the name pronounced, as they ordinarily wrote foreign names, but in these names, having this well known ending, according to the rule the master of cuneiform orthography taught. It is a singular thing that the element in every case known to me in tablets from Babylonia, is written *Ja-a-ma.* Inasmuch as the Israelites had become so numerous that Jahweh occurred more frequently than some of their own

Jahweh in Cuneiform Literature 249

deities in personal names, the supposition seems at least plausible.

Hebrew names with the divine element as initial, are more rare in the Babylonian literature, as they are in the Old Testament; for which reason a similar treatment would not be found necessarily expedient; although the scribes did recognize *Jāḫô* as a deity, because in some cases they used the determinative *ilu*, "god," before the element. Furthermore, the scribe of the late period represented the Hebrew *He* by *ḫ* which was not done in the names from Assyria. As mentioned before, the consonant was scarcely heard. Perhaps, however, we have also in *Jāḫô* a writing adopted by the guild of scribes.

An interesting example of a similar practice is to be found in the writing of the plural sign after the character for god in Hebrew names that are compounded with *El*, which are found in the contract literature also of this period. The Babylonian word for god is *ilu*. The Hebrew shortened form in names was *El*, although in its full form it is *Elohim*. The Babylonian scribe, having recognized the difference between the pronunciation of the Hebrew *El* and their *ilu*, may have desired to represent it. The scribes doubtless knew that the Hebrew word for god, *Elohim* was plural. As Hebrew names compounded with *El* were also exceedingly numerous in this period, it is not unreasonable to suppose that in their schools, in their efforts to distinguish between the Hebrew and Babylonian word for god, and also in order to avoid using the sign meaning *ilu* for the Hebrew *El*, as had formerly been done, they added the plural sign.[1] This combination carried with it the idea of plurality, which was so expressive of the Hebrew word for god.

---

[1] Professor Barton came to similar conclusions in his discussion of the Palestinian names written with *ilu* and the plural sign, which occur in the Amarna tablets. See *American Oriental Society's Proceedings*, April, 1892, p. CXCVI.

XI

THE AMARNA LETTERS

No discovery in recent years has had a greater bearing upon questions of historical criticism, or has thrown so much welcome light upon Palestine, as the find of over three hundred inscribed clay tablets in Egypt. They were discovered in 1887, about one hundred and eighty miles south of Cairo, at a site known as Tel el-Amarna. It was at this place that Amenophis IV in the fifteenth century B. C. had established the capital of Egypt. In digging for marl one of the fellahîn came upon a crumbling wooden chest which contained the tablets. Some were in a very fragmentary condition. In order to increase the income from their sale some of the larger tablets were broken into pieces, and this has naturally increased the difficulties of the decipherer. Most of the tablets have been secured for museums. About one hundred and eighty were acquired for the Berlin Museum, eighty for the British Museum, and sixty were retained at Boulac, in Egypt; while a few remain in the possession of private individuals.

It was soon ascertained that these inscriptions represent the official archives of two kings of

Egypt, Amenophis III, and Amenophis IV, who lived in the fifteenth century B. C. They contain letters and reports written to the kings of Egypt by their officials in Palestine, Phœnicia, and Syria, and by friendly rulers of Eastern nations. They were not written in the Egyptian tongue, as might have been supposed, but in the Babylonian language[1] and in the difficult cuneiform script. They show that the Babylonian was the official language of diplomacy in Western Asia at that time; and that this period was not prior to all knowledge of writing in Palestine; they offer evidence of an advanced literary activity, and also of a very fair civilization among the people of that country.

Amenophis III (the Greek for *Amen-hotep*) began to rule at the age of sixteen. His throne name was Nibmare (*Neb-ma't-Re*), which means "Re (the sun god) is lord of truth," but in the inscriptions he was addressed Nimmuria and Nibmuaria. The only campaign that he is known to have conducted was in the fifth year of his reign against the Ethiopians. He erected temples at Karnak and Luxor, besides the famous Colossi of Memnon, on the west bank of the Nile, not far from Thebes. He married Gilukhepa, a sister of Dushratta, king of Mitanni; and also the Egyptian Teie, who was the mother of the son (Amenophis IV) that succeeded him.

---

[1] A few are written in a foreign language, but in the Babylonian script.

The Amarna Letters 253

The throne name of Amenophis IV, who is known as the heretical king, was *Nefer-khepru-Re*, which means, "Beautiful is the Being of Re." In these archives he is addressed as: Napkhurîa, Napkhururia, etc. He married Tadukhipa, princess of Mitanni, who was a niece of his father's wife, Gilukhepa. While in the Asiatic home of his wife he became infatuated with the worship of the sun. This he endeavored to have supersede the worship of the Egyptian gods. In consequence, he incurred the enmity of the priests of Amen in Thebes; and he finally found it desirable to set up his new worship elsewhere. The Court was therefore removed from Thebes to Tel el-Amarna, where the king built a new city. He changed his name from Amenhotep to Khu-en-Aten, "Spirit of Aten." The new capital he named, Khut-Aten, "Horizon of Aten." The names of his daughters were also compounded with Aten. In this exclusive worship of the sun, monotheistic ideas seem to have prevailed. His religion, according to the inscriptions, was more expressive of devout feelings than the state religion. But his innovations did not last long, for after his death a reaction set in. His sepulcher was profaned, his mummy was torn to pieces, his city was destroyed, and his innovations were set aside. Those who continued to cling to his heresy were driven away or killed. Civil war followed.

Two of the tablets discovered contain Babylonian mythological texts. On one the words are separated with dots in black ink, and on the other with red. They were doubtless used as exercises in learning the cuneiform languages and script. One contains what is known as the Adapa legend, and the other refers to the consort of the god Nergal and her messenger Namtar. Several of the tablets have endorsements written upon them in ink, recording the time of their arrival, besides the name of the sender.

A few of the letters are addressed to Amenophis III, but most of those discovered were addressed to Amenophis IV, who in changing his place of residence seems to have taken with him some of his father's archives. The letters show that these two Pharaohs enjoyed friendly relations with foreign rulers of Babylonia, Assyria, Mitanni and Alashia. The rulers of these nations seem to have regarded each other as equals. The following opening lines of a letter will illustrate how they addressed each other:

> To Napkhururia, king of Egypt, my brother:—Burna-Buriash, king of Karduniash, your brother. It is well with me. May it be very well with you, your wives, your house, your sons, your horses, and your chariots.

Four of the letters were written by Kadashman-Bêl I (formerly read Kalimma-Sin), a Cassite ruler in Babylonia. Among the archives also is a large tablet written by Amenophis III to Kadashman-Bêl, which is either a copy of one sent, or a tablet which had not been despatched. The correspondence between these rulers is largely taken up with references to domestic matters, and the interchange of presents. The Babylonian ruler was anxious to receive gold from Egypt, while the Egyptian had asked for the Asiatic king's daughter in marriage. The latter did not feel assured that his sister, whom his father sent, was alive and well treated. He complained also to Amenophis that he had upbraided his ambassadors, charging them with having said that another woman which he had sent was not beautiful. This the Egyptian denied having said. The latter, in another letter, repeats his request for the Babylonian king's daughter, which request was granted later on. Kadashman-Bêl makes a similar entreaty, desiring to have the Pharaoh's daughter in marriage. The latter having refused, the Babylonian wrote: "If there is any beautiful woman there send her. Who shall say: 'She is not a king's daughter'?" The reluctance shown by Amenophis in giving his daughter in marriage to Kadashman-Bêl was in accordance with his claims of divinity. Some of the Pharaohs of this dynasty married their own sisters, not considering that there were any others living their equals. These concubinal affairs are curiously mixed up with business matters. The Egyptians seemed to possess plenty of gold, as at this time the Nubian mines were being worked. In his letters, Kadashman-Bêl made repeated requests for the precious metal in return for presents which he sent, or as a dowry.

Six or more of the letters were written by the

Babylonian king Burna-Buriash II to Naphurria (Amenophis IV). Exchanging of presents and matrimonial affairs also make up a large portion of their correspondence. Among other things he complained of his caravans being plundered in the Egyptian king's land, Canaan (*Kinakhi*).

> They (the agents of Amenophis) have killed and appropriated their money. . . . Canaan is your land, and you are the king. I have been violently dealt with in your land. Make good the money they have stolen; and the people who have killed my servants, kill them and avenge their blood.

As we shall later see, the conditions in Palestine were in a serious shape for the king of Egypt, who at this time held the suzerainty of that land. Burna-Buriash also requested the king of Egypt not to give encouragement to his own vassals, the Assyrians, who were endeavoring to gain independence from Babylonia, reminding him that on a previous occasion his father Kurigalzu, had not given ear to the Canaanites, who sought his aid when they rebelled against Egypt.

Ashur-uballit, king of Assyria, is represented by one letter in the archives, which was written to Amenophis IV. The desire for the yellow metal seems also to have been the burden of his message.

Dushratta, king of Mitanni, whose sister was married to Amenophis III, wrote five of the letters to his brother-in-law. He also asked for "much gold." He was willing to have it regarded as

The Amarna Letters

purchase money for his daughter, whom the Pharaoh wanted for his son's wife. After the death of Amenophis III, Dushratta addressed a letter to his widow and several to his son. In the one to the former, he pleads that the pledges made by her husband be fulfilled. Many complaints against each other seem to have been made by the two potentates, and it is probable that later a rupture in their relations took place. Mitanni at this time seems to have included the territory from Cappadocia into Assyria, including Nineveh.

A number of letters are addressed to the king of Egypt by the king of Alashia, who fails to mention his name. They are largely of a business character. In exchange for his copper and building wood which he sent as presents, he requests silver, oil, and manufactured articles. Alashia is indentified with Cyprus, as that country is called in Egyptian Alas.[1] This being true, the expression in one of the letters from that country referring to Nergal indicates some influence of the Babylonian religion in that land.

Of special value, in the interest of the Old Testament, are the letters from Phœnician and Canaanite vassals, princes, and governors. These comprise the bulk of letters. Through them we gain much data for the historical geography of Palestine, and

---

[1] See Jeremias, *Das Alte Testament, im Lichte des alten Orients*, p. 154 and, W. M. Müller in *Orientalistiche Litteraturzeitung*, Aug. 15, 1900, p. 288. Elishah of Genesis 10:4 is doubtless also to be regarded as the name of that country.

also much light upon the state of civilization at that early date. The situation as indicated by these tablets is in remarkable accord with the books of the Old Testament referring to this age. Moreover, for the first time we learn that the native princes and governors who wrote these letters were subject to Egypt. The conquests of Thothmes III had brought this region under Egyptian sway. But while Egyptian rule had been supreme, its authority was rapidly declining. From what follows it will be seen that the Egyptian king left the governors to their fate. Their repeated requests for reinforcements or assistance seem to have been totally disregarded. Aliens everywhere had disaffected the people. The Hittites were encroaching upon the land. Rebellion and uprising against Egypt had openly been made, and little seems to have been done to maintain the Pharaoh's authority. Each prince or king protested his loyalty and fidelity and submission. The neighboring ruler was accused of being the rebel. Accusations against each other form a considerable part of this correspondence, as well as efforts to justify their actions. Back of it all was the desire of these rulers to throw off the Egyptian yoke. A number of them were in league with the Hittites and the Habiri (*Ḫabiri*) people, who were encouraged to make inroads upon the land. We shall first consider briefly the letters that were written in Northern Palestine, then those that came from Southern Palestine.

The Amarna Letters

These letters are naturally addressed differently from those of the friendly powers. For example, Rib-Addi of Gubla (the Gebal of Psa. 83:7) in a verbose phraseology addresses the king thus: "To my lord, my sun. Rib-Addi your servant. At the feet of my lord, my sun, seven times and seven times I fall." In other letters the writer, in writing concerning himself, uses the words: "the dust of thy feet," "the dust under the sandals of thy feet," "the ground on which thou walkest," "the groom of thy horse," "thy dog." Rib-Addi wrote no less than sixty of the letters to Amenophis IV, some of which in his appeals for success are most pathetic. The burden of his letters is the charge that native princes, who are supposed to be subjects of Egypt, are in league with the Hittites and the Suti and the Habiri. Rib-Addi criminates especially two vassals, Abdi-Ashirte and his son Aziru, for playing into the hands of the king's enemies. In fact, they have by the help of these allies captured many cities.

Japakhi-Addi writes:[1] "Why do you neglect Simyra? For all the lands are fallen away to Aziru, from Gebal as far as Ugarit; and Shigata is revolting and also Ami," etc. Akizzi of Qatna asks for troops to protect Nukhashshi from Azira and the Hittites. He speaks of the king of the Hittites as being in the land, and that he endeavored to treat with him.

---

[1] Winckler, *Keilinschriftliche Bibliothek* V. No. 123.

Many other complaints are made against Aziru, as well as his father and other princes.

Finally, Khanni, a messenger, was sent by the Egyptian king to look into affairs. Aziru heard of his coming, and went to Tunep where he remained until the messenger departed. Then he wrote protesting his loyalty, and expressed his great regrets at having missed seeing Khanni. An attack by the Hittites had called him away from the city.

To all charges that have been made by the Pharaoh he had plausible answers. Concerning the city Simyra, that he is charged with having destroyed, he claims that that was necessary in order to prevent its falling into the hands of the enemies; and the cities he was then occupying, was in order to defend them against the Hittites.

A similar clamor for assistance came from faithful princes in Southern Palestine. In the North the enemies were designated as Egyptian vassals who had the assistance of the Hittites; a people called the *Sagas* (or Khabiri) as well as the Suti. In the South the enemy is referred to as the Habiri. They had the support of several native vassals of Egypt, among whom were Milkilu and the sons of Labaya.

The chief opposition to the inroads of this people was made by a faithful vassal named Abdi-khiba, who wrote from the city called Urusalim, which is Jerusalem. Nine of his letters have been preserved, the burden of which is that the Habiri have the assistance of some of his vassals; they are conquering the land. "The land of the king is going to ruin. If you do not listen to me all the dependent princes will be lost . . . . . let my lord, the king, send troops." "The king has no longer any territory, the Habiri have devastated all the king's territory." "If troops come in this year, the territory will remain my lord's, the king's, but if no troops come, the territory of my lord the king is lost." Again he writes: "Behold this action is the action of Milkilu and that of Labaya's son, who are delivering the king's lands to the Habiri." Another letter reads:

> To the king, my lord, speak as follows [namely] Abdi-khiba, your servant. At the feet of the king, my lord, seven times seven I fall. Behold the deed which Milkilu and Shuardatum have done against the land of the king, my lord,—they have engaged the soldiers of Gazri [Gezer] the soldiers of Gimti [Gath] and the soldiers of Kilti; they have taken the district of the holy city. The territory of the king is lost to the Habiri people, and now indeed the city of the territory of Jerusalem,—its name is Bît-Nin-ib, a city of the king, is lost to the people of Kilti. Let the king listen to Abdi-khiba thy servant, and let him send troops, in order that I may bring back the land of the king to the king. For if there are no troops, the land of the king will be lost to the Habiri people This deed of Shuardata and Milkili . . . . and let the king care for his land."

The Hittites are not mentioned in the letters from Southern Palestine. The native princes seem to be in league with the Habiri. It would appear that Labaya had in this part of the country formed a confederacy somewhat similar to the one in the

North. His chief opponent, Abdi-khiba, doubtless was silenced in some way. After the king's relations with him had been severed, he was captured, but on the way to Egypt he escaped; after which he continued to tear asunder the Egyptian rule.

In the reign of Amenophis III, the king's authority was generally unquestioned, although the letters from Babylonia to his son and successor show that Canaan had already become restless, and some of the princes were anxious to revolt. The Canaanite vassals, in the reign of his successor, realized that the government at home was exceedingly weak; this was largely due to the disaffected priesthood, because of the king's introduction of the new religion. They also realized that a rebellion was imminent, and did not hesitate to break away from Egyptian authority. Even those who preferred to remain loyal, certainly realized that the situation was hopeless, and in time went with the crowd. While little is known of what followed, it would seem that after the confusion the princes became entirely independent, except those who had allied themselves with the Hittite king. Such a dissolution of authority was easy, as Egypt apparently had made no attempt to establish its own form of government in that land. The impress made upon their culture was so slight that very little influence, up to the present, has been recognized.

These letters afford a most welcome insight into the relations of the great nations, and especially

The Amarna Letters

into the affairs of Palestine in the second millennium before Christ. While the letters are written in Babylonian there is every indication that the language of Palestine at this time was Hebrew. There are interesting glosses in the tablets written in Hebrew. For instance after *shadî*, the word for mountain in Babylonian, its Hebrew equivalent *harri* is written; after *halqat*, *abada*, "perish"; after *ipira*, *apara*, "dust," and other glosses are inserted side by side with the Babylonian words. The scribe was either not sure that he used the right word, or being afraid the reader would not understand, inserted these glosses in the Canaanite language, or Hebrew, which in all probability was his native tongue.

Of the one hundred and fifty cities mentioned in these letters, about one hundred have been identified. Besides the many towns mentioned in the letters which throw light upon Old Testament places and which enable us to reconstruct a new geography of Palestine for this period, an interesting fact was ascertained in the decipherment of the letters referring to the city Jerusalem. The common understanding was that prior to the time of David the name of the city was Jebus, although Jerusalem is used for the early period in the Old Testament (Joshua 10:1, etc.). These letters show that Jerusalem, which is mentioned by that name, was perhaps the older, being written Urusalim. In the period of the Judges the Jebusites having made it their stronghold, gave it the name Jebus. The letters show that in that early period the city was a place of great importance among the cities of Southern Canaan.

At this time Canaan, written *Kinaḥni* and *Kinaḫḫi*, represented the whole of Syria, including Palestine, east and west of the Jordan. The district mentioned in the farthest north was known as *Narima* or *Nakhrima*, which is the Naharaim of the Old Testament.

Especially important has been the discussion with reference to the invaders who assisted the native princes in their efforts to overthrow the Egyptian rule. The Habiri, who are frequently mentioned as invading the South, are in all probability identical with the *SA-GAS*, who were invading the North. The latter term having the determinative prefixed which indicates a class of men, has the ideographic value *ḫabbatu*, "robber." In one letter *SA-GA-AS* is followed by *ḫabati*, which would then be in apposition. Labaya in southern Palestine, who is one of those charged by Abdi-khiba as being unfaithful to the king of Egypt by intriguing with the Habiri, evidently speaks of that people in a letter to the king, when he used the term *SA-GAS*. This must be regarded as strong evidence in proving that they are identical.

The question is, Who are the Habiri people mentioned in these letters as entering Palestine? It was early suggested that they were the Hebrews

The Amarna Letters

entering Western Canaan under Joshua. This view has been strongly opposed by some scholars, who have regarded it as an untenable assumption. Some admit that the identification of the word Habiri with Hebrew is quite possible, but that a more likely conjecture would be that the Habiri were the predecessors of the Israelites; their name being connected rather with a hypothetical Heber, referring to Heber of the clan of Asher (Gen. 46:17). Others hold that neither the name nor the date are what we should expect, as the Hebrews were known to foreign people as the Israelites, and that at this time they were in Egypt. Another argument used was that Milkilu, a native prince in the South, played the leading part in opposition to the established authority, and not Joshua; besides, the kings of Jerusalem, Gezer and Khasor, mentioned in the letters, are not the same as referred to in the Old Testament. Another is, that the Habiri cannot be said to be the Hebrews; as both were in the same general stream of migration. Again others have suggested identification with the Habirai, that is, the Habiraeans, a generic term for the inhabitants of Elam, or with the Cassites. Others have said, the term means "confederate," "companion;" that it is a general term for an ally. A few scholars, however, continue to cling to the idea that the Habiri and the Hebrews are identical.

From a philogical point of view the identification of Habiri, *i.e.* (*Ḫabiri*) and *'Ibri* (the word, in the original translated "Hebrew") is quite possible. The Hebrew character *Ajin* in Palestinian names written in cuneiform is usually reproduced by Kheth, *e.g.*, *Ḥumri*, *Ḥazatu*, are examples of names which begin with an *Ajin* in Hebrew. Examples to illustrate the change from ʻ*Abiri* into ʻ*Ibri* are known. Compare those which have been cited by Professor Hommel,[1] *e.g.*, *maliku=milku*; *namiru=nimru*. Then also the time of their entering Palestine synchronizes practically with the Hebrew chronology for the conquest under Joshua (see below). It would therefore seem reasonable that an identification of these invaders with the Hebrews after their tutelage in Egypt, was in the highest degree probable.

The principal objection to the identification seems to be in what the opponents say is the "amazing discrepancy" between the approximate date of the letters and the date of the Exodus. Let us weigh carefully this argument, inasmuch as the conquest under Joshua, according to the Hebrew chronology, as just stated, nearly synchronizes with, or shortly followed, the invasion of Palestine by the Habiri.

Since the discovery of Pithom, the treasure city built by the Hebrews, Rameses II has been generally regarded as the Pharaoh of the Oppression, and Merneptah II, his son and successor, as the Pharaoh

---

[1] The Ancient Hebrew Tradition, p. 230.

of the Exodus. In consequence, the Exodus instead of having taken place in the fifteenth century B. C., is brought down to the close of the thirteenth century. With exceedingly few exceptions, scholars and the general student accept this as practically settled. Rameses II is generally pronounced the Pharaoh of Oppression. The following are the only reasons offered, which are of any value, for this identification and change in the Hebrew chronology, and all else that it involves.

Edouard Naville, in 1883, in his excavations at Tel el-Maskhutah ("mound of the statue") determined that the ancient name of the place was Pithom (*Pi-Tum*) "the abode of the god Tum." This is in all probability the city where the Israelites were forced to build storehouses for the Egyptians. Rectangular chambers of various sizes, with thick walls of crude bricks which had been laid up with a thin layer of mortar were found. A temple in the southwestern corner of the city was excavated, and the course of the heavily built city wall was traced. From a few inscriptions discovered, besides the statue of Rameses II sitting between two gods, which has given rise to the modern name of the place, Naville says, "the founder of the city, the king who gave to Pithom the extent and importance we recognize is certainly Rameses II. I did not find anything more ancient than his monument. It is possible that before his time there may have been here a shrine consecrated to the worship of Tum, but it is he who built the enclosure and storehouses."[1]

After carefully reading Naville's accounts of his excavations, one cannot help being impressed with the fact that his conjectural conclusions are entirely too dogmatic on the basis of the work he accomplished. In the first place he says, "I excavated to the bottom of chamber 1 and 2 (see his accompanying map); but seeing that they had been intentionally filled up, it seemed useless to go on emptying them, so I confined the work to digging deep enough to trace the direction of the walls, without attempting to go to the bottom. . . . . I laid bare the upper part of the walls of several of the storechambers, which I do not doubt extended over the greater part of the space surrounded by the enclosure." In other words he informs us that he excavated a few of these chambers, but only two of them to the original soil; yet we are led to believe from his accounts of the excavations that hundreds of these chambers existed at Pithom. The oldest construction, in the part of the city nearest to the canal has suffered, he informs us, to such an extent that it would be hopeless to trace any kind of plan. On the data gathered from these tentative soundings —certainly not a systematic excavation of the site—one might properly conclude, as he tells us, that Rameses II built the storehouses which he

---

[1] The Store City of Pithom, p. 13.

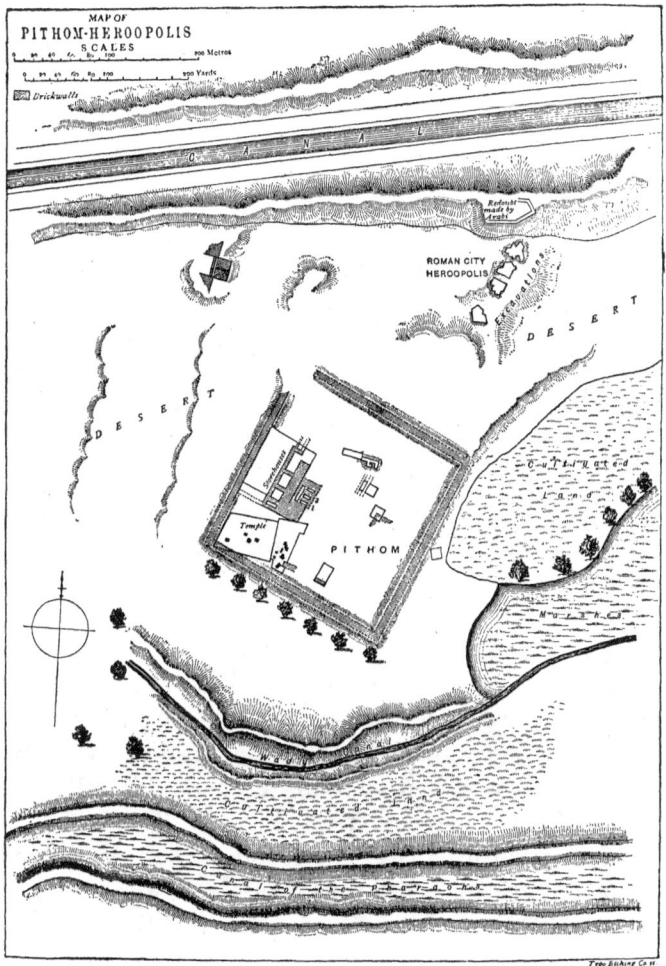

Naville's map of Pithom, the store-city.

examined, although he does not inform us that he found any stamped bricks of Rameses II in their construction. Granting also that this great ruler built the enclosure of the city, or at least part of it, including the temple; how can he speak in such a positive, unconditional way as to the founding of the city, and especially when the greater portion of the city remains untouched. Rameses II may be "the king who gave to Pithom the extent and importance we recognize," but the portion of the city towards the canal, which he left untouched, and which he says represents the oldest part of the city, may yield inscriptions which will force us to different conclusions. Even Naville, from the examinations he made, must have had reasons for saying, "it is possible that before his time there may have been a shrine consecrated to the worship of Tum."

It is a known fact that excavators find in almost every quarter in Egypt, however remote and obscure, that Rameses II has restored and built upon the work of his predecessors, even usurping their work and making it appear as his own. He is even charged with having credited himself with most of the achievements of the great Thothmes III in enumerating places he conquered from which it is practically certain he did not even receive tribute. About thirty miles from Pithom is the modern Tanis. The city is identified by some as the biblical Rameses, where Israel lived in servitude. It was called Pa-Ramessu Meriamun (*i.e.*, the place of Rameses II). But while the city was built by Rameses, who is even called its "second founder" by Naville, it had been in existence for more than a thousand years prior to his time, having been built as early as Amenemhet I, of the twelfth dynasty. The early name of the place was Zoan (Numbers 13:22), and if it is the Rameses where the Israelites lived, it was doubtless known by that name in later days; and, in the Old Testament, the name Rameses is used because when this account was written, that was the name with which the people were familiar. Such adaptations or glosses are numerous in the Old Testament. The same must be said of the passage in Genesis 47:11, where we are told that Joseph placed his father and brethren in the land of Rameses. In his day there scarcely was a place called Rameses, as the first Pharaoh by that name did not live until several centuries later. Naturally the city in question may not have been Zoan, but one of the others which have been pointed out as bearing the name of Rameses. From this it will be seen that the reasons why Rameses II should be considered the Pharaoh of the Oppression, are exceedingly precarious. While on the other hand there is a whole series of reasons why the old date of the conquest should remain practically unchanged.

Thothmes III (1503–1449) in every respect fulfils the requirements of the character of the oppressor portrayed in the Old Testament. He carried on fourteen campaigns in Syria, conquering all the kingdoms of Palestine, and brought the land under his suzerainty. On the pylons of Karnak, he has given a list of three hundred and fifty places in Palestine, Syria, and thereabouts, which he

Thothmes III.

conquered. One hundred and nineteen of these are within and about Canaan. As a builder, he has made himself famous. To his reign belongs also the familiar picture which graphically describes the taskmaster with a rod standing over the brick-

The Amarna Letters

makers, the inscription of which states that the laborers are prisoners whom Thothmes III brought home for the work in his father's temple, Amen, in Thebes.

In the succeeding reign of Amenophis II, some cities revolted, but they were speedily punished.

Brickmakers in Egypt. From a mural painting of a tomb.

Thothmes IV ruled but a very short time. During the reign of Amenophis III, Canaan remained submissive with the exception perhaps of Aziru, who even as early as this ruler caused trouble, but one of the Amarna letters clearly indicates the restlessness of the princes, and even their intrigues looking towards revolting. In the reign of the heretical Pharaoh we know from the letters that Egypt's control over Palestine was greatly relaxed, and that the recognized ruler made no effort to sustain his domination of the land (see p. 262), and to all appearances it was completely lost to Egypt. The remaining four or five rulers of this dynasty were exceedingly weak, and doubtless never entered Palestine.

Nothing can be gathered from the records of Rameses I, and Sety I, to show that Canaan was any longer an Egyptian province. Besides extending his conquest in Northern Syria, Sety I conquered Pahil, which is eighteen miles south of the Sea of Gallilee, and also Bath-Shar, which is supposed to have been four miles north of Hebron. Pa-Kan'ana is also mentioned, which may be a little south of Hebron. The annals of Rameses II inform us of his many conflicts with the Hittites in the early part of his reign; and although he marched frequently through Palestine, and may have attempted to break up the confederacy, he seems only to have conquered here and there a town: Ashkelon, Shalam, Merom, and Dapur, which is supposed to be Tabor. In other words these cities, if all are rightly regarded as being in Palestine, could have been conquered by the Egyptians, and the Israelites, if in the land, would not have been molested, for in the Old Testament we do not learn that they had anything to do with these places. There is nothing in the annals of

Rameses I, Sety I, and Rameses II to show that Israel was not in Canaan during these reigns. But on the other hand, in the reign of Sety I and Rameses II, according to Professor W. Max Müller, the tribe of Asher (written 'A-sa-ru) is already located in western Gallilee. Efforts naturally are made to explain away the importance of this fact by making conjectures similar to those made in connection with the following.

The crowning discovery having a bearing on this question was made by Petrie, in finding the stele of Merneptah, the successor of Rameses II, which shows that Israel in his time was already in Palestine, and that this ruler was not the Pharaoh of the Exodus. On the back of an inscription of Amenophis II, he had inscribed a hymn of victory, in which he praised himself for his glorious achievements.

> The kings are overthrown, saying: "salâm!" Not one holds up his head among the Nine Bows. Wasted is Tehenu (Libyans), Kheta (Hittites) is pacified, plundered is Pekanan ("*the Canaan*") with every evil, carried off is Askalon, seized upon is Gezer (Judges, 1:29), Yenoam is made as a thing not existing. Israel is desolated, his seed is not; Palestine has become a widow for Egypt. All lands are united, they are pacified, are in peace; every one that is turbulent is bound by king Merneptah, given life like Re, every day.[1]

This inscription shows that the Israelites were in Canaan in the early part of his reign, which makes

---

[1] See Breasted, *Egypt in Ancient Records*, Vol III, p. 263.

it impossible to consider him the Pharaoh of the Exodus, and his predecessor, Rameses II, the Pharaoh of the Oppression, unless the forty years in the wilderness be considered a myth, inasmuch as this stele was set up in Merneptah's fifth year. The word "Israel" in this inscription does not refer to a single city, where, as has been suggested, the descendants of the Israelites might have been settled who had been left behind in Canaan, the rest having migrated to Egypt; or, who might have returned after the famine; but to the people Israel in general, for the word has before it the determinative for a class of men, while the other names have the determinative which signifies that they are countries or cities. In the verse following that with the name Israel, Palestine stands as if it were in parallelism to it. It is possible, as some one has suggested, that the poem refers to Israel while in the wilderness south of Canaan; but if the invasion proper followed shortly afterwards, should we not expect to find reference to Egyptian supremacy over Palestine in the Old Testament, and especially as we learn that Merneptah had invaded Gezer, which Joshua had conquered.

To meet the conclusions to which this discovery forces us, as well as the other, concerning the tribe of Asher, the theory has been advanced that a portion of Israel left Egypt before the Exodus, and settled in Palestine. If such were the case, and they were of sufficient numbers to be mentioned, if only in a

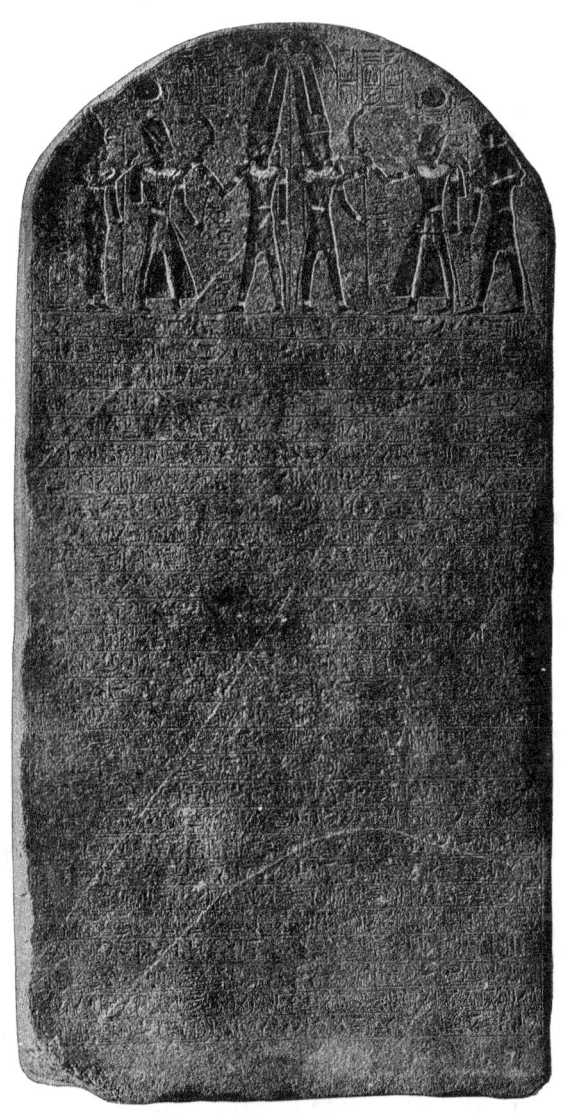
Stele of Pharaoh Merneptah, mentioning Israel.

general way, as synonymous with the term Palestine, we surely should expect some reference to them in the history of Joshua's invasion.

Another very important consideration in this connection is the chronology of the Old Testament. It is generally recognized as a most difficult subject, and that it presents many difficulties. It has become the fashion to discredit it on the slightest pretext, in fact, very often without any reason. Shifting the Exodus two centuries later, and putting it after Rameses II, necessitates the lengthening of the Hebrew chronology for the period before and shortening it after the Exodus. In the period, however, between Abraham's migration, if the date 2100 B. C. for Hammurabi be accepted, and the date about 969 B. C., which is generally fixed for the founding of the temple, the monuments and ancient writers offer us remarkable synchronisms with the Old Testament all along the line, providing the view stands which has been held formerly, that the Exodus took place in the eighteenth dynasty instead of the nineteenth, as is declared by those influenced by Naville's discovery at Pithom. Starting from 2100 B. C., the 220 years in addition to the 430 of the sojourn, would bring the Exodus to 1450 B. C. Going backward from 969 B. C., the date for the founding of the temple, and using the 480 years of 1 Kings 6:1 (the Septuaguint makes it 440 years) we should reach 1449 B. C., for the Exodus; in other words practically the same date. Assuming that the

The Amarna Letters

accepted date of the Exodus is not disturbed by the discovery that Rameses built or rebuilt Pithom, and that he was not the Pharaoh of Oppression, the letters found at Tel el-Amarna, referring to the Habiri invasion synchronize in a general way with the Hebrew conquest under Joshua. And inasmuch as there is no philological difficulty in regarding them as identical with the Hebrews, the question whether they actually are, becomes exceeding interesting.

The impressions made by the appeals of the princes for assistance in these letters would lead us to suppose that the invasion, while perhaps of a serious character, could easily be controlled, if only Amenophis would send a few troops. Naturally they had the protection of walled cities and their own organized forces, which would enable them to protect themselves against a goodly number. We are not led to believe that the Hittites referred to can be regarded necessarily as an army of the Hittite king. Moreover, it seems as if the impression of an invasion was a ruse to mislead Amenophis, and that the operations of these allies were welcomed, and perhaps invited by the princes who desired to revolt. Rib-Abbi calls them allies of Abdi-Ashirti, the servant (literally dogs) of the king of Mitanni, of Kashi, and of the Hittites.

Again, the invaders are called the Suti, Habiri and Hittites. These surely did not represent any organized efforts on the part of kings, but they were doubtless bands of invaders. In like manner it would be unreasonable to regard the Habiri as the Hebrews entering Western Canaan under Joshua, for as has been stated, Adonizedec in the Old Testament is the king of Jerusalem (Joshua 10:1); and not Abdi-khiba, as in the letters; or Horam is king of Gezer and not Yaphi; or Yabim of Hasor and not Abdi-tirshi; or Yaphi is king of Lachish, and not Zimrida. But this conjecture is reasonable. In view of the fact that these allies represent bands of marauders of various peoples, the Habiri were Hebrews who had left the main body, perhaps while on the other side of the Jordan, or, more probable, while in the wilderness. That they pushed ahead, seems reasonable, and, by making alliances with the Canaanites who were about to break away from Egyptian control, made the way for the conquest which followed much easier. It left the princes politically divided up as they were prior to Thothmes' invasions. In this disturbed state, the Egyptians having been expelled the conditions were such that the country was ripe for an invasion. The kings of Egypt following Amenophis IV were weak, and made no attempt, so far as is known, to reëstablish their lost prestige. It is therefore quite reasonable to conjecture, owing to the peculiar conditions prevailing during the reign of Amenophis IV, and also because of the civil war which followed his death, that the land was practically lost to Egypt, about the close of his reign. This is about the time, or shortly afterwards that the Hebrew chronology fixes the conquest by Joshua.

The Pharaoh of the Exodus would then be Amenophis II or III, preferably the former. It is a strange coincidence that though this ruler sat on the throne at least twenty-six years, nothing is known of his reign after the fifth year. Although disasters are not as a rule, recorded on the ancient monuments, this may be the reason why no reference to the Exodus has been found in the Egyptian inscriptions. Thus the old view, as formerly held by Egyptologists, as well as by Manetho and nearly all the ancient historians, who have handed down the traditions current among the Egyptians, seems altogether reasonable, namely, that the expulsion of the lepers, meaning Israel, took place in the reign of Amenophis II.

Home scene in the camp of Arab workmen at Nippur. In the foreground an oven (the Old Testament *tannûr*) is seen.

XII

BABYLONIAN TEMPLE RECORDS OF THE SECOND MILLENNIUM BEFORE CHRIST

From the beginning of the eighteenth century B. C., to the close of the thirteenth, foreign kings, known as the Cassites, ruled over Babylonia. Already in the ninth year of Samsu-iluna, about 2000 B. C., these foreigners invaded Babylonia, but were driven out, to return a little later, when they established themselves firmly in the land, and founded a new dynasty.

It is not known as yet to what group of languages their tongue belongs. Efforts have been made to show that it is an Indo-Germanic language. Nor has it been determined from whence these people came. Some think they are connected with the Kissians, others associate them with Elam, while still others locate their native land to the north of that country. It is not improbable that the Hyksos, who ruled Egypt at that time, have some connection with their contemporaries, the Cassites; who ruled Babylonia.

The temple of Bêl at Nippur seems to have received considerable attention from several of these rulers. In its restoration and enlargement, in the latter half of the second millennium B. C., the work of the Cassite rulers Kadashman-Bêl, Kuri-Galzu, and Rammân-shum-uṣur is quite conspicuous. Many inscribed bricks of these kings have been found in the ruins of the Temple Ekur. Besides their devotion to the temple buildings, they dedicated a large number of inscribed votive objects to the patron deities of Nippur; namely, *Bêl, Ninib,* and *Nusku*.[1] They are in lapis-lazuli, magnesite, agate, ivory, feldspar, turquoise, glass in imitation of lapis-lazuli, etc. A good many of these dedicatory objects, which had belonged to the temple, were found[2] in a jeweler's shop of the late period. Perhaps found during excavations for some late construction, these objects were sold to the jeweler, who intended to use them as raw material in the manufacture of gems, but his establishment was suddenly destroyed, and the valuable stones buried. The following translations[3] of inscriptions afford illustrations of these votive objects, most of which are quite small.

An ivory knob, perhaps of a scepter, contains

---

[1] The oath formulæ of contracts of the second millennium B.C., besides the fact that a number of votive objects are dedicated to *Nusku,* as well as to *Bêl* and *Ninib,* show that Nippur regarded all three as special patron deities. See my Documents from the Temple Archives of Nippur, Vol. XV, p. 2.

[2] See Peters, *Nippur,* Vol. 2, p. 77.

[3] Copies of these votive inscriptions are to be found in Hilprecht, *Old Babylonian Inscriptions,* Part 1.

on its rounded top an inscription in Sumerian: "To Bêl, his lord, Burna-Buriash, king of Babylon, has presented it." Similar inscriptions are found on little disks of lapis-lazuli, some of which are an inch to two inches in diameter, and about three-eighths to a quarter of an inch in thickness. The inscriptions of several of these disks mention the name of the stone upon which they are written; namely, *ugnu*. As a result, this familiar word was finally determined to mean lapis-lazuli. Another inscription reads: "To Nusku, his sublime minister, his lord, Kadashman-Turgu has made the bright *ashme* of lapis-lazuli and presented it for his life." As the little object is in the form of a disk, it has been inferred that *ashme* means "disk."

A very interesting object is a little irregular agate tablet, which was also found in the jeweler's shop. It is about two inches by two, and about one-half inch in thickness, through which a small hole is bored. On the one side it contains an inscription of Dungi, about 2650 B.C., which reads: "To the goddess Ninâ, his lady, for the life of Dungi the powerful hero, king of Ur, Siatum." The balance is broken away. The other side is inscribed: "Kuri-Galzu, king of Karduniash, conquered the palace of *Shasha* (Shushan of Esther 1:2) in Elam, and presented [it] to (the goddess) Bêlit, his lady, for his life." In other words, the history of this little tablet is as follows: Dungi had it inscribed and presented to the goddess Ninâ, presumably in Erech. Later it was carried to Elam. Ashurbanipal informs us that a statue of the same goddess had been carried to Elam by Kudur-Nankhundi, 2285 B. C., who with his hordes invaded Babylonia. He brought back the statue of the goddess, and restored it to her shrine in Erech. Doubtless this little tablet had been carried away to Elam at the same time. Kuri-Galzu, about 1250 B. C., conquered Elam, and

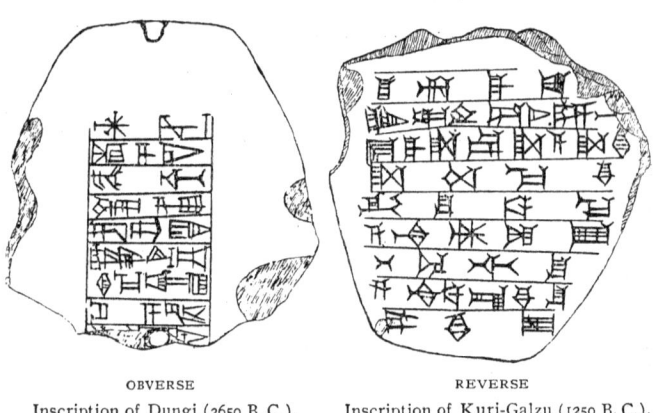

OBVERSE
Inscription of Dungi (2650 B. C.).

REVERSE
Inscription of Kuri-Galzu (1250 B. C.).

among other booty brought back with him this little tablet. Again it was dedicated to a Babylonian goddess, but this time to Bêltis, the consort of Bêl, at Nippur. In the late days of Babylonian history, it found its way into the jeweler's shop, with other inscribed pieces of valuable stone. The gem cutter's labors being interrupted, the little tablet was buried. Its discoverer has caused it to be removed once

Babylonian Temple Records 287

more from Babylonia, its last resting-place being in the Imperial Ottoman Museum at Constantinople. It is, of course, not impossible that some day it will again be returned to Babylonia.

Another interesting object which was found near the temple area is a fragment of a votive battle-axe.

Prayer of Nazi-Maruttash on imitation of lapis-lazuli.

It contains a beautiful prayer of Nazi-Maruttash. Unfortunately the dedication and conclusion are wanting, but when complete doubtless read: [To Bêl (or some other god) his lord], Nazi-Maruttash, the son of Kuri-Galzu, to hear his prayer; to be favorable unto his supplications; to accept his sigh, to protect his life, to lengthen his days, [does he present this bright lapis-lazuli axe]. It would be interesting to know whether the restoration in brackets is correct, and that he actually called it lapis-lazuli; for it is only an imitation of that stone, being made of glass, and colored with cobalt. If that is true, he cheated his god.

Other votive objects, for example, a large irregular block of lapis-lazuli dedicated by Kadashman-Turgu, and a small one by Kadashman-Bêl, besides small tablets of different shapes, were found, having been at one time the property of the temple. While other Babylonian temples of this period have not been disinterred, and the cities where the Cassite rulers lived is unknown, unless perhaps Dûr-Kuri-Galzu, it seems as if Nippur received considerable attention at the hands of these foreign rulers. Whether other Babylonian temples were embellished, and favored by them, as was Ekur, future excavations will determine.

Besides these votive objects and bricks, only a few other inscriptions have been published belonging to this dynasty, notably several boundary-stones, or deeds of territorial grants. Most of these have been found in Susa by de Morgan, having been carried away by the Elamites. The discovery at Nippur, therefore, of about 18,000 clay tablets and fragments of tablets, large and small, baked and unbaked, belonging to this dark period, must be heartily welcomed by scholars; although the inscriptions only represent the records of the temple

Babylonian Temple Records 289

revenues, and their disbursement. But, while they are disappointing in not throwing much light upon historical questions, they throw considerable upon the nomenclature and incidentally upon religious questions, as well as enable us to gather much data for a better understanding of the inner workings of an ancient temple, especially as regards its maintenance. While there is no connection whatever with the Hebrew temple, which belongs to a later period, these documents will at least illustrate how the administrative affairs of such an institution were conducted, especially when it was maintained by the tithes of the people.

On the second campaign of the excavations at Nippur, in 1890, Doctor Peters discovered a large collection of thoroughly-baked tablets, a good many of which were dated in the reigns of these Cassite rulers. They were found at a little distance from the southwest wall of the palace, known as the "Court of Columns," in the western half of the city. About three years later, Doctor Haynes resumed active explorations at this as well as at another point, in the southern part of the city where excavations had also been previously made. Thousands of tablets and fragments were recovered from the ruins of these mounds. Several rooms of an ancient palace were explored, which turned out to be archive rooms where the temple records were kept. The tablets were preserved in the very position in which they were left when the building was destroyed.

He found some "placed on their edges, reclining against each other, like a shelf of leaning books in an ill-kept library of to-day. In other instances the tablets were found in great confusion, showing that at the time when they were buried, they had fallen [perhaps from wooden shelves] into the débris which covered them."[1] Most of these tablets are unbaked.

All the dated tablets belong to the latter half of the second millennium before Christ. Most of the tablets found belong to the reigns of the following rulers: Burna-Buriash II, Kuri-Galzu II, Nazi-Maruttash, Kadashman-Turgu, Kadashman-Bêl II, Kudur-Bêl, Shagarakti-Shuriash, and Bitiliash. A great many do not bear dates, and others do not mention the name of the king, but only the year, month, and day of the reign in which they were written. These can be assigned generally to the reigns mentioned, because they were found intermingled with the others, in the same archives; because they have the same general appearance as regards the form and texture of clay; but especially because the same officers mentioned in them appear in those having complete dates.

After studying these tablets, I came to the conclusion[2] that they are temple administrative ac-

---

[1] From the diary kept by Doctor Haynes on the scene of operations.

[2] See Documents from the Temple Archives of Nippur, Vols. XIV and XV of the Babylonian Expedition of the Uni-

Babylonian Temple Records 291

counts, which were kept in connection with the collection and disbursement of the revenues gathered for the maintenance of the sanctuary. In other words, they are records of temple taxes collected from the outlying towns and districts about Nippur; commercial transactions conducted by the officials of the temple, in which they used the revenues as capital; and pay-rolls of all in the temple service, from the head official of the storehouse, the priest, the warden, down to the lowest servant.

Those dealing with the receipt of revenues throw little light upon the question as to how the taxes were levied. The revenues are designated as the full tax, the maintenance tax, or so many *qa* tax (*i.e.*, from four to twelve *qa*), etc. This *qa* is a fraction of the *gur* (=180 *qa*), a dry measure; but in these records it refers to animals and liquids, as

---

versity of Pennsylvania. The documents are written in the Babylonian language, with the exception of certain Sumerian phrases, which were frequently used. At Nippur the temple documents of an earlier period seem to have been written entirely in Sumerian. At Telloh upwards of 30,000 tablets from the temple archives have been found. These are written in Sumerian. Several publications of them have already appeared: Arnold, Ancient Babylonian Temple Records (1896); Reisner, *Tempelurkunden aus Telloh* (1901); Thureau-Dangin, *Recueil de Tablettes Chaldéennes* (1903); Virolleaud, *Comptabilite Chaldéenne* (1903); British Museum Series of Cuneiform Texts; Barton, Haverford Library Collection of Cuneiform Tablets (1906). Hundreds of Neo-Babylonian documents of the same general character have been published by Father Strassmaier, under the title Babylonische Texts.

well as cereals, for the tax was paid in kind. It may refer to a percentage of the amount harvested by the people of the district; or it may have been *per capita*. It is, however, more likely an income tax, which had been levied upon the lands in and about Nippur for the maintenance of the temple, a custom with which we are familiar in modern times in certain countries. By the number of *qa* mentioned, we are to understand perhaps that the 4 *qa* tax was for fallow lands, or for the minimum which those less prosperous were allowed to pay; while the 10 *qa* or full tax, was for arable lands. In other words, the lower amount was what the poor man was permitted to pay, a privilege enjoyed not only in Babylonia, but in Israel as well.

In a number of tablets, the purpose of the tax is set forth; for instance, in some it is recorded as having been given for the priests; in others, for temple servants, or salaries of the storehouse officials; or for the maintenance expenses in general.

That these documents are records of temple revenues is clear from expressions found in them. Payments, for instance, are made out of the funds called "the temple stipends;" or out of the "full tax of the house of god." Then also they are made to the "male and female temple servants," besides the priests, temple-gatemen, singers, seers and seeresses, etc.

A great many towns are mentioned whence the income was received. They were apparently hamlets

Topographical map showing towns, canals, and a road in the vicinity of Nippur. On the left edge an additional town is represented.

and villages belonging to the environs of Nippur. On a topographical map[1] discovered by Doctor Haynes somewhere at Nippur, during the third campaign, the relative positions of no less than eight towns are given, indicating also canals and a road upon which they were situated. Three of the towns of this map are mentioned in these records. Doubtless in the archive room where the temple records were kept, a complete set of such maps of the entire district about Nippur was to be found, especially of those towns whence the incoming revenues were derived.

The taxes collected were deposited in the town storehouse or treasury, where they were stored until needed. A good many of the towns seem to have had granaries. Several large storehouses existed in Nippur, two of which, perhaps, are to be seen on another topographical map, which is of Nippur proper. If this conjecture, after the map has been cleaned and studied proves correct, they were situated to the north of the temple (see page 111). In most of the records, the storehouse whence the property was taken is mentioned, as well as the kind of tax. These facts were doubtless recorded to show what disposition had been made of the revenues. In fact, the recording of such data served a number of purposes.

---

[1] Published by the writer in the *Transactions of the Department of Archeology, University of Pennsylvania*, Vol. 1, part 3, p. 223f.

Babylonian Temple Records   295

To illustrate the general character of these records, the following translations are offered. The first two record the receipt of revenues.

> Corn, the full tax, which Khunnubi [the agent] brought from the town Kalbia. 33 *gur* from Bît-Marduknishu, 33 *gur* 150 *qa* from Bît-Gimillum. Total 67 *gur* 120 *qa*. The month Sivan, day ninth, year twenty-first. (Vol. XV, No. 113)[1].
>
> 25 *gur* of grain of the 10 *qa* tax from the town Kandure Sin-issakhra [the agent] brought to the temple (literally house). The month Shebet, year fifteenth. (Vol. XV, No. 89).

These two officials, who figure very prominently in these texts, doubtless acted as agents in the collection of certain revenues which were due, but which had not been paid.

The following refer to business transactions conducted by the officials in the interest of the temple, with the revenues as capital. Loans of various kinds were made by the temple officers. When the people, for instance, needed assistance, they went to the temple to borrow grain in order to sow their fields. Interest, contrary to what some have claimed, was exacted from them. In some of the records of loans, this condition is stipulated. The time fixed for the payment of such loans was generally on the day of harvest.

---

[1] These references are to tablets published in Documents from the Temple Archives of Nippur, dated in the reign of Cassite rulers, Volumes XIV and XV of the Babylonian Expedition of the University of Pennsylvania.

One *gur* of grain, of the full tax, in *shapiltu*, with interest, from the storehouse, is at the disposal of Burra-Ishtar, son of Ushbi-Sakh. On the day of his harvest, the grain and its interest, he shall pay.

Before Sin-issakhra, [the witness], before Rammân-êresh the measurer. The month Ab, year twelfth. The *sisiktu* [instead of the seal] of Burra-Ishtar. (Vol. XV, 30).

This is a case tablet. The tablet proper does not have the names of the witnesses, nor does it refer to the substitute *sisiktu* which had been used instead of the seal. On the case is a clearly-defined small hole, made while the clay was soft, by something called *sisiktu* (see page 175).

1 *gur* 12 *qa* of grain of the 6 *qa* tax in *shapiltu* is in the possession of Sin-damaqu. The horse-feed he shall pay; whereupon his seal he shall break. The month Shebet, day twenty-eighth of the year fifteenth. Seal of Sin-damaqu. (Vol. XV. 49).

Seal impressions were occasionally made on the tablets of this period. This one may have been encased, but it has the general appearance of being a tablet which had not been enveloped. The expression "break the seal" meant the destroying of the tablet which recorded the debt and which had upon it the impression of the man's seal. Doubtless when the debt was satisfied the case bearing the individual's seal was broken off, but the tablet proper was preserved in the archives as a record of the transaction.

The following is an inventory of sheep and goats

Records of cattle and sheep herds leased to individuals by the storehouse officials. The first line of the tablet on the left contains a hitherto unknown character which is to be read *lu* "bull."

(temple property) which the officials rented to an individual for stock raising. The document fully stipulates what the amount of rent was to be. It is dated in the fifth year of Nazi-Maruttash:

> Forty-seven sheep [male], twenty-eight large females, seven [male], seven suckling females. Total, eighty-nine sheep, thirty-four large goats [male], thirty-one female, seven male kids, eight female goats. Total, eighty goats. Sum total, one hundred and sixty-nine *Kleinvieh*. [For one hundred and sixty-nine] sheqels of wool; (*i.e.*, for) one sheep, one sheqel; forty-four and one-half minas of wool; twenty minas of goat wool; they are at the disposal of Rabâ-sha-Ninib. All his hides he shall weigh; sinews and fat of sheep, two perfect goat hides; one perfect garment, he shall pay. (Vol. XIV, No. 48).

The bulk of these archives are receipts for amounts paid to the temple officials in salaries, for general supplies, or for work done. In other words they are pay-rolls. The privilege of service in the temple was in many cases hereditary. Certain families were entitled to fill offices, because of service that was rendered the state or the temple by them or by an ancestor. In the days of Arioch two individuals, Sin-imguranni and Sin-uzili, had their rights confirmed, which were for five days' service each year in the temple of Bêlit, and eight days in the shrine of Gula, respectively. Other references to similar rights to act in the capacity of an official are on record. There was a whole host of tradesmen and functionaries in connection with the temple. Besides the priest, elder, seer, seeress, sorcerer, singer, etc., there were the farmer, weaver, miller, carpenter, smith, butcher, baker, potter, overseer, scribe, measurer, watchman, etc.

In this series of documents, *i.e.* which contain payments of salaries there are two tablets which are quite similar, the one having been written two years after the other. One individual, however, had died during the intervening time. The salary of one man had been reduced from 36 *qa* to 24 *qa* per month, while that of another had been raised from 30 *qa* to 36 *qa*. Only one name is changed. A man is replaced by a woman at the same salary of 30 *qa* per month. These tablets record the payments made for the first seven months of the year. The grant to render service may have been only for that length of time each year.

These rights were negotiable, as they could be sold, traded, or pledged, doubtless subject to a reversion to the owner at a fixed time. In these pay-rolls there are certain individuals whose names occur repeatedly in the same document. Doubtless they made a business of leasing temple allowances from individuals, furnishing substitutes where it was necessary to render service. Certain grants that are on record carefully stipulate that the right could not be sold, but became hereditary.

A great many names in the pay-rolls have *Mâr* or *Mârat* prefixed, meaning "son" and "daughter," like Scotch names with *Mac*. In case a son of Irîmshu-Ninib filled the office, he was called *Mâr–*

Irîmshu-Ninib, representing thus the name of the head of the family, who may have been deceased. The transliteration, and in part translation on pages 302 and 303, is of one of the finest specimens of this class of documents that has found its way to Philadelphia (see opposite page). It records the payment of grain and dates as temple stipends for twelve months.

In the first line the names of the months are given. In the first six columns are recorded that which was paid for the first six months. In the seventh, the total (*naphar*) for the first half year is given. In the fourteenth, the total for the second half year; and in the fifteenth the amount for the entire year. In the next column, *awîlûtum* means "men." In this column, the stage in life of the individual whose name appears in the following is given. If he or she were a member of a family the relation of the recipient to the head of the family is indicated. *KAL* means "adult;" *SAL*, or the feminine determinative, "woman;" *KAL-TUR*, "adult son;" *SAL-TUR*, "adult daughter;" *KAL-TUR-TUR*, "adult grandson;" *TUR-GAB*, "boy;" *SAL-TUR-GAB*, "girl." In this column also are found the words *BAD*, "deceased," and *HA-A*, "fugitive." It will be noticed that no amounts are recorded as having been paid the individuals before whom these two words are written. At the top of the last column, *MU-BI-im* means "his name," but here stands for "their names." In this column the names of the beneficiaries are recorded. In a number of instances,

Temple stipends for the 13th year of Nazi-Maruttash, recording monthly payments.

[Ninanna]	Sin gu	Shugurra	Dūmu	Aya	Ulūlu	mahar	Tashrītu	Arahsamnu	Kislīmu	Tebītu	Shabātu	Addaru	mahar shi'um	aha qāt libbi abulli i-na libbi shi'i sha Zarat-Mu u sabappu mahrum	mahar shi'um	mahar	amēlūtu-tum	MU-BI-um	
72qa	72qa	72qa	72qa	72qa	72qa	72qa	72qa	72qa	72qa	72qa	72qa	72qa		2qur 72qa	4qur 144qa	KAL	mSin-da-ma-qu, "overseer"	
72qa	72qa	72qa	72qa	72qa	72qa	72qa	72qa	72qa	72qa	72qa	72qa	72qa		2qur 72qa	4qur 144qa	KAL	mSin-mu-shab-shi, "temple servant."	
72qa	72qa	72qa	72qa	72qa	72qa	72qa	72qa	72qa	72qa	72qa	72qa	72qa		2qur 72qa	4qur 144	KAL	mIp-pa-e-a w(ditto)	
72qa	72qa	72qa	72qa	72qa	72qa	72qa	72qa	72qa	72qa	72qa	72qa	72qa		2qur 72qa	4qur 144	KAL	mIdinnum-Shamash, "keeper"	
30qa	30qa	30qa	30qa	30qa	6 ya	1 gur	30qa	30qa	30qa	30qa	30qa	30qa		1 gur	-2 gur	SAL or l	Tam-bi-Da-du, "his wife."	
24qa	24qa	24qa	24qa	24qa	24qa	144. qa	24qa	24qa	24qa	24qa	24qa	24qa		144 gur	1gur 108qa	SAL-TUR	Da-li-lu-sha, "his daughter" "seeress"	
18qa	18qa	18qa	18qa	18qa	18qa	108 qa										KAL-TUR	mArdu-Nusku, "his son," ušu Tashrītu horridum	
12qa	12qa	12qa	12qa	12qa	12qa	72 qa	12qa	12qa	12qa	12qa	12qa	12qa		72 qa	144 qa	KAL-TUR-TUR	mNusku-ki-ma-u-pur, "his [grand] son"	
72qa	72qa	72qa	72qa	72qa	7-2qa	2qur 72qa	72qa	72qa	72qa	72qa	72qa	72qa		36 qa	72 qa	TUR-GAB	mGab-mar-ta-ash, "his son"	
48qa	48qa	48qa	48qa	48qa	48qa	1gur	108qa	48qa	48qa	48qa	48qa	48qa		2qur 72qa	4gur 144qa.	KAL	mA-na-ASk-cm-i-al-kal, "grandcr"	
24qa	24qa	24qa	24qa	24qa	24qa	144 qa	24qa	24qa	24qa	24qa	24qa	24qa		3gur 108qa	3gur 36qa	SAL or l	Iah-tar-br-li-a-z-n	
30qa	30qa	30qa	30qa	30qa	30qa	1 gur	30qa	30qa	30qa	30qa	30qa	30qa		144 qa	1gur 108qa	KAL-TUR	mUshab-sh-gu-mi-a-ma-sh, "her son," horridru	
12qa	12qa	12qa	12qa	12qa	12qa	72 qa								1 gur	-2 gur	KAL-TUR-TUR	mDu-uk-kn-tu-tu, ASH(?) "her [grand] son"	
12qa	12qa	12qa	12qa	12qa	12qa	36 qa	12qa	12qa	12qa	12qa	12qa	12qa		72 qa	144 qa	SAL-TUR	Ba-an-un-du, "her daughter," "seeress ''	
6qa	6qa	6qa	6 qa	6 ya	6qa	36 qa	6qa	6qa	6qa	6qa	6qa	6qa		36qa	72 qa	SAL-TUR-GAB	Hu-ta-lu-tum. "her daughter"	
48qa	48qa	48qa	48qa	48qa	48qa	1gur	48qa	48qa	48qa	48qa	48qa	48qa		1gur 36qa	3gur 36qa	TUR-GAB	I-na-rish-Marduk-d-nu, "her son"	
18qa	18qa	18qa	18qa	18qa	18qa	108 qa	18qa	18qa	18qa	18qa	18qa	18qa		108 qa	1gur 36qa	SAL or l	Btiti-balātu-i(risbi,-ish)	
12qa	12qa	12qa	12qa	12qa	1.2 qa	72 qa	12qa	12qa	12qa	12qa	12qa	12qa		72 qa	144 qa	KAL-TUR-TUR	mLul-la-mar-Nusku, "her son," "weaver"	
6qa	6qa	6qa	6qa	6qa	6qa	36 qa	6qa	6qa	6qa	6qa	6qa	6qa		36 qa	72 qa	SAL-TUR-GAB	Rabô-sha-41-i-bo-ru, "her daughter"	
48qa	48qa	48qa	48qa	48qa	48qa	1gur	48qa	48qa	48qa	48qa	48qa	48qa		1gur 108qa	3gur 36qa	SAL or l	Di-ra-ih-tu-mar, "her daughter"	
48qa	48qa	48qa	48qa	48qa	48qa	1gur	48qa	48qa	48qa	48qa	48qa	48qa		1gur 108qa	3gur 36qa	SAL or l	Mi-sha-ri-tum I-na-Ak-ka-di-rab-bat	

Transliteration (in part translation) of the Document, found on the previous page,

	6qa	6qa	6qa	6qa	6qa	6qa	6qa	6qa	36qa	6qa	6qa	6qa	6qa	36qa	72qa	SAL-TUR-GAB	
25																BAD SAL-TUR-GAB	ᵐIn-na-mar, "her daughter"
																BAD KAL	Amtu-Nusku, "her daughter"
																BAD KAL	ᵐKa-durah-man-Sak, BIR-SHI-LUM qât ᵐBu-ub-bu.
																BA-A KAL	ᵐKur-me-e, "gate watchman"
																BA-A KAL	ᵐU-na-tol, "grinder"
30																BA-A KAL	ᵐGub-mar-to-ash, "grinder"
																BA-A KAL	ᵐKu-ub-shi-io-Sak, "grinder"
																BA-A KAL	ᵐKa-qa-du-mu, "gateman"
	72qa	72qa	72qa	72qa	72qa	72qa	72qa	72qa	2gur 72qa						4qur 144qa	KAL	ᵐU-qi-shi-io-Sak, "grinder"
	72qa	72qa	72qa	72qa	72qa	72qa	72qa	72qa	72qa 32qa	72qa	72qa	72qa	72qa	2pur 72qa	2qur 72qa	KAL	ᵐArdu-imu XIIIlan KA-ZID-DA
	72qa	72qa	72qa	72qa	72qa	72qa	72qa	72qa	2gur 72qa	72qa	72qa	72qa	72qa	2pur 72qa	4qur 144qa	KAL	ᵐA-bu-uah-ki, BIR-SHI-LUM
35	30qa	30qa	30qa	30qa	30qa	30qa	30qa	30qa	1 gur					1 gur	2 gur	SAL or I	U-si-u, "his wife."
	36qa	36qa	36qa	36qa	36qa	36qa	36qa	36qa	1gur 36qa	36qa	36qa	36qa	36qa	6gur 36qa	2gur 72qa	KAL-TUR	ᵐPi-ri-io-ni, "his son"
	24qa	24qa	24qa	24qa	24qa	24qa	24qa	24qa	144 qa					144 qa	1gur 108qa	SAL-TUR	U-ri, "his daughter"
	12qa	12qa	12qa	12qa	12qa	12qa	12qa	12qa	72 qa	12qa	12qa	12qa	12qa	72 qa	144 qa	SAL-TUR-GAB	ᵈRammân-na-do, "his daughter," "seeress."
									72qa	72qa	72qa	72qa	72qa	2pur 72qa	4qur 144qa	KAL	ᵐTu-kul-ti-Rammân-bragga.
40									30qa	30qa	30qa	30qa	30qa	1 gur	1 gur	SAL or I	Bu-tî-Rammân, "his wife"
																BA-A	(Bi-il-ti-nu-tum, "his daughter"
										12qa	12qa	12qa	12qa	72 qa	72 qa	SAL-TUR-GAB	Eri-r-tum, "his daughter"
																KAL	ᵐHu-um-ba-no-pi-ir, bârshu.
45																KAL-TUR	ᵐNap-shi-ru-Nusku
																KAL	ᵐI-na-shiri-Marduk-alak-barrânu
																KAL	ᵐA-b-iddina(-na)
marginal 5gur 18qa									31gur sha ina libbi ahê'im sha ᵐHu-na-bi nadnat					36gur 108qa 672gur 108qa sha ina libbi ahê'im abulli ahê'im sha Za-rat-IMᵏⁱ u suluppu sha Tâmtu			38	
50	5gur 18qa															SAL or I	A-ba-ta-ti-shu, "bride."
[She'im GISH-BARI 6qa sha ultu orbuNisannu sha shattu 13tan oti orbuAdaru sha shattu 13tan Na-at-Ma-ru-ti-ta-ash i-na libbi ahê'im sha qât ᵐHu-na-bi i-na libbi ahê'im abulli i-na libbi ahê'im sha Za-rat-IMᵏⁱ u suluppu sha Tâmtu nadnat(-nv).

recording the payment of Temple Stipends for twelve months.

the office represented by the individual follows the name, as gate-watchman, weaver, seeress, etc. Whole families are mentioned as receiving stipends. The name of the individual in line five is followed by wife, daughter, two sons, and a grandson.

In line eight, after the name is written *ultu Tashrîtu ḫarrânu*, "from Tishri, road." Nothing was paid the individual from that month. It is not improbable that he had leave of absence; perhaps he was on a mission in the interest of the temple. Others (see line 13, etc.) were absent for the entire year.

Beneath *napḫar* in the seventh column the line means, "what was received from Khunabi," the bursar. The lines beginning beneath the second *napḫar* in the same line read: "grain which is out of the gate [storehouse], which is out of the grain received from the town Zarat-Im. In the forty-seventh line, the totals paid to all during the first month are given; also the total for the first six months; and the total for the second six, which is followed by the sum total. The little note in connection with the total for the first six months reads: that "which was paid out of the grain of Khunabi." The next note reads "that which was out of the grain of the gate storehouse, from Zarat-Im, and dates from Tâmtu. The number 38 in the next column refers to the actual number in the service. In all there are forty-six names in the list, but eight were dead or fugitives. The last two lines read:

These two documents are dated in the 7th and 9th months of the 14th year of Nazi-Maruttash. They record payments made to the heads of the same families mentioned in the larger document of the previous year (see p. 301), but only for a month and a fraction.

"Grain of the 6 *qa* tax, which is from the month Nisan of the thirteenth year, unto Adar, of the fourteenth year of Nazi-Maruttash; from the seed which was given into the hands of Khunabi; from the grain out of the gate [storehouse], of the seed from Zarat-Im, and dates from Tâmtu." This lengthy record is therefore a statement of the temple bursar of amounts paid to a group of temple beneficiaries for a period of one year, as well as the sources from which the revenues were received. What relation the recipients bear to the entire number of temple functionaries is not known. In several other documents of the following years, which were only for a month and a fraction, this same group of persons, with some changes, received stipends. But instead of giving the name of each member of the families, the word *qinnu*, "family," precedes the name of the *pater* or *mater familias*, to whom the full amount was paid. Doubtless at the end of the year statements similar to the previous one discussed were drawn up for the entire year.

A large number of the smaller documents, found among the archives, are records of salaries which were paid to the head officials of the institution.

> 31 *gur* 30 *qa* of grain, food for horses, out of the maintenance tax; 19 sheep, 21 lambs, salary, from the month Tebet unto the fourth day of Nisan (for) Innannu. Month Nisan: day fourth, year first. (Vol. XV, No. 1.)
>
> 2 *gur* 60 *qa* grain out of the maintenance tax, 2 sheep, 2 lambs as salary for Innannu. (Vol. XV, No. 2.)

Babylonian Temple Records 307

Innannu was one of the head officials of the storehouse. With the possible exception of one passage in which "scribe" follows the name Innannu, no title is found in connection with his name, which occurs hundreds of times. He is represented as

Receipts or records of payments made by the administrative department of the temple. Hundreds of documents of this size and character were found in the archives.

receiving taxes, making disbursements and loans. During the time he administered affairs, he seems to have been at the head of the department. The name of others who succeeded him become well known from the texts, only, however, in business transactions. Practically nothing of a personal character concerning these individuals becomes known to us through the inscriptions that have been published.

Usually the seal impression of another is made upon this class of documents, evidently by an officer who delivered the articles mentioned at the residence of the official, and who was required to leave the impression of his seal upon the record of payment which was held by the bursar. This was a guarantee that the delivery officer had paid the amount.

Some of the pay-rolls were quite lengthy. They seem to have been copied frequently from year to year from earlier lists and then what was paid was checked off. The nature of the writing material, being clay, made it necessary to write the tablet at one sitting. Of course it was possible to wrap the tablet in a damp cloth, and lay it aside temporarily, thus preventing it from hardening. This is clearly shown to have been done, as is determined by cloth marks, and also by the marks made upon the tablets in checking off the amounts paid; for some were made after the tablets were almost hard. But the indications are that the scribes usually finished writing tablets before they laid them aside. Some lists, as above, contain many names and amounts which were paid to individuals; in some cases what was received for a number of months. To indicate what was actually paid small holes, round or semi-spherical, before the name or amounts were made.

Record of salary payments made to priests in the Temple service. The small holes are checkmarks used to check off the amounts paid.

These I have determined to be check-marks.[1] It is not unlikely that the upper end of the stylus was used to make these indentures.

These documents, as well as many others discovered in other ancient Babylonian cities, show how carefully the business affairs of the temple were conducted. Among the records also are a number of letters representing the official correspondence of the heads of this executive department of the temple, but these have not yet been deciphered.

It will be readily seen that these administrative documents show that the affairs of the Babylonian temple of the second millennium B. C. were conducted along lines similar to those of some modern religious institutions with which we are acquainted. It is not improbable that the temple at Jerusalem was conducted in a similar manner; and that were we able to recover any of the records, which in all probability were written on perishable material, they would resemble in many ways those found at Nippur and other Babylonian cities.

The study of these documents has resulted also in the determination of some technical details, such as the discovery of two new cuneiform characters and their values, besides additional values for hitherto unknown signs, a large number of new Cassite words, and more than a score of names and epithets

---

[1] See Documents from the Temple Archives of Nippur, Vol. XIV, p. 16.

Record of payments made to the Temple and different shrines of Nippur.

of gods. Among the published documents also are a number of private contracts, the provenience of which is unknown, but which may have come from the office of the temple recorder; and also an interesting tablet, which is a report of an examination of a sheep's liver for divination purposes. It is quite probable that it is a report of an examination to a high functionary, perhaps the king, who abode in Dûr-Kurigalzu near Nippur, which preceded some official act, and in regard to which it was important to determine in advance the disposition of the gods.

XIII

THE ASSYRIAN HISTORICAL INSCRIPTIONS

To Assyria more than to any other country do we look for archeological data which furnish points of contact by yielding parallel accounts of events recorded, as well as by the help of which the pages of the Old Testament are illuminated. It is to the Assyrian period that a considerable portion of the Old Testament refers. No less than six Assyrian rulers are mentioned by name: Tiglathpileser (or Pul), Shalmaneser (IV), Sargon, Sennacherib, Esarhaddon and Asnapper (Ashurbanipal). It must be regarded as an interesting fact that nearly every reference made in the Old Testament to these rulers is in some way touched upon in their annals.

With the exception of the invasion by Shishak (Shashank I) recorded in 1 Kings 14: 25 and following, and which is also recorded on the temple wall at Karnak, Israel was left unmolested by Egypt after the time of Pharaoh Merneptah. Babylonia had become a second rate power. Assyria, of which we hear for the first time in the days of Hammurabi, had by this time developed into a world-conquering nation, and was in a position to play an important rôle among the nations.

Under Tukulti-Ninib (890-885) Assyria entered upon the most brilliant period of its history. Babylonia was annexed. The forced rule lasted seven years, at the end of which time the subjects of Tukulti-Ninib, under the leadership of his own son, rebelled. In the civil war which followed, the king was killed. His son and successor, Ashur-nâṣir-apal (884-860), did not attempt to continue the rule over Babylonia, but carried his work of conquest into the North and West. Tyre and Sidon, when he reached the shores of the Mediterranean, paid him tribute. Samaria at this time was not molested, but the disintegration of the surrounding kingdoms was bound sooner or later to involve the Israelites as well, when the ambitious enemy of the Tigris valley, in his efforts to extend his rule throughout Western Asia, directed his attention to the overthrow of their fortified cities. The beginning of the end of Israel took place in the reign which followed.

Shalmaneser II (860-824) devoted a good deal of his long rule to the establishment of his power in the West. In the mountains of Armenia, at a place called Kurkh, south of Diarbekir, a long monolith inscription was erected by the king, in order to commemorate his deeds. This is now in the British Museum. In it he informs us that after setting out

Assyrian Inscriptions

from the Euphrates, in the sixth year of his reign, he approached Khalman (Aleppo), where he received

The Assyrians besieging a walled city.

tribute. He then advanced to the cities of Irkhuleni of Hamath:

316   Light on the Old Testament

> Adenu, Barga, Argana, his royal city, I conquered; his spoil, his property, the possessions of his palaces I brought forth; to his palaces I set fire. I departed from Argana, and came to Qarqar. Qarqar, his royal city, I destroyed, I devastated, with fire I burned. 1,200 chariots, 1,200 saddle-horses, 20,000 men of Adad-'idri (biblical Ben-hadad II) of Damascus, 700 chariots, 700 saddle-horses, 10,000 men of Irkhuleni of Khamath, 2,000 chariots, 10,000 men of Ahab of Israel (A-kha-ab-bu mât Sir-'i-la-ai), 500 men of Gue, 1,000 of Mutsri, 10 chariots, 10,000 men of Irqanat, 200 men of Matinu-Ba'li, of Arvad, 200 men of Usanata, 30 chariots, 10,000 men of Adunu-Ba'li of Shianu, 1,000 camels of Gindibu'u, of Arbu, 1,000 men of Ba'sha, son of Rukhubi of Ammon; these twelve kings he took to help him; to make war and battle they came to meet me. With the splendid forces which Ashur the lord had given, with the mighty weapons, which Nergal, who marches before me, had presented, I fought with them; from Qarqar to Gilzau their defeat I established. 14,000 soldiers, their fighting men with the sword I laid low with [my] weapons, etc.

In this inscription we have the first mention of Israel that has been found in the Assyrian inscriptions. The information gained is especially valuable, as the alliance with the other kings and the conflict with Shalmaneser II is not recorded in the Old Testament. The obelisk, mentioned below, gives a résumé of this campaign, and fixes the number killed at 20,500; and still another inscription at 25,000. As usual, the Assyrian losses are not given. There is little doubt but that the armies of the allies were defeated, and even the confederation broken up; but as there is no claim of territory having been acquired; or that tribute was exacted; or that booty was carried away, the real issue was not as advantageous to the Assyrians as the chronicler would have the reader of his annals infer.

No reference is made in the Old Testament to Ahab's alliance with Syria, or to other kings who were routed by Shalmaneser. The account given in 1 Kings 20 concerning the conflict of Ahab with Ben-Hadad must be understood to belong to the period prior to their alliance against the Assyrian king. The book of Kings represents Ben-Hadad surrendering to Ahab with a rope about his neck, after which he promised to restore the cities taken from Israel by his father, and to allow Ahab to build streets in Damascus. The latter doubtless readily agreed to such conditions because he recognized that difficulties were in store for the Western nations at the hands of Assyrians; and he felt that for prudential purposes it was better for him to permit Syria, which lay between him and Assyria, to maintain its strength; and to be allied with that nation, rather than be at war with it. When, therefore, Shalmaneser entered this region on a campaign of conquest, Ben-Hadad, Irkhuleni, Ahab, and others were ready to meet him. The alliance however, seems to have been broken up by the defeat which Shalmaneser inflicted upon them.

In the identification of *Aḫabbu* with Ahab, in this inscription, we have an additional chronicle of the kings of Israel, which may have had very far-reaching consequences had Shalmaneser been entirely successful; for Israel might then have lost its independence. The Hebrew chronicler does not mention the event. Perhaps it was because the people were not in sympathy with such an alliance, and the battle had involved only the army, which fought far beyond the confines of the land. Israel, under Jehu, paid tribute to Shalmaneser, and this also was omitted in the brief extracts which are preserved in the Old Testament of the annals of these reigns.

In the Old Testament, the king of Syria is called Ben-Hadad, while in the Assyrian inscriptions he is called Adad-'idri. The full name of the king doubtless was Ben-Hadad-'idri. The Assyrian has preserved the latter part of the name, while the Hebrew simply the name of the deity. Names compounded with Ben-Hadad are known from the contract literature, for example: Ben-Addu-natan, and Ben-Addu-amara.

Five years later the land of Hamath is again attacked. Shalmaneser is again confronted by twelve allies, under the leadership of Ben-Hadad II of Damascus and Irkhuleni of Hamath; but the king of Israel is not among them. The Assyrians claim to have slain ten thousand in this battle but again no important advantage is gained. The conclusion we must draw is that the allies were able to resist the advances of the Assyrians. Several years later another attempt was made, after his army had been greatly reënforced; and he informs us that he again accomplished their defeat. But for the same reasons, no other conclusion can be reached, but that the battle proved a draw. Four years later, Shalmaneser tested once more their prowess, but with better success. Ben-Hadad II was no more. Hazael, the usurper, ruled in his stead. The alliance with the other kings apparently had been broken up. Hazael alone determined to resist the Assyrians, and at Saniru took a stand (842 B. C.) On a slab found at Calah, Shalmaneser gives an account of his victory.

> In the eighteenth year of my reign, for the sixteenth time I crossed the Euphrates. Hazael of Damascus trusted in the mass of his troops, and mustered his army in great numbers. Saniru, a mountain peak, which is at the entrance of the Lebanon mountain, he made for his stronghold. With him I fought; his defeat I established. Six thousand soldiers, his warriors, with arms I brought low. 1,121 of his chariots, 470 of his riding-horses, with his camp-baggage, I took from him. In order to save his life, he made off. After him I went. In Damascus, his royal city, I besieged him. His plantations I cut down. As far as the mountains of Hauran, I went. Cities without number I destroyed. I devastated, [and] with fire I burned. Their spoil, beyond reckoning, I carried away. As far as the mountain Ba'lirasi, which is a promontory of the sea, I went. The image of my royalty on it I set up. At that time, I received the tribute of the Tyrians and Sidonians, [and] of Jehu, the son of Omri.

In accordance with 2 Kings 8: 15, Hazael is mentioned by Shalmaneser as the successor of Ben-Hadad. It seems that the allies of Damascus had

320   Light on the Old Testament

enough. Tyre and Sidon preferred to send gifts instead of continuing the conflict. Jehu, the usurper,

The black obelisk of Shalmaneser II.

perhaps in the hope of freeing himself from the Syrians, and also because of the alarming advances of the formidable Assyrian, was willing to send

Assyrian Inscriptions

costly gifts. This, apparently, was the first step towards the downfall of Israel, for the advantage thus gained by the Assyrians assumed greater and greater proportions, until that people was finally absorbed.

On the famous black obelisk which Layard discovered at Nimroud, Shalmaneser depicted himself in bas-relief, receiving tribute from Jehu. He calls him "son of Omri," or "of the house of Omri;" not knowing that Jehu had usurped the throne by overthrowing the dynasty of Omri. It is possible also that by the term "Omri" he means "Israel;" as for many years the country was known in Assyria as *Mât Omri*, "Land of Omri." The inscription over the line of bas-relief referring to Israel reads:—

> Tribute of Jehu, son of Omri: silver, gold, a golden bowl, a golden ladle, golden chalices, golden buckets, lead, a staff for the hand of the king, spear-shafts(?) I received.

Hazael, being defeated, fled to Damascus, where he was besieged by the Assyrians, but was not conquered. Three years later, the sixth and final, but unsuccessful, attempt was made to establish the supremacy of Assyria over Damascus.

Jehu, in seeking favor of Assyria by paying tribute, did not gain any special advantages over the old enemy Syria; for in 2 Kings 10:32 f we learn that Hazael greatly humiliated Israel after

Shalmaneser had withdrawn. The same is true of Jehoahaz, Jehu's son; for Syria, under Hazael's son, Ben-Hadad III, reduced Israel, "and had made them to be trodden down like the dust."

For about forty years the West-land was left unmolested by Assyria. Shamshi-Adad (824–812) succeeded Shalmaneser. Although the kingdom had been expanded farther than at any previous time, it now became so contracted that the rulers controlled scarcely anything beyond the immediate surroundings of their capitals.

In 2 Kings 13:5, we learn that Jehoahaz, in his dire extremity because of the oppression of Syria, "besought the Lord." "And the Lord gave Israel a saviour, so that they went out from under the hand of the Syrians." The name of the deliverer is not mentioned, but it doubtless was Adad-nirâri (812–783). In an inscription he tells how he brought into submission the princes of the four quarters of the world, and how he conquered many lands, among which was Syria.

> As far as the great sea of the rising sun, from above the Euphrates, the land of the Hittites and Amorites to its entirety, the land of Tyre, the land of Zidon, the land of Omri, the land of Edom, the land of the Philistines as far as the great sea of the setting sun, I subjected to my feet. Tribute and presents I placed on them. Against the land of Damascus I marched; Mari, the king of Damascus I shut up in Damascus his royal city. The terror of the majesty of Ashur, his lord, overwhelmed him; he embraced my feet, [and] became a vassal. 2300 talents of silver, 20 talents of gold, 3000

The second line of bas-relief which extends around the four sides of the obelisk, recording the payment of tribute by biblical Jehu who prostrates himself before Shalmaneser.

talents of copper, 5000 talents of iron, variegated cloth, linen, an ivory bed, a seat with inlaid ivory, a table, his possessions, his property beyond reckoning in Damascus his royal city, in his palace I received.

In this inscription we learn how Israel was able to prevail over the old enemy, Syria. The deliverer, *i.e.*, the Assyrian king, exacted tribute from Israel. Syria, however, was at last crushed.

The successor to the Assyrian throne, Shalmaneser III, followed up the advantage gained over Syria. Ashur-dan, the next ruler, did the same. But Assyria beyond this was inactive in the West-land. Because of this and the chastisement given Syria, and because of the decline of that nation, Israel was able to regain its lost prestige. In consequence, Jeroboam II extended the borders of Israel farther than had been done at any previous or subsequent time. His conquest included Hamath, Damascus, and Moab. His armies were planted on the banks of the Euphrates. The commercial interests of the nation were greatly increased, the resources greatly enlarged. In short, it was a brilliant burst of prosperity prior to the calamity which was to befall the nation. It was also during this period that Uzziah of Judah, who was on friendly terms with Israel, was able to conquer the Philistines, and his country was extended to the south, so that in this direction his kingdom reached practically the old boundaries of Solomon's rule. Not since the division of the kingdom had the tribes been able to

Assyrian Inscriptions 325

extend their political influence as they did during this period; nor had they previously realized such prosperity. Unquestionably this was due to the inactivity of Assyria and the fact that the old enemy, Syria, was crushed.

It was during this period that there was an eclipse of the sun in the month of Sivan. In the Assyrian Eponym chronicle there is recorded for the ninth year of Ashur-dan the following: "Bur-Sagale, of Guzanu. Rebellion in the city of Ashur. In the month Sivan there was an eclipse of the sun." Astronomers fix the date at June 15, 763. The eclipse at this unfortunate time was regarded as an evil omen. Disorder at home, and in neighboring districts, which were under the suzerainty of Assyria, continued for over five years; when at last, "peace in the land" was recorded. It may only be a coincidence but Amos, who was a contemporary, made reference to an eclipse in his prophecies: "I will cause the sun to go down at noon, and I will darken the earth in the clear day" (Amos 8:9).

After the death of Jeroboam II, which was during the lifetime of the prophet Hosea, the northern kingdom became the prey of factions; and in consequence became weakened. His son Zachariah ruled but six months, and was followed by Shallum. The latter reigned one month, when he was assassinated by Menahem.

Ashur-dan, king of Assyria, was succeeded by Ashur-nirâri (753-745), who made several expeditions, but not to the West-land. He ruled ten years, when Tiglath-pileser III (745–727) came to the throne. In the Old Testament he is known also as Pul, although in 1 Chronicles 5:26, the writer considered Tiglath-pileser and Pul as two persons. For many years no Assyrian king by the name of Pul was known. The late Professor Schrader had correctly argued that Pul and Tiglath-pileser were one and the same person. Later, Dr. Pinches was able to prove conclusively that this theory was correct. He showed that the Babylonian chronicle says:

> In the third year of Ukîn-zêr, Tiglath-pileser marched against Akkad, laid waste Bît-Amukani and took Ukîn-zêr captive. Ukîn-zêr reigned three years in Babylon. Tiglath-pileser ascended the throne in Babylon. In the second year of Tiglath-pileser he died in the month of Teteb.

The Ptolemaic Canon shows that Ukîn-zêr and Pulu (Poros) together ruled five years over Babylonia. Hence it follows that Pulu and Tiglath-pileser are the same. Pulu as a proper name is known also in the inscriptions. Whether this was an official name the ruler received in Babylonia, or whether it was his original name, as is more likely, is not known. The question as to how he came to the throne also needs more light. He is generally supposed to have been a usurper, having perhaps been a general in the army.

He succeeded to the throne at a time when the country was in an unsettled state, but he made his

Assyrian Inscriptions 327

reign one of the most important in Assyrian history. The historical inscriptions recording his annals have been handed down in a mutilated condition. The events, however, can be arranged in chronological order by the help of the Eponym Canon. We learn that his first efforts were directed against Babylonia, Chaldea, and Armenia. Nabonassar had been the acknowledged king of Babylon, but now Tiglath-pileser assumed the ancient title of the entire country, including Shumer and Akkad. He next brought into subjection the rulers of Ararat, Arpad, etc. About this time he began to make trouble for Syria and North Phoenicia. The Canon for 738 B. C. records the brief statement: "He captured the city of Kullanu. This is supposed to have been in the vicinity of Hamath, which would make it identical with Calno of Isaiah 10:9. The name of Azariah is mentioned four times in the inscription, but unfortunately, owing to its fragmentary condition, little can be gathered from the references. It would seem that Judah had formed an alliance with Hamath, in order that they might mutually protect themselves against the advances of the Assyrians. While those in league with Judah seem to have suffered, Azariah himself did not become involved. In an inscription, Tiglath-pileser mentions Azariah as follows:

> Nineteen districts of the city of Hamath, together with the towns of their environs along the coast of the sea of the setting sun, who in sin and wickedness they

328   Light on the Old Testament

(the people) took up for Azrijau (Azariah), to the boundary of Assyria I added. My commander-in-chief as governor I set over them.

Besides the nineteen places which were captured, a long list of kings is mentioned as having paid

The biblical Tiglath-pileser or Pul standing before a besieged city.

tribute, among whom are: "*Raṣunnu* (Rezin, 2 Kings 16:5) of Damascus, *Menihimme* (Menahem) of the city of the Samarians, and *Ḥirummu* (Hirom) of the city of the Tyrians." In 2 Kings 15:19, we learn that "there came against the land Pul, the king of Assyria; and Menahem gave to Pul one thousand talents, etc." Neither the Bible nor the inscriptions say that Tiglath-pileser fought with Menahem. In the former, the silver is paid "to confirm the kingdom in his hand," whereupon "the king of Assyria turned back and stayed not there in the land" (2 Kings 15: 20). In the inscriptions Menahem is only mentioned as having paid tribute.

In 2 Kings 16:5, we learn that Rezin, king of Syria, and Pekah, king of Israel, warred with Ahaz, and besieged him in Jerusalem. For a season he was able to withstand their efforts; but there being those at the capital who were hostile to him, and his country having been overrun by the enemy, he sought the assistance of Tiglath-pileser, by sending him presents of gold and silver. The king of Assyria readily hearkened unto him, as he doubtless saw danger in the organized efforts of Israel and Syria; and at the same time he was desirous of making Ahaz a vassal. He went up against Damascus, and took it; and carried the people captive to Kir; and slew Rezin.

In the following inscription Tiglath-pileser records his treatment of Rezin.

> . . . Like a hind . . . he entered the great gate of the city. His chiefs alive with my hands I took, and upon stakes I caused them to be raised up, and made them a show for this land. 45 camps . . . I collected, and shut him up like a bird in cage. His plantations, . . . which were innumerable I cut down, and did

not leave one . . . Hâdara, the house of the father of Rezin of Damascus, in which he was born, I besieged, etc.

The fact that Rezin eventually lost his life at the hands of the Assyrian king must be supplied from the Old Testament (2 Kings 16:9), owing to the fragmentary condition of his annals.

In 2 Kings 15:29, 30, we are informed that "in the days of Pekah, king of Israel, came Tiglath-pileser king of Assyria, and took Ijon; and Abel-beth-maacah and Janoah and Kedesh, and Hazor and Gilead, and Galilee, all the land of Naphtali; and he carried them captive to Assyria. And Hoshea the son of Elah made a conspiracy against Pekah the son of Remaliah, and smote him, and slew him, and reigned in his stead." In an inscription Tiglath-pileser records substantially the same thing.

. . . . the city of *Gal-'[ed]* (Gilead ?) . . . the city of *Abilakka* (Abel-beth-maacah?) which is of the boundary of the land of Beth-Omri (Israel) . . . the broad, in its entire extent, to the territory of Assyria I annexed; my commander-in-chief as prefect I appointed over them. *Ḥânûnu* (Hanno) of Gaza, who fled before my arms, escaped to the land of Egypt. Gaza I captured; its possessions, its treasures, its gods I carried away . . . and the image of my royalty I erected. . . . Beth-Omri (Israel) . . . the whole of its inhabitants its possessions to Assyria I deported. Pekah their king they smote. *Ausi'* (Hoshea) as king, over them I appointed. Ten talents of gold, 1,000 talents of silver together with their presents I received from them.

Assyrian Inscriptions 331

There is a gap between the reference to Israel and what follows. The annalist greatly exaggerated the results of his campaign if he intended that the statement, "the whole of the inhabitants of the land of Omri," should refer to Israel. The Old Testament mentions the names of the cities and districts whose inhabitants were carried by him into captivity; but the capital of "Omri" which was Samaria, is not mentioned as being depopulated, either in the inscriptions or the Old Testament, until later.

In an inscription belonging to the closing years of his reign, he mentions the receiving of tribute not only from the kings of northern cities, but also from Sanipu, of Bēth-Ammon, Salamanu of Moab, Metinti of Askelon, *Jauḥazi* (Ahaz) of Judah, Kaushmalak of Edom, and Ḥanûnu (Hanno) of Gaza. While there is no reference in the Assyrian inscriptions to explain Tiglath-pileser's movements against Israel and Syria, this fact confirms the statement (2 Kings 16: 7), that Ahaz sought the assistance of Tiglath-pileser in order to free himself from Israel and Syria. The inscription recording the tribute belongs to one of the succeeding years.

The voluntary homage paid the Assyrian king, in his dire extremity to rid himself of Syria and Israel, was the first prominent move towards the downfall of Judah. The desired relief was gained, but as Assyria was entering upon a long period of subjugation and oppression, the deliverance which he obtained only served to remove a barrier for subsequent conquest, which meant eventually the overthrow of Jerusalem.

That Ahaz should pay a visit to Tiglath-pileser, the mighty conquerer of the West-land, at Damascus, as is recorded in 2 Kings 16: 10, seems perfectly natural, for he was the master of this entire region.

In the closing years of his life his attention was directed to a league formed by the Chaldeans with the Arameans, who had designs upon Babylon. Tiglath-pileser appeared on the scene; the Chaldeans were subdued, and he became the king of Babylon, over which he ruled for two years.

The biblical Shalmaneser IV (727–722) followed Tiglath-pileser. He also was an adventurer, as no relationship with his predecessors is mentioned. Little is known from the inscriptions of his short reign of five years, except the brief statements in the Babylonian Chronicle and the Eponym Canon. The former states: "On the 25th of Tebet, Shalmaneser sat on the throne in Assyria. The city Shamara'in he destroyed." Unfortunately, the Eponym Canon is mutilated, and in consequence is of little value.

The Old Testament and Josephus furnish additional data concerning the reign of this ruler. In 2 Kings 17: 3–5, we learn that Shalmaneser came up against Hoshea, who "became his servant and gave him presents. And the king of Assyria found conspiracy in Hoshea for he had sent messengers to

So, king of Egypt." Shalmaneser imprisoned him and besieged Samaria. Josephus, as well as commentators in former years, understood the passage, "in the ninth year of Hoshea the king of Assyria took Samaria, and carried Israel away into Assyria" (2 Kings 17:6), to refer to Shalmaneser. The inscriptions of Sargon, the successor of Shalmaneser, definitely show that he, or rather his representatives, deported Israel in the first year of his reign, in consequence of which he is "the king of Assyria" who is referred to by the Hebrew chronicler. In the Eponym Canon, the name Samaria might be supplied in some of the incomplete lines. The name of the city destroyed in the Babylonian Chronicle is read by some *Sabara'in* instead of *Samara'in*, as the characters for *ba* and *ma* are almost identical; but in view of the fact that in the succeeding reign the Hebrew *Shomeron* (Samaria) is written *Samerîna*, in the inscriptions, which is nearly the same; and because Shalmaneser, while he did not destroy the city, laid siege to it, and perhaps destroyed some of its outlying districts, there can be little doubt but that Samaria is meant. The city, however, did not fall until later, as is determined by the inscription of Sargon.

So, of Egypt, or, vocalizing the Hebrew letters, differently, and reading *Sive*, king of Egypt, doubtless refers to Shabaka, the Ethiopian who founded the twenty-fifth dynasty. Sargon refers to *Sib'e*, whom he calls the *tartan*, or commander-in-chief of the Egyptian army. If the Hebrew *Seve* and the Assyrian *Sib'e* are intended to represent Shabaka, then either the Hebrew writer in calling him king, anticipated his becoming such, or the Assyrian annalist was not aware that he had become king.

Another adventurer followed Shalmaneser. He is known as Sargon II (722–705), which name he very likely assumed. He called himself "Sargon the Later" in distinction from the name of the illustrious Sargon I, who lived about 3800 B. C. The latter's full name, as found in his inscriptions, is *Shargâni-shar-âli:* but in all probability it had been handed down in a form something like the name the usurper assumed. His name is sometimes written *Shar-ukîn*, "[a god] has appointed a king" and again *Shar-kênu* "the legitimate king." Both meanings would lead us to suppose that he desired to impress his subjects with the legitimacy of his appointment as ruler. His adopting a Babylonian name instead of an Assyrian, as his two predecessors had seen fit to do, may have had some diplomatic signification.

With the exception of the reference to Sargon in Isaiah 20:1 his name was lost to history. It was really preserved in the Ptolemaic Canon as Arkeanos, but although an initial Sigma, according to a well-known law in Greek, sometimes appears as the rough breathing, Arkeanos was not identified with Sargon.

An inscription of Sargon, (722-705), found at Nimroud, bears the following:

One of the two-winged bulls which stood at the entrance to the palace of Sargon
(see page 14)

336   Light on the Old Testament

From the beginning of my sovereignty until the 15th year of my reign Humbanigash, the Elamite of the city Der, I accomplished his defeat. Samerina (Samaria) I besieged I captured. 27,290 people, dwelling in it I carried away. 50 chariots I collected from them and the

SARGON II (722-705 B.C.) Captor of Samaria.

rest [of the people] I allowed to retain their possessions. My commander-in chief I placed over them, and the tribute of the former king I placed upon them. Hanno king of Gaza, [and] Sib'e the tartan of Egypt advanced against me in Rapikhi (Rapkia) to make war and battle. I

Assyrian Inscriptions 337

accomplished their defeat. Sib'e feared the sound of my arms and fled, and his place was not found. Hanno, the king of Gaza I took with my hand. The tribute of Pir'u king of Egypt, Samsê, queen of Aribi (Arabia), It'amara of Saba'ai (Sabeans), gold product of the mountain, horses [and] camels I received:

The reference to the subjugation of Humbanigash in the opening lines of this inscription does not necessarily mean that an assault upon Elam was made as his first act. According to the Babylonian Chronicle, this took place in the second year of Sargon's reign. The first act of his army doubtless was the capture of Samaria, and the carrying of the children of Israel into captivity; the final drama in the history of Israel. Sargon's account of his deportation of 27,290 of Samaria's inhabitants is supplemented by the biblical record (2 Kings 17:6) which informs us that he "placed them in Halah (perhaps near Haran) and by the river Ḫabor (the Khabour), and in Gozan, and in the cities of the Medes."

In a text of Sargon parallel to the above this statement is added: "I settled there the men of countries conquered [by my hand]." 2 Kings 17:24 is an interesting commentary on this passage. It reads: "And the king of Assyria brought men from Babylon and from Cuthah (Kutu), and from Avva, and from Hamath, and from Sepharvaim, and placed them in the cities of Samaria instead of the children of Israel, and they possessed Samaria, and dwelt in the cities thereof." In a record belonging to the time about seven years later, he says: "The tribes of Tamud, Ibâdid Marsiman and Khayâpâ, Arabian tribes, inhabitants of the desert, of whom no sage or scholar had known, who had never paid tribute to any king I smote in the service of Ashur my lord; and the rest of them I carried away and settled in Samaria."

The Nimroud inscription above referred to mentions among other cities, Samaria, as being in league with Jau-bi'di, who had designs on the throne of Hamath. He had the assistance of Sib'u of Egypt and Hanno of Gaza. Jau-bi'di was captured and flayed alive. It is difficult to understand who is meant by Samaria unless the remnants that had not been deported, or some of those settled there.

In another inscription also he mentions people of the land of Philistia, Judah (Jaudu), Edom and Moab as depending upon "Pir'u king of Egypt a prince who could not save them," in other words, a "bruised reed." The inscription is fragmentary and does not relate the outcome of this dependence.

Sennacherib (705–681 B. C.) succeeded his father Sargon, who before his death had turned over to him the responsibility of keeping under subjection the northern Armenian provinces. Sennacherib seemed to lack his father's ability in managing the heterogeneous elements of which the great nation was composed. In military ability he was not wanting, but instead of conciliating the vanquished and replacing the turbulent, he finally became the ruler of a sparsely populated desert; as he not only destroyed cities and towns, but he murdered the inhabitants. On his accession to the throne, he doubtless appreciated the fact that Babylon would be difficult to control. He evidently foresaw the difficulties which later did arise, and which finally resulted in the overthrow of Assyria. In consequence, from the very beginning he ignored their authority, and did not accept titles and honors from their priesthood. At this slight, the Babylonians became indignant; and proclaimed king over them a man of humble origin, Marduk-zâkir-shum by name. A month later the indefatigable Merodach-baladan, who had been defeated by Sargon, appeared on the scene. In a sedition which followed, Marduk-zâkir-shum was killed, and Merodach-baladan was once more proclaimed king. He sent an embassy to Elam and to Hezekiah (2 Kings 20: 12–19), the ultimate purpose of which, although the annalist supposed it was in connection with his sickness, seems to have been to encourage the western states to rebel against Assyria. The showing of the treasuries perhaps implies that Hezekiah indicated to the emissaries what his strength in this particular was.

Sennacherib wasted no time in putting down the rebellion in Babylonia. He proceeded to Kish, where the Chaldean king was entrenched. Merodach-baladan's army was defeated, and he fled for safety. Sennacherib entered the gates of Babylon which were thrown open to him, pillaged the royal

Boundary stone of biblical Merodach-baladan, in which he makes a grant of certain lands to one of his dignitaries. Above his pointed crown the inscription reads: The picture of Merodach-baladan, king of Babylon.

Assyrian Inscriptions

treasury, and placed Bêl-ibni on the throne. In his second campaign, Sennacherib invaded the country of the Cassites and the Iasubigalleans. In his third campaign, he directed his attention to the rebellious subjects in the West-land. The Assyrian army had not been in Palestine for about ten years. The people in consequence felt more or less secure, and were anxious to throw off the yoke of Assyria. The embassy sent to Jerusalem by Merodach-baladan and the uprising in Babylonia, had doubtless succeeded in arousing the anti-Assyrian party to renewed activity. Hezekiah had been victorious over the Philistines (2 Kings 18:8). In order to withstand sieges in dry seasons a conduit had been built (2 Kings 20:20), to bring water within the city walls. In view of these circumstances, although strongly opposed by the prophet Isaiah, the Egyptian party prevailed upon the king to send gifts (Isa. 30:1-4) to Egypt, seeking the aid of that country. Anxious to restore lost prestige in Palestine, the desired aid in throwing off the yoke was again promised. Whether this rebellious spirit had spread to Phoenicia is not known, but at Ekron the elders of the city cast Padi, the Assyrian king and vassal into irons, and had Hezekiah imprison him in Jerusalem.

To put down the uprising, Sennacherib lost no time. He entered the land from the north, and first struck at Sidon. In what is known as the Taylor cylinder, which was discovered at Nineveh in 1830, together with an inscription on one of the colossal bulls which Layard brought from Kunyunjik, besides a duplicate, we have Sennacherib's own account of this invasion.

> In my third campaign I went to the land of the Hittites. Luli, king of Zidon, the fear of the splendor of my lordship overwhelmed him, and he fled to a distant place in the midst of the sea (variant Cyprus). His land I subdued. Great Zidon (Josh. 19:28), Little Zidon Bit-Zitti, Sarepta (1 Kings 17:9), Makhalliba, Hosah (Josh. 19:29), Achzib (Judg. 1:31), Accho (Judg. 1:31), his mighty cities, fortresses, pasture and irrigated lands, houses of his assistance, the dreadfulness of the arms of Ashur, my lord, overwhelmed them, and they submitted unto me. Ethbaal (1 Kings 16:31) upon the royal throne I placed over them, and a perpetual yearly payment of the tribute of my lordship I imposed upon them.
>
> As for Menahem of Samsimuruna, Ethbaal of Zidon, Abdili'ti of Arvad (Ezek. 27:8), Urumilki of Gebel (Ezek. 27:9), Mitinti of Ashdod, Pudu-el of Bēth-Ammon, Chemosh-nadbi of Moab, Malik-rammu of Edom, and all the kings of the West land, rich presents, their heavy gifts, for the fourth time brought to me, and kissed my feet.

The humiliation of Zidka is then recorded, as well as the subjugation of his cities.

> And Zidka of Ashkelon, who had not submitted to my yoke, his ancestor's gods, himself, his wife, his sons, his daughters, his brothers, the seed of his father's house I tore away and carried to Assyria. Sharludari, the son of Rukibtu, their former king, I placed over the people of Ashkelon. I put upon them the giving of tribute, presents for my lordship; and he shall draw my yoke.

Assyrian Inscriptions

In the course of my campaign Bêth-Dagan (Josh. 15:41), Joppa, Beni-berek (Joshua 19:45) (and) Azuru, the cities of Zidka, which had quickly thrown themselves at my feet, I besieged I conquered, their spoil I carried away.

The kings of Egypt with their armies, are summoned, but in front of Eltekeh (Josh. 19:44) Sennacherib accomplished their defeat. Some think that the word translated Egypt, which is Muṣri, means rather Northwest Arabia.

The governors, chiefs and people of Ekron, who threw into chains Padi a lord of the law and oath of Assyria, and had given him to Hezekiah of the land of the Jews, and who as an enemy shut him up in prison, feared in their hearts, and called forth the kings of Egypt, warriors, bowmen, chariots, horses of the king of Melukha, a force without number; and they came to their help. In the vicinity of Eltekeh they set a line of battle before me. They asked their weapons [to decide]. By the assistance of Ashur, my lord, I fought with them, and I accomplished their defeat. The chief of the chariots and the sons of the king of Egypt together with the chief of the chariots of the king of Melukha in the midst of the battle I took alive with my hands. Eltekeh, Tamnâ I besieged, I took I carried away their spoil.

To Ekron I rode, and the governors [and] princes who had transgressed I killed, and I bound their corpses upon stakes around the city. The inhabitants of the city who had done sin and evil I reckoned as spoil. The rest of them who had not committed sin and ignominious acts, whose sin they did not have I pronounced their amnesty. Padi, their king from Jerusalem I brought out and I caused to enter upon the throne of lordship over them. The tribute of my lordship I placed upon them.

> As regards Hezekiah, the Judean, who did not submit to my yoke, forty-six of his mighty cities, strongholds, together with innumerable small places of their environs, by the battering of rams and the assault of the siege engines, . . . I besieged, I conquered, 200,150 people, small and large, male and female, horses, mules, asses, camels, oxen and sheep without number, from their midst I carried out and reckoned as booty. Himself (that is Hezekiah), like a bird in a cage in Jerusalem his royal city I penned him. Trenches against him I threw up, and those coming from the gate of their city I forcibly turned back. His cities which I had sacked, I cut off from the country, and I gave them to Mitinti of Ashdod, Padi, king of Ekron and Tsil-Baal, king of Gaza, thus reducing his territory. In addition to the former tax, to pay yearly, I added a tribute of subjection to my royalty, I placed upon them. Himself Hezekiah, the fear of the splendor of my lordship overwhelmed him. The courage of the Arabians and his faithful soldiers whom he had brought in for the defense of Jerusalem, his royal city, failed. Together with 30 talents of gold and 800 talents of silver, precious stones, . . . his daughters, women of his palace, . . . to Nineveh, my royal city, I caused to be brought after me; he sent his ambassador to offer tribute and perform homage.

This is perhaps the most remarkable parallel account to the Old Testament records which is found in the Assyrian inscriptions. With the Hebrew story of Sennacherib's invasion as recorded in Isaiah 36:1 ff. and 2 Kings 18:13 ff. all biblical students are familiar. Sennacherib's account naturally differs considerably from it, as it is written from an altogether different standpoint. But it corroborates many details, as well as supplements and gives a

Cylinder of Sennacherib.

clearer view of the whole situation. That the Assyrian account should record the exact amount of gold paid by Hezekiah, namely thirty talents, is remarkable.

In view of the fact that Josephus, who quotes from Berosus, makes the attack upon Jerusalem to have taken place on his return from Egypt after he had spent some time there besieging Pelusium, some scholars hold that Sennacherib made two invasions to this region, and that the one immediately follows the other in the Old Testament. That on the former he received the tribute; and that the ignominious defeat took place on the latter, which belongs to the last eight years of his life, *i.e.*, after the period covered by the Taylor cylinder. The fact is, it looks highly probable if Berosus is right in speaking of a battle at Pelusium, and also that Sennacherib lived only " a little while " after his disastrous defeat, which the Old Testament also seems to imply, although no Assyrian records thus far bear out the theory.

Another argument can be found in the fact that the annals of Sennacherib do not mention Lachish, although he had the capture of the city depicted on a huge bas-relief. That he gloried in this event seems reasonable to suppose. That it should not be mentioned in his annals if it took place on his third campaign, seems somewhat difficult to understand. In 2 Kings 19:9, Tirhakah is mentioned as the king of Ethiopia with whom

Assyrian Inscriptions 347

Sennacherib came into conflict. If there was but one invasion, the Hebrew annalist anticipated his title; for although in the early period of Sennacherib's reign he was in charge of the Egyptian forces, Shabaka, his uncle, was the reigning Pharaoh.

If it is insisted upon that there was but one invasion of the West-land the fact that no reference is made to the ignominious defeat of Sennacherib's army by night would occasion no difficulty. Such would be unlooked for in Assyrian annals. Only that is mentioned which is calculated to magnify the great achievements of the army and the valor of the king. But instead of it there are sonorous phrases concerning what was successful, and what is mentioned which was not so, is couched in words to give the impression that the results were the same. The fact that he did not capture Jerusalem, doubtless the leading city in the revolt, but instead simply beleaguered it, and penned up Hezekiah in the city, like a bird in a cage, shows conclusively that the campaign did not terminate in as successful a manner as the annalist would have his readers infer. The pillaging of his suburbs and cutting off his territory was not such an important feat.

The Hebrew account, on the other hand, while it enlarges upon the miraculous deliverance of the city, which explains why Sennacherib never made a second attempt, fearing the God of the Hebrews, at the same time mentions the fact that Hezekiah had confessed that he had offended, and that he had paid immense sums to buy off Sennacherib. In this connection Herodotus says that when the Assyrians were encamped before the Egyptians at Pelusium within sight of the enemy, an army of field-mice destroyed the bowstrings, etc., of the Assyrian army, which resulted in their being routed, and many slain. Josephus, quoting from Berosus, in explaining the disastrous defeat, relates how God had sent a pestilential distemper upon Sennacherib's army, which was under the Rabshakeh. In other words, Egyptians as well as Jews, as is shown by the echoes of the calamity, rejoiced in the victory.

On his return to Nineveh Sennacherib had carved a series of slabs representing in bas-relief his assault and capture of the city of Lachish. This fact is not mentioned in the Old Testament, although Sennacherib is said to have been at Lachish when his officials called upon Hezekiah at Jerusalem. In one portion of the relief, the walls of the city are represented, upon which are bowmen, slingers, and those who hurled lighted torches upon the portable sheds in which the battering rams were worked. From the entrance of the city near the center, captives are seen issuing forth, and soldiers carrying impaled bodies of men. The steps and guard-house of the great gate of this period were discovered in the excavations by Bliss at Lachish. Sennacherib's army is represented as being on the slope of the hill with engines, spearmen, bowmen, and slingers. Ladders for scaling the wall are seen. On the top

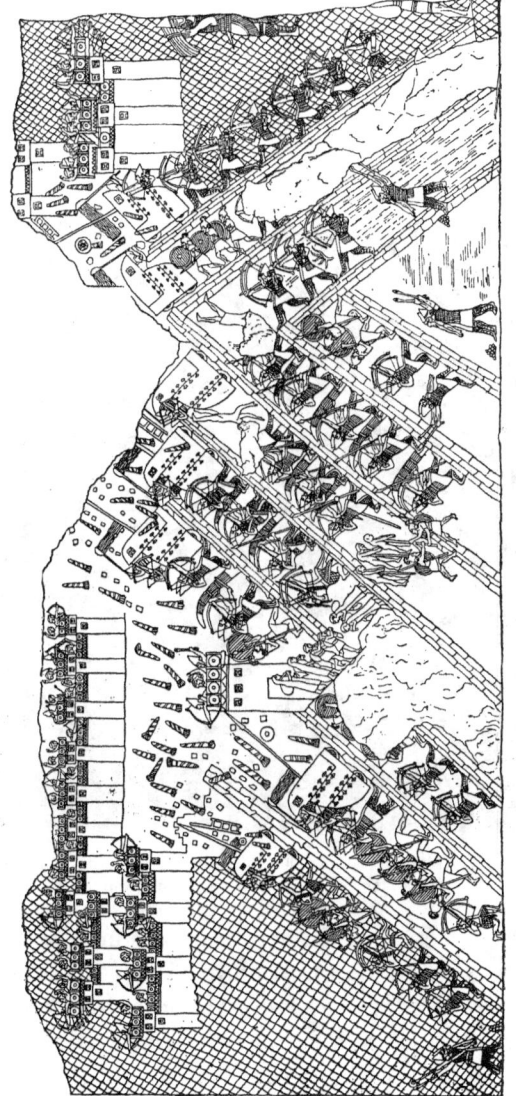

Storming of Lachish by Sennacherib's army.

of each engine a man is seen, pouring water over its roof, in order to prevent it from catching fire from the burning brands.

In another portion of the slab Sennacherib had

One of a series of sculptured slabs, showing Sennacherib seated upon his throne before the city of Lachish, receiving tribute.

himself depicted in a great throne chair, with bow and arrow in his hand. Before him are his officials, perhaps represented as reporting upon the results of the attack. Over them is the inscription: "Sennacherib, king of the world, king of Assyria, sat on a throne-chair and caused the spoil of Lachish to pass before him." Behind these officials are captives with pronounced Hebrew features. Behind the victorious king stand eunuchs with "fly flaps;" behind these is his tent. Over it an inscription reads: "Tent of Sennacherib king of Assyria." Below is the king's chariot, and soldiers killing captives.

According to the inscriptions only one son is implicated in the parricide which brought this reign to an end, although it is quite possible that another was involved, as is recorded in the Old Testament, which says, that Sennacherib was assassinated by his two sons Adrammelech and Sharezer (Isa. 37: 38). In the Babylonian Chronicle the following occurs:

> On the 20th of Tebet, Sennacherib, king of Assyria, was killed by his son in a rebellion. For [23] years Sennacherib had reigned over the kingdom of Assyria. From the 20th of Tebet until the 2nd of Adar there was an insurrection in Assyria. On the 8th of Sivan Esarhaddon, his son sat on the throne.

Esarhaddon (681–668) accomplished what his father and Sargon had failed to do, namely defeat Egypt and make it an Assyrian province. He felt that the conquest of the land and the humiliation of the king was the only possible remedy for the constant interference of Egypt with Assyria's control of Palestine and Syria. His first attempt, in 673 B. C., was unsuccessful. Seven years later he invested

Tyre whose king, Baal, had identified himself with Tirhakah. The Egyptian army was defeated and the king escaped to Memphis. In returning from Egypt, when his army reached the Nahr el-kelb along the coast-road, he had cut in the rocks beside the triumphal stele of Rameses II, his own, in which he recounted his achievements. Also, on a large triumphal stele which he erected at Zinjirli, he had himself represented in colossal size, while before him in diminutive form is Tirhakah (2 Kings 19:9), who is identified from his negroid features; and also Baal of Tyre. They have rings through their lips, to which cords are attached. These Esarhaddon with great complacency holds in his left hand, while he holds a cup near his mouth with the other. In the inscription, which is in the Berlin Museum, he says:

> Tarqu, the king of Egypt and Kush from Iskhupri as far as Memphis, his royal city, a march of fifteen days, I smote his warriors in great numbers. Himself I attacked five times with the point of the spear in a mortal combat. Memphis, his royal city I besieged for half a day; I took it, I laid it waste, I burnt it with fire. His consort, his other concubines, Ushanakhuru his son and the rest of his sons and daughters, his possessions, his treasuries, his horses, his oxen, his flocks without number, I carried away to Assyria. The root of Kush I tore up out of Egypt, and not one of the least did I permit to return. Over the whole of Egypt I placed afresh kings, governors, prefects, officials, overseers, regents. The tribute of my sovereignty, [to be paid] yearly without fail, I imposed upon them.

Esarhaddon holding biblical Tirhakah, king of Egypt and Baal, king of Tyre with thongs passing through their lips.

Esarhaddon does not mention in his inscriptions that he took Manasseh to Assyria, but he does say that when he was about to build a new palace he caused twenty-two kings of the land of the Hittites, along the sea coast, and the islands to furnish him with building material, among whom was Manasseh:

> I filled up the platform. I mustered the kings of the Hittite land and across the sea. Ba'lu king of Tyre, Menasê (Manasseh), king of the city Jaudu (Judah) Qaush-gabri king of Edon. Musuri king of Moab, Tsil-Bêl king of Gaza, Metinti king of Ashkelon, Ikasamsu king of Ekron, Milki-ashapa, king of Gebel, Matan-Bêl, king of Arvad, Abi-Bêl, King of the Samsimuruna, Budu-ilu, king of the city Bēth-Ammon, Akhi-Milki, king of Ashdod, 12 kings of the sea coast. Ekishtura, king of the city of Idalion, Pilâgura king of Kitrus, Kîsu king of Sillua, Itûandar, king of the city Paphos, Eresu, king of Sillu, Damasu king of Kurium; Atmezu king of Tamassus; Damûsi king of Qarti-khadasti, Unasagusu, king of Lidir, Butsusu king of Nuria, 10 kings of the land of Cyprus within the sea; altogether 22 kings of the land of the Hittites the sea coast and midst of the sea, all of them, etc.

Esarhaddon met his death on the road to Egypt, intending to reconquer his vassals who had rebelled, and follow up his former victories. To him and his son is due the credit for resuscitating Babylon, which his father had endeavored to obliterate. At Nippur also his work is manifested by inscribed bricks bearing his name. In consequence of this interest in the land there was no Babylonian revolt during his reign. He was succeeded by his two

Ashurbanipal depicted on a stone votive stele as the high priest or canephorus. The inscription records his pious acts such as rebuilding temples.

sons, Ashurbanipal ruling Assyria and Shamash-shum-ukin, Babylonia.

Ashurbanipal (668–626) is generally believed to be "the great and noble" Asnapper, Ezra 4: 10, who settled in Samaria the Dinaites, Apharsathchites, Tarpelites, Apharsites, Archevites, Babylonians, Shushanchites, Dehaites, Elamites, and men of other nations. In a list of twenty tributary kings corresponding to that of Esarhaddon, Manasseh (written Minse) of the land of Judah is again mentioned. In 2 Chronicles 33 : 11 ff. we are informed that the captains of the host of the king of Assyria took Manasseh with hooks and bound him with fetters, and carried him to Babylon. The king was either Esarhaddon or Ashurbanipal. If the former, the triumphal stele described above becomes especially interesting. Later, because of his repentance, Manasseh was restored unto his kingdom. It is interesting to note in the inscriptions that Ashurbanipal accorded similar treatment to Necho, the vassal king of Memphis and Sais, who had joined Tirhakah in his revolt against Assyria. He had been brought to Nineveh bound in chains; but having gained the confidence of Ashurbanipal he was sent back to Egypt with marks of special favor, and reinstated upon his throne. Manasseh's bondage and treatment, which is recorded only in the book of Chronicles, is thus paralleled by the experience of another subject king.

The words uttered by the prophet Nahum in his

So-called garden scene of Ashurbanipal and his consort.

prediction concerning the downfall of Nineveh, when he said,"Art thou, Nineveh better than No Amon" finds an interesting explanation in the inscription of Ashurbanipal. No, meaning "city," is the name of Thebes, while Amon (or Amen) was the chief god worshiped in that city. Tirhakah had been conquered by Esarhaddon. He advanced against the rulers appointed by Assyria and took possession of Memphis. Ashurbanipal went to Egypt to suppress the insurrection. Tirhakah's forces were defeated. He fled by ship to Thebes ($Ni'i$, "No"), which city Ashurbanipal took. Shortly afterwards Urd-amani succeeded Tarqu. Ashurbanipal again entered Egypt. But when the king "saw the onslaught of my mighty battle, he left Ni'i (No) and fled to Kipqip. This city (*i.e.* No) in its entirety, in reliance upon Ashur and Ishtar my hands conquered." In other words, the rapacious Assyrians spoiled the city. It is this to which the prophet refers (Nahum 3:8).

Several short reigns followed Ashurbanipal in the twenty remaining years of Assyrian rule, namely that of Ashur-etil-ilâni, Sin-shum-lîshir and Sin-shar-ishkun. But Nineveh at last met her doom. Nabopolassar, the Chaldean ruler of Babylonia, made an alliance with the Umman-Manda or Medes, and Sennacherib's destruction of Babylon was avenged. The city was razed to the ground, never to be rebuilt, and its treasures were carried away. The Medes took possession of Northern Assyria and

Hunting scene of an Assyrian king.

the Armenia vassal states; Babylonia took Southern Assyria and the title to the West-lands including Palestine, Syria, and Egypt.

"Thy shepherds slumber, O king of Assyria: thy worthies are at rest: thy people are scattered upon the mountains, and there is none to gather them. There is no assuaging of thy hurt; thy wound is grievous; all that hear the bruit of thee clap the hands over thee; for upon whom hath not thy wickedness passed continually?" (Nahum 3: 18, 19.)

XIV

THE NEO-BABYLONIAN HISTORICAL INSCRIPTIONS

The time had arrived for the supremacy of the valley to change hands. The coalition of the Medes and Babylonians had secured their independence from Assyria. Nabopolassar, who was of Chaldean origin in all probability, had been installed as viceroy by the Assyrian king Ashur-etil-ilâni-ukîn, and was continued in that position by his successor Sin-shar-ishkun, the last king of Assyria. He made an alliance with the Medes, strengthening it by the marrige of his son Nebuchadrezzar to the daughter of Astyages, the Median king.

Necho II succeeded to the throne of Egypt about the time Assyria was near its end. He constructed a war fleet for the Mediterranean and the Red Sea. He saw an opportunity to establish Egyptian control over Palestine and Syria. (2 Kings 23: 29–30.) He advanced with his army to the plain of Megiddo, where Josiah with an inferior force recklessly threw himself against him. Josiah was defeated and mortally wounded. With this stroke Necho was able to capture the entire land; and he moved north as far as Riblah, in the land of Hamath.

Jehoahaz, the son of Josiah, was chosen king; but Necho sent him a prisoner to Egypt. Eliakim his brother, who assumed Jehoiakim as his throne name, was appointed ruler. A tribute of one hundred talents of silver and one talent of gold was imposed upon him. (2 Kings 23:31-35). But the fall of Nineveh gave the vigorous Babylonians the title to this land; and Necho's plans were interfered with. Nabopolassar despatched his son Nebuchadrezzar against the Egyptians, whom he defeated at the battle of Carchemish on the Euphrates; and the coveted territory was again wrested from Egypt. The news of his father's death, however, prevented Nebuchadrezzar from following up his victory. He made a hurried march across the Syrian desert, and on reaching Babylon was proclaimed king.

Five years later he turned his attention to the West-land. The princes readily submitted to their new master. "And the king of Egypt came not again any more out of his land, for the king of Babylon had taken from the river of Egypt unto the river of Euphrates all that pertained to the King of Egypt." (2 Kings 24:7). "Jehoiakim became his (*i.e.* Nebuchadrezzar's) servant three years: then he turned and rebelled against him" (2 Kings 24:1).

In 2 Chronicles 36:6, it is recorded that Nebuchadrezzar bound him in fetters and carried him to Babylon, and Jehoiachin reigned in his stead. After a short reign of three months he had Nebuchadrezzar beleaguering Jerusalem. Jehoiachin, and his mother, the princes and officers threw themselves on the mercy of the conquerer. He deported them,

Inscribed brick of Nebuchadrezzar with stamp in Aramaic. Inscription reads: Nebuchadrezzar, king of Babylon, the restorer of Esagila and Ezida, the first son of Nabopolassar, king of Babylon.

together with all the mighty men of valor, making ten thousand captives, and all the treasures of the temple and palace. Those that he allowed to remain were, "the poorest sort of the people of the land." Mattaniah, whose name was changed to Zedekiah, was placed upon the throne. Again Egypt made overtures, and promised assistance to the king if he would renounce Babylonia. In the ninth year of Zedekiah's reign, Nebuchadrezzar laid siege once more to Jerusalem, as the king had revolted. This event coincides with the accession of Pharaoh Hophra, who marched to the assistance of his confederate. The Babylonians raised the siege long enough to punish the Egyptians, who returned to their country (Jer. 37:5 ff). In two years, after a stubborn resistance, the city fell, and the king who had escaped by night from the city was captured. The faithless vassal was taken to Nebuchadrezzar at Riblah, where his son was killed before his eyes, after which he was blinded, and sent to Babylon in fetters. (2 Kings 25:6 f.). A second deportation followed, when the walls of Jerusalem were broken down. Over the remnant that remained, which was composed of the poorest classes, Gedaliah was appointed governor. Several months later he was murdered by his own countrymen, who then fled to Egypt.

A good many lengthy records known as building inscriptions have been found belonging to Nebuchadrezzar, but no historical inscriptions corresponding to the annals of the Assyrian kings. It is not improbable that some day these will be found. In consequence, little or no light from Babylonian

Neo-Babylonian Inscriptions 365

sources has been thrown upon the situation. It is interesting, however, to note that while these records make no reference to his political activity, they represent him to be a man in every respect similar to the way he is characterized in the Old Testament. In the first place, he was a great builder. He built the two great walls of the city, called Imgur-Bêl and Nimitti-Bêl. He built immense quays in the banks of the Euphrates, besides developing otherwise the facilities for handling the commerce. He dug wide moats about the walls, so that it was as if the sea surrounded the city. The great procession street between the temple Esagila in Babylon and Ezida in Borsippa, was elevated above the houses of the people, and greatly beautified. This wide street was called Aiburshabu ("May the enemy not prevail"). It was enclosed by two walls, which were beautified with glazed

A king putting out the eyes of a prisoner.

The Lion of Babylon in tiles.

tiles¹ in which lions, life size, were represented in colors. These were enclosed in borders of rosettes. The streets were paved with stone slabs which contained a brief inscription concerning the builder. It was on this street which led from the most sacred

God Marduk (Merodach).
(Found at Babylon.)

God Rammân (Addu).

part of the temple through the city across the Euphrates to the other temple, that on New Year's day, Marduk (Merodach) was taken on a visit to

¹Koldeway, the director of the excavations at Babylon, found enough fragments of these tiles to reconstruct a complete figure of one of the lions, which is given in the illustration on opposite page.

his son Nabû (Nebo), the patron deity of Borsippa. The latter accompanied the former back to his shrine.

Nebuchadrezzar also built the palace of his father, and in addition erected another adjoining it. The temple of Marduk, as well as the temples in Borsippa and Sippara, were rebuilt and adorned. These and many other important structures, for example the hanging gardens, were built in Babylon. With the

Inscribed cylinder of (biblical) Nebuchadrezzar referring to his restoration of the Tower of Babel and the building of the edifices in Babylon.

exception of a fragment of a bas-relief, which is supposed to represent the gardens, nothing has been found in the sections of the city excavated to prove that they existed. We are dependent for our knowledge of them upon the Greek historian. For millenniums the bricks used in the construction of Nebuchadrezzar's buildings, which bore his name and titles, have been used by builders in the neighboring cities. Babylon has been a veritable brick quarry.

Neo-Babylonian Inscriptions 369

In these cities can be found in great numbers bricks which bear the name of the famous builder, many of which had been used in his restoration of the Tower of Babel (see page 102), as well as the temple walls and palaces of the city.

Babylon of this age was largely the creation of Nebuchadrezzar. Sennacherib endeavored to annihilate it, but Esarhaddon, Ashurbanipal and others rebuilt it. Nebuchadrezzar, however, laid out the city on a scale unknown before and since his day. As a builder he will be renowned until the end of time. All this gives a realistic significance to the passage in Daniel (4:30): "Is not this great Babylon, which I have built for the royal dwelling-place by the might of my power and for the glory of my majesty?"

Nebuchadrezzar was not only a great builder but an intensely religious man, as is indicated not only by his inscriptions, but by the Old Testament as well. Consider, for instance a prayer which he offered to his god Marduk: "O, eternal Sovereign, Lord of everything that exists! As it seemeth good unto thee direct the name of the king, whom thou lovest, whose name thou hast called. Lead him in the right path. I am the prince, who is obedient unto thee, the creature of the land. Thou hast created me; the governing of mankind thou hast entrusted to me. According to thy grace, O Lord, which thou hast bestowed upon all mankind, cause me to love thy sublime dominion. The fear of thy god-head divinity implant in my heart; yea, grant unto me whatsoever seemeth good unto thee, O thou who hast created my life." If Jahweh had been addressed in this prayer it could have been used by any devout Jew.

His works were prompted by a religious sentiment. From the records which are extant, we do not get the idea that he considered the chief occupa-

Contract tablet dated in the reign of Evil-Merodach with reference note written in Aramaic.

tion of a monarch to be that of conquest and domination. While he deported people to Babylonia, it was because no other policy seemed to obtain. There are no indications of intolerant despotism. His subjects were not ravaged; but on the contrary, there seems to have been a disposition to be generous towards them, and to improve their condition.

Evil-Merodach (562–559 B. C.), his son, who is mentioned in the Old Testament as improving the condition of Jehoiachin in the thirty-seventh year of his captivity (2 Kings 25: 28 ff), followed Nebuchadrezzar, and ruled two years. Berosus, who lived early in the third century, says, "he governed public affairs lawlessly and extravagantly." In all probability he was easy going and mild. He was slain in a revolt which was headed by his brother-in-law, Nergal-sharezer (559–555 B. C.), who succeeded him. It is thought that he is the same who is mentioned by the prophet Jeremiah (39: 3), as being at the capture of Jerusalem at the close of Zedekiah's reign. Four years later his young son Lâbâshi-Marduk ascended the throne, but he was murdered nine months later by a body of conspirators, who chose as his successor Nabonidus, the father of Belshazzar.

Nabonidus (555–538 B. C.) had been a general of the army during the reigns of several of his predecessors. It is quite likely that he was one of the chief intriguers who caused the death of the former king. According to the Babylonian Chronicle, or the Annals of Nabonidus, we learn a few important facts concerning him, and his son Bêl-shar-uṣur, the biblical Belshazzar. The latter had been regarded as a mythical personage until the discovery of tablets mentioning him as "son of the king." Moreover, he seems to have taken a prominent part in governmental affairs, at least in connection with the army, as is indicated in the Chronicle.

This valuable record unfortunately is only partly

preserved. In the seventh year we learn that the "king was in Tema; the son of the king (Belshazzar), the princes and the army were in Accad." In consequence, on New Year's day when the great festival called *akîtu* was celebrated, the king "to Babylon did not go; Nebo to Babylon did not go; Bêl did not go forth; the *akîtu* was omitted." Their absence interfered with the annual procession of the gods

Cylinder of Nabonidus, king of Babylon, containing a prayer for his son Belshazzar.

on the great street Aibur-shabû, between the temple Esagila and Ezida, as it was necessary for the king to head the procession. Sacrifices, however, were offered in the temples. In the ninth year the same state of affairs seems to have existed. During this year the king's mother died. The official period of mourning for her by the people is mentioned in the Chronicle. In the tenth and eleventh years, the feast was also omitted, due to the absence of the king, his son, and the nobles. The fragmentary Chronicle next refers to the seventeenth and last year of his rule.

It was not because Nabonidus was an irreligious man that he neglected to be in Babylon on these occasions so that the festivals could be observed; for we learn from his inscriptions that his pious acts such as building and restoring temples, etc., were especially numerous. It does seem, however, that he was more interested in historical or antiquarian investigations than he was in the religious feasts. He seems to have delighted in the search for knowledge. In restoring temples he usually excavated to their foundations, in order to ascertain who had laid them. He made diligent search for the ancient records that had been deposited in the foundations. In recording his own labors on cylinders, he usually made reference to what he had learned in reading these inscriptions, mentioning at the same time the condition in which he had found them, as well as something about the builder.

Evidently the priests and the people were not interested in his researches, and perhaps even looked with disfavor upon the excavations which were necessary to ascertain the desired data. They were especially displeased because he neglected to attend the feasts. In consequence, they readily welcomed a change of affairs, and as a result the throne passed from the Babylonians to the Achaemenians. The Chronicle for the seventeenth year reads:

> . . . Nebo from Borsippa to go forth . . . the king entered the temple *E-dur-kalamma.* In the month . . . and the lower sea a revolt . . . Bêl came out; the *akîtu* festival according to the custom . . the gods of Marad, Zagaga and the gods of

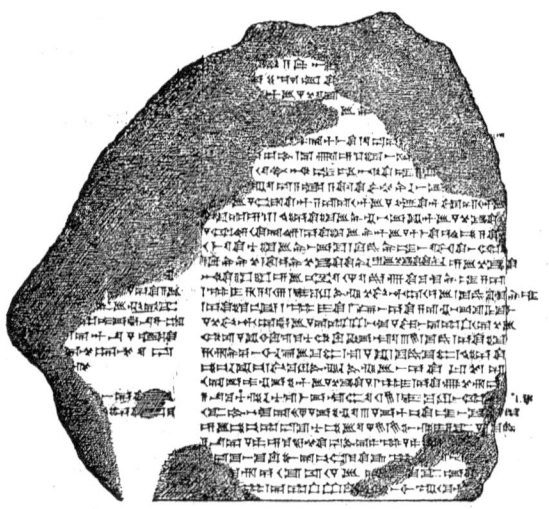

Chronicle recording the death of Belshazzar.

Kish, Bêltis and the gods of Kharsagkalamma entered Babylon. Unto the end of Elul, the gods of Borsippa, Cutha and Sippara did not enter. In the month Tammuz, Cyrus when he made battle in Kesh (Opis), on the banks of the river Zalzallat, with the soldiers of Accad, conquered the inhabitants of Accad. When they assembled, the people were killed. On the 14th, Sippara was taken without a battle. Nabonidus fled.

On the 16th, Gobryas, the governor of the land of Gutium, and the soldiers of Cyrus entered Babylon without a battle. Later Nabonidus was captured because he tarried in Babylon. To the end of the month the shield bearers of Gutium guarded the gates of Esagila. No arms of any kind were taken into Esagila or into the shrines; nor was the standard carried in. On the third day of Marchesvan Cyrus entered Babylon. Difficulties were cleared (?) Peace was established for the city. Cyrus proclaimed peace to all Babylonia and from the month Kislev unto Adar the gods of Accad whom Nabonidus had brought to Babylon returned to their cities. In Marchesvan, by night, on the 11th, Gobryas in . . . and the son of the king was killed. From the 27th of Adar, until the 3rd of Nisan there was lamentation in Accad. All the people bowed their heads. On the 4th day Cambyses, the son of Cyrus, went to *Eshapakalamma summu*, etc.

We learn from the Chronicle that Cyrus, king of Anshan and Persia which he had also conquered, began his conquest of Babylonia at Opis. This was in the year 538 B. C. He captured Sippara without fighting. Two days later the gates of Babylon were thrown open to his army under Gobryas, and Nabonidus was imprisoned. About three and a half months later Cyrus entered the city, and proclaimed peace to the inhabitants. A week later Gobryas entered . . . (tablet is injured), and Belshazzar, the son of the king, was slain.

In view of this Chronicle, it is now generally asserted that Herodotus' description of the strategy by which Babylon was taken, namely, by turning the waters of the Euphrates, which enabled the army to gain entrance by passing beneath the arches that spanned the river, is to be regarded as nothing more than a romance. Further, they say, in disagreement with the fifth chapter of Daniel, there was no violence when the city was captured; Belshazzar was not king, neither was he or his father the son of Nebuchadrezzar.

While it is not impossible that in some way he was connected with the royal house, nothing has been revealed to show that any relationship existed with the famous builder. Further, it is not likely that there was any. In his inscriptions he does not claim any connection. He says Marduk had appointed him sovereign by reason of his faithfulness. His father's name was Nabû-balatsu-iqbi, whom he simply calls *rubû emqu*, "wise prince." If he could have made any claims of royal lineage he would have done so. There are other difficulties of a historical character in the book, for which no satisfactory explanations have as yet been offered, but according to what follows, one important difficulty disappears; at least the kingship of Belshazzar is made quite possible.

Belshazzar, according to the inscriptions, is not known as a king, although it is quite clear that he was peculiarly associated with his father in the rule of affairs. In the Chronicle the actions of the king, his son, and the nobles are usually recorded. Some see in this fact an explanation of the promise to make Daniel the third ruler in the kingdom, in case

Neo-Babylonian Inscriptions

he was able to interpret the handwriting on the wall; but the fact must be recognized that Nabonidus was at this time dethroned, and if Belshazzar regarded himself king, according to what follows, then the rulers in order could not be: Nabonidus, Belshazzar, Daniel.

While the inscriptions do not recognize Belshazzar as king, it is not at all impossible that he was regarded as such by a percentage of the Babylonians, at least for a short time, and not without legitimate reasons. Cyrus's army entered Babylon, and Nabonidus was imprisoned. But how about Belshazzar, the king's son, who figured so prominently in governmental affairs? Three and a half months later Cyrus enters the city, when doubtless he is acknowledged to be the king. A week later the army under Gobryas entered a certain place, and Belshazzar is slain. The feast of Belshazzar could have taken place in Borsippa or any other city; *i.e.* it did not take place necessarily in Babylon. Commentators have fixed this event in that city, although the city is not mentioned in the fifth chapter of Daniel. It is, however, not unlikely that it did take place right in the city of Babylon. We know enough about the city and its buildings, at the present time, to understand how it was possible that in that city, which was very great in extent at the time, a large number of his followers could congregate, and even fortify themselves. The Chronicle mentions the fact that, prior to Cyrus's appearing in person, the gates of Esagila were guarded, and that no arms were taken into the sanctuary. It is not so likely that Belshazzar and his nobles were assembled there, but it is quite possible that they had fortified themselves in the great palace which Nebuchadrezzar had built; in which case it would be the palace referred to in the Book of Daniel. The king's palace was separately fortified, and protected by walls and moats,—in other words it was a fortress within a fortified city. After Nabonidus, who was the rightful heir to the throne, had been dethroned, it is altogether reasonable to suppose that Belshazzar's faithful followers proclaimed him king; and that he reigned in this peculiar way for nearly four months.

The dating of contracts shows that the people did not recognize Cyrus as king until after he had entered the city. In contracts published by Father Strassmaier there are no less than twelve dated in the reign of Nabonidus after he was imprisoned, in fact up to the day before Belshazzar's death; and one even later. On the other hand there is one published contract dated in the reign of Cyrus which is supposed to belong to the month prior to his entrance in the city, but the tablet is effaced, and the date uncertain. The first tablet, the date in which his reign is mentioned, was written on the 24th of Marchesvan, *i.e.* twenty-one days after Cyrus had proclaimed peace in Babylon. These facts show that Cyrus was not generally acknowledged to be king until after he entered Babylon, three and a half months after his army had dethroned Nabonidus. And although during this period the scribes continued to date legal documents in the reign of the dethroned king, it is quite reasonable to believe that at least some regarded Belshazzar as the ruler, and also that tablets may be found dated during his short reign. (See also page 397, on the feast of Belshazzar.)

The latter part of the Chronicle, although quite fragmentary, is supposed to refer to the burial of Belshazzar with royal honors. Cyrus, in accordance with his policy, caused his son Cambyses to lead the cortège and, according to Berosus, appointed Nabonidus governor of Karmania.

Cyrus adopted the title, "king of Babylon, and king of countries." This included Anshan and Persia. He claimed to be the legitimate successor of his predecessor. Cyrus selected an auspicious time for his invasion of Babylonia. The people apparently welcomed a change, but it is somewhat surprising that a foreign king should have been so acceptable. In order to make himself secure, it was Cyrus's policy to cater to all classes by favoring them from a religious point of view, although he worshiped Ormuzd. He seems to have succeeded in making the Babylonians believe that he was more loyal to their deities than was Nabonidus. Foreign people that had been brought to Babylonia were allowed to return to their native lands, and take with them their gods. In this way he became the popular head of the kingdom.

Unfortunately no historical records of the reign of Cyrus and his son Cambyses have as yet been found, except a fragmentary cylinder inscription which Rassam found in Babylon. It was written in the year of Cyrus' accession. In it he described the way he desired the world to understand his acts.

The Dragon of Nippur.

He claimed to have been legitimately raised up to take the place of Nabonidus, the impious usurper. He desired to have the people believe that he was a defender of their religion. The existence of strange gods brought to the capital by Nabonidus, which gave offense to the priests, offered him the opportunity to show how considerate he was to foreign peoples by returning them to their respective shrines,

Neo-Babylonian Inscriptions 381

and especially by sending the peoples held in bondage to their native homes. Naturally the Jews did not have gods but "vessels of the house of the Lord, which Nebuchadrezzar had brought forth out of Jerusalem, and had put them in the house of the gods" (Ezra 1:7-11). The inscription of Cyrus reads:

" . . . By an unrelaxing yoke he destroyed all of them. At their lamentation the lord of the god was

The Dragon of Babylon.

enraged exceedingly . . . their boundary; the gods that dwelt in their midst forsook their abode in wrath that he (Nabonidus) had brought them into Babylon. Marduk before . . . He went about to all the districts where their abodes were established, and had regard for the people of Sumer and Accad who were like the dead . . . he had compassion upon all the lands. In all of them he sought for [and] beheld him. He searched for an upright prince, the desire of [his] heart, whom he took by his hand, Cyrus, king of Anshan he called his name; for the kingship of the whole world he proclaimed his name.

The land of Quti the whole of the Umman-manda he made submissive to him. The black-headed people whom he (the god) caused his hands to subdue, in justice and righteousness he cared for them. Marduk, the great lord, the protector of his people beheld joyfully [his] deeds of piety and his upright heart. His march to his city Babylon he commanded; he caused him to take the road to Babylon; like a friend and comrade he walked by his side. His wide extended troops whose numbers were like the waters of a river, could not be known, with their weapons girded on, marched beside him. Without a fight or a battle he made him enter Babylon. His city Babylon he spared from distress. Nabonidus who did not reverence him he delivered into his hand. The people of Babylon —all of them the whole of Sumer and Accad, the nobles and governors submitted themselves before him, they kissed his feet, rejoiced for his sovereignty, their countenances brightened.

The lord who by [his] assistance revived the dead, in distress and need he relieved (?) all—they gladly honored him, and observed his word. I am Cyrus, the king of the world, the great king, the mighty king, king of Babylon, king of Sumer and Accad, king of the four quarters [of the earth], son of Cambyses, the great king, king of Anshan; grandson of Cyrus the great king of Anshan; great grandson of Teispis the great king, king of Anshan; that enduring seed of royalty whose reign Bêl and Nabû loved; for the happiness of their heart they desired his reign. When I entered Babylon peacefully amidst rejoicing and shouts, in the king's palace I took up the seat of lordship. Marduk the great lord, the big hearted . . . son of Babylon . . . . me, and daily I venerated him. My vast army went about in Babylon peacefully. The whole of the people of Sumer and Accad. I did not permit to be . . .

Cylinder of Cyrus.

> Within Babylon and all its cities with consideration I looked upon the sons of Babylon . . . . like without heart . . . . The yoke which was not honorable, was removed(?) I quietly relieved their sighing, I soothed their sorrow. Marduk the great lord rejoiced over my deeds of piety, and inclined graciously. To me Cyrus, the king who worshipped him and Cambyses the son, the going forth of my heart and all my troops and . . . .

The reference to the deliverance of the Jews in the first verse of the book of Ezra, which took place, "in the first year of Cyrus," is thus verified by this inscription. That they were allowed to take with them their sacred vessels (Ezra 1:7), is also substantiated by the fact that Cyrus returned to their respective shrines the deities brought into Babylonia. Naturally, temple utensils as well as statues of gods were included. That Cyrus should issue also a proclamation for the rebuilding of the temple (Ezra 1:1, 4) seems to be in strict accordance with his policy. Nearly two generations had passed, in which time there was a great increase of Jews in Babylonia. Doubtless many had become prosperous and influential. The published contracts, dated in the reign of Nabonidus show that many Hebrews had entered into contract relations with the Babylonians. It is therefore quite reasonable to think that Cyrus in his efforts to please this portion of the inhabitants would readily issue such a decree. And that the prophet should represent him as saying that, "the Lord God of heaven had given him all

Portrait sculpture of Cyrus, at Meshed-Murghâb.

the kingdoms of the earth" (Ezra 1:2 ff), is exactly what Cyrus endeavored to have the different peoples believe; namely, that their respective gods were favorable to him.

Cyrus made his son Cambyses a co-regent the year before his death (530 B. C.). He gave him the title "King of Babylon," while he retained "king of countries." About this time, the Babylonians began to realize that they preferred one of their own nation to rule them; and in consequence dissatisfaction arose. While Cambyses was in Egypt ruling that country, a Median named Gomates proclaimed himself king, having made the claim that he was the son of Cyrus, whom Cambyses had killed. The Babylonians called him Barzia. A number of contract tablets have been found which are dated in his reign. Media and Persia, besides Babylonia, temporarily acknowledged him king. Cambyses, who was in Egypt, turned his steps in haste towards Babylonia, but when he reached Syria he committed suicide.

A prince of the same house, although more Persian than Median or Elamitic, named Darius (521-486 B. C.) took the throne; and in a short time was able to put down Barzia, who ruled about eight months, as well as several other pretenders who had mounted thrones in various parts of the empire. His victory over these pretenders and the revolted provinces he had inscribed in their language upon the rocks of Behistun. He extended his empire

Neo-Babylonian Inscriptions 387

by conquest until the kingdoms which acknowledged his rule numbered twenty-three. Two unsuccessful attempts had been made to invade Greece, the second effort coming to an issue in the battle of Marathon, 490 B. C. An uprising in Egypt and his death prevented a third attempt.

Darius, the greatest of Persian kings was a strict

The impression of the cylinder-seal of Darius. The trilingual inscription, in Old Persian, Median, and Babylonian, reads: "I am Darius, the great king."

monotheist, worshiping Ahurmazda or Ormuzd, "the maker of heaven and earth, and the creator of man." On a magnificent seal, for the impression of which see the accompanying illustration, he is depicted hunting lions under the protecting care of his god. The inscription, which is written in Persian, Median and Babylonian reads: "I am Darius the great king." Darius I, or Hystaspes, was succeeded by his son Xerxes, whom he appointed to succeed him.

In the English of the Old Testament this ruler is known as Ahasuerus. In the inscriptions, his name is written *Aḫshiwarshu, Akshiarshu, Hishiarshi,* etc., which is quite similar to the Hebrew, *Ahashwerosh.* After this identification had been made, and the social and political conditions, as portrayed in the book of Esther were found to be those of the Persia of this time, the theory maintained by certain scholars, that Esther is a work of fiction, lost its force. Further, the excavations of Dieulafoy in the mounds of Susa, where he uncovered "Shushan the palace" (Esther 1:2), discovering also one of the dice with which the people at that time "cast Pur, that is, the lot" (Esther 3:7), make the story so realistic, that we cannot but feel that it rests upon historical facts.

The palace of Xerxes was restored by his son and successor to the throne, Artaxerxes I (464–424 B. C.). This ruler was favorably disposed towards the Jews. In his seventh year he made a decree empowering Ezra to go to Jerusalem with all those who desired to accompany him, and take with them all that they could collect, besides making extensive grants in order that he could put affairs in good shape, and offer sacrifices. During the reign of Artaxerxes I and Darius II, the Sons of Murashû conducted their business transactions in and about Nippur (see next chapter). More than one third of the contracts thus far published, of these brokers, were drawn up with Hebrews who continued to live in Babylonia after the exile.

Before his death Artaxerxes restrained those who were engaged in rebuilding the temple (Ezra 4: 21-24). He was succeeded by his son Xerxes II, who reigned only two months when he was murdered by Sogdianus, an illegitimate son of Artaxerxes. After he had ruled seven months, he was murdered by another illegitimate son, who is known as Darius II, or Nothus (423-404); the same that resumed the rebuilding of the Temple at Jerusalem.

After the thousands of undeciphered clay tablets that have been excavated have been forced to yield their contents, additional light here and there will doubtless be added, by the aid of which some historical difficulties will vanish but doubtless new ones will arise—and the veracity of the Old Testament writings will be more firmly established.

XV

BABYLONIAN LIFE IN THE DAYS OF EZRA AND NEHEMIAH

Many of the Hebrews returned to the land of their ancestral homes after Cyrus had liberated them. In the reign of Artaxerxes, about fifteen thousand more went to Palestine with Ezra (about 458 B.C.). A great many of the Jews, however, preferred to remain in the Tigro-Euphrates valley, and continue to live among the Babylonians; some of whom had become more or less influential. Nehemiah had been one of these. He had made himself useful in the court at Susa, so that he became the king's butler. It was in the twentieth year of the reign of Artaxerxes I (some scholars say Artaxerxes II), after Nehemiah had heard of the condition of his compatriots in Jerusalem, that he petitioned the king to send him to the "city of the sepulchres of his father." Artaxerxes appointed him civil governor of the district; and with the usual bodyguard, he dispatched him on his mission (about 445 B. C.).

The discovery of a literature[1] in Babylonia

---

[1] Several thousand contract tablets of this period have been published by Father Strassmaier and others.

Babylonia in Days of Ezra 391

belonging to this very time, which throws light upon the social customs and manners of the people with whom the Hebrews had daily come in contact, must be welcomed by all biblical students. This literature is of special interest when in it are found many of the names of those that remained in Babylonia, who are the descendants of the Jews to whom Ezekiel preached, along the banks of the

A dog and her puppies, in terra-cotta.

Chebar. In these late Babylonian inscriptions we therefore look for that which, in a measure, illustrates the life of the Hebrews themselves, in the post-exilic period; for many of those that returned, after being liberated by Cyrus, had been born in Babylonia; and most of those that had returned with Ezra were of the fourth generation after Nebuchadrezzar had deported them.

It was in the spring of 1893, that Doctor Haynes, who directed the excavations of the third expedition, carried on by the University of Pennsylvania at Nippur, discovered on the western side of the canal Shatt en-Nil, twenty feet below the surface of the mound, the archive-room of a business house which flourished during the reigns of Artaxerxes I (464–424 B. C.), Darius II (423–404 B. C.), and the first part of the reign of the following ruler, namely, Artaxerxes II. The room was about eighteen feet long by nine feet wide. Only a small portion of the walls remained standing, the roof having fallen in, and the walls destroyed, doubtless not long after the time of the latest dated tablet. The ground floor of the room was literally covered with tablets and fragments. About seven hundred and thirty, including fragments, were gathered. Nothing remained to show how the archives had been kept, but it is presumed that they had been laid in rows upon wooden shelves. When the roof of the building fell in, the tablets were buried.

They were simply sun-dried, having been made of clay, well kneaded and washed from grit. This increased the adhesive power of the clay, and gave the tablet the appearance of being baked, and at the same time offered an exceptionally smooth surface for the writing.

The tablets, as a rule, were carefully inscribed, a great many of which are remarkable for the care bestowed upon them by the scribes. Most of these documents were written for the sons and grandsons of Murashû, namely: Bêl-khâtin, who transacted business until 437 B. C., Bêl-nâdin-shum, whose name is not mentioned after 416 B. C., Rîmût-Ninib, and Murashû, sons of the former, and a Murashû, son of the second mentioned.

A number of them were inscribed in the interests of their servants, or slaves, and the slaves' servants. It is not stated whether these servants or slaves transacted business for themselves, or in the interest of their masters. As is well known, it is quite possible to understand that they carried on business for themselves. The fact that their tablets are found with the archives of the family, implies perhaps some intimate connections in their business transactions with different members of the family.

Each tablet is drawn up in the interest of one particular person. Only in a single tablet do we find any connection between the sons of Murashû. In this instance, an order presented to one of the sons is paid by another. Beyond the fact that they had a common ancestor, and the tablets were found together in the archive-room, there is nothing to show the existence of a firm, in those thus far published. It is possible to understand, of course, that these ancient brokers were carrying on a business which had at some previous time been established by an ancestor named Murashû, like the house of Egibi of Babylon; or by the first named of the sons of Murashû, and even that a firm existed;

but there is no definite information on this subject which has been gathered from the tablets that have been deciphered.

Of great value are the brief Aramaic legends found on these archives. They were either scratched deeply into the clay, or lightly with some kind of an instrument. In a number of instances the remains of a black color in the inscription show that they had been scratched with some kind of a pen. In consequence, some are exceedingly faint, and only here and there a character is legible, to indicate the former existence of an inscription. It would seem reasonable to conjecture that all the tablets of these archives originally had Aramaic inscriptions.

The word "docket" has in the past been incorrectly applied to these brief legends. The act is that of docketing, but the proper term in legal parlance for the writing is "endorsement." In other words, after the tablet was written in the cuneiform script in the legal language, which in this case was Babylonian, endorsements were written upon them, as for instance, a lawyer of the present day endorses a deed or contract, by stating its character, etc., as a reference note in filing the paper. In some instances the Aramaic endorsements describe the nature of the document, *e.g.*, "The document of the land of the *nagaraja* (carpenters) which Khîdûri, son of Khabṣir gave to Ribât, son of Bêl-êrib, for (literally 'in') rent." (See illustration on opposite page.) In other cases it simply records

the name of the obligor or recipient, for example:
"Document of Lâbâshi," or "Document of Akhushunu, son of Bêl-êṭir."

The question arises, why were these endorsements
not written in cuneiform, the regular script of the

Deed with an Aramaic endorsement or reference note.

Babylonian language, instead of Aramaic, the
language of Armenia. Without any doubt it points
to the fact that the endorsements were written
in the tongue of the record keeper, or more probably
in the language of the man in whose interest the

tablets were written. In other words, the Murashû sons, or their archivarius, were of Aramean origin, or Aramaic was their tongue. As we shall see (page 404), the country was filled with Western Semites.

There are many known facts concerning the use of Aramaic in Babylonia, Assyria, and Palestine, which in the centuries before and after the exile are suggestive of a very general usage of the language. We can infer that Aramaic was the language of diplomacy in the time of Sennacherib from the episode which occurred between his officials and those of Hezekiah who were standing on the walls of Jerusalem, when Eliakim of the latter, said: "Speak, I pray thee, to thy servant in Aramaic for we understand it: and speak not with us in the Jews' language, in the ears of the people that are on the wall" (2 Kings 18:26). Recall also the edicts of the late period which were made in Aramaic, or the letter which Bishlam and the rest of his companions wrote unto Artaxerxes, "which was written in the Aramaic character, and set forth the Aramaic tongue" (Ezra 4:7). In Babylonia, bricks inscribed with Aramaic legends, which took the place of those written in the cuneiform script, have been found; also some in Babylonian and Aramaic, (see illustration, p. 363). Bas-reliefs, seal cylinders, weights, etc., which contain Aramaic inscriptions have also been found. In Assyria, as well as in Babylonia, many contract tablets, exclusive of the Murashû documents, have been found with Aramaic endorsements,[1] some dated as early as the time of Sennacherib. The fact that portions of the Old Testament written in the post-exilic period are in Aramaic, and that eventually it became the language of Palestine, would indicate, perhaps, that the people had learned this language during their exile; although there is considerable Aramaic influence in the pre-exilic Hebrew literature. On taking these and other things into consideration in connection with the fact that a large percentage of the names found on the tablets of this period are West Semitic, of which a great many are Aramean, we become impressed with the extended usage of the Aramaic language throughout this region, and especially in Babylonia.

The cuneiform script continued to be used until the third or second century before Christ, and even later. The scribes continued to study Babylonian as the literary and legal language of the country, and employed it in writing contracts, letters, etc., but it is reasonable to conjecture that the usage of the language was on the decline as early as the sixth century B. C. The tongue of the common people seems to have been Aramaic, which eventually crowded out the Babylonian with its most difficult cuneiform script. The intercommercial use of the

[1] These have been gathered in a volume by Professor J. H. Stevenson of Vanderbilt University, entitled, Assyrian and Babylonian Contracts.

language, the fact that many Western Semites had emigrated to this region, besides the descendants of war captives and merchants who lived there, and that for writing purposes the Aramaic, with its short alphabet was infinitely easier to learn than the difficult cuneiform script, with its five hundred characters, nearly all of which have many phonetic and ideographic values, give us reasons for the theory that the Aramaic gradually supplanted the Babylonian as the spoken language of the land.

The use of Aramaic in Babylonia offers an interesting commentary on the story of Belshazzar's feast. When commentators considered the language of Babylonia to be Chaldean, the same as the language in which post-exilic portions of the Old Testament are written, there was no difficulty with reference to the handwriting on the wall being in that tongue. When later it was learned that this language was Aramaic, and that as far as was known, it had nothing to do with the language of Chaldea (*i.e.* Babylonia), and further, that the language of the country was the Babylonian and the script was the cuneiform, there seemed to be a serious discrepancy; for the night in which Belshazzar was slain, the handwriting upon the wall of the king's palace was in Aramaic. But when we realize that in Belshazzar's time the language which the lords knew in their official capacity, as well as that which the average man very probably understood, was the Aramaic, we have reasons why the Chaldeans spoke to the

Babylonia in Days of Ezra 399

king in Aramaic (Dan. 2:4), and why the inscription on the wall was written in that language. Doubtless the characters were clearly intelligible to all who were present, but it required a Daniel, in his prophetic spirit, to interpret them.

The Aramaic endorsements incised or written upon the clay tablets are valuable also in that we are able by their help to improve readings of the cuneiform characters, especially in proper names. Through the study of these legends the pronunciation of one well known Babylonian god was determined, as well as the consonantal writing of another. The name of a god commonly called Ninib, being the son of Bêl, and one of the patron deities of Nippur, is found quite frequently as an element in the names from that city. Few scholars, however, believed that the name of the god *Nin-ib*, which reading is Sumerian, was to be read the same in Babylonian. It occurred to me that as the god was prominently worshiped at Nippur the name could be ascertained through the medium of the Aramaic endorsements, if a name, compounded with the so-called Ninib, occurred in them. The first thing to be determined was, whose name should be expected in an endorsement written upon a contract. It became clear that if only one name occurred in a short legend, like, "Document of Lâbâshu," the name of the obligor was to be expected. Accordingly several tablets with endorsements were found, in which the obligor's name contained as an element

400 Light on the Old Testament

the god *Nin-ib*. In the case of two, the names were very poorly preserved. The reading turned out to be something altogether different from anything that had ever been suggested. After considerable study I came to the conclusion that the consonants of the name were to be read, either ' *n w sh t* or ' *n r sh t*. Although practically convinced that the middle character was W(aw) and not R(esh), I presented both readings with preference for the former. As to the vocalization of the characters, and the

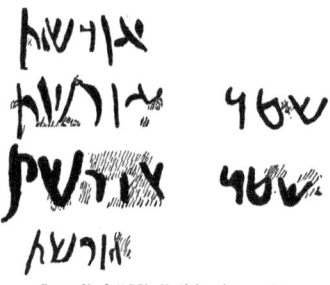

So-called " Ninib " in Aramaic.

identification of the name in cuneiform or other literatures, I did not offer my views, not being convinced of the correctness of anything which suggested itself to me. Another scholar followed by reading the characters ' *n r sh ḫ*, and regarded the name as identical with Nisroch of the Old Testament (2 Kings 19: 37). This is impossible. The readings of all other scholars, with one exception, conformed either to one or the other which I had offered. The exception referred to, *i.e.*, *b l p r sh t*=*bêl pirishti*

Babylonia in Days of Ezra 401

"lord of decision," is also an impossible reading. Others read: *Enu rêshtu*, "the chief lord;" *Enu-erishtu*, "lord of decision;" *Urashat*, the feminine of Urash, *In-arishti*, as the Semitic equivalent of *Nin-urash*; and *'nwusht=namushtu=namurtu*, which was regarded the same as "Nimrod" of the Old Testament. The latter by Professor Jensen, although questioned by some scholars has been accepted by others. Additional light on the subject will be heartily welcomed.

The other deity whose name had been read *Shadû-rabû* (*i.e.*, KUR-GAL) or Bêl is written in Aramaic ' *w r*, for which I proposed the reading *Amurru*, which is the name of the land of the Ammorites, as well as their chief god. The name of the god and land is written ideographically MAR-TU. This foreign deity played an important rôle from early times in the Babylonian religion. In a volume of texts recently published by Professor Peiser of Königsburg, the correctness of my theory was fully established. The name of an individual in the archives which he published is written with the characters read *KUR-GAL* (*-êrish*), *MAR-TU* (*-êrish*) and in an abbreviated form *Amurri*(*-a*). In other words, the name of the god, which is the first element of this name, is written in three ways, the last of which, taken into consideration with the Aramaic, shows that the others are to be read *Amurru*.

In practically every period of Babylonian and

Documents of the Murashû Sons with endorsements or reference notes written in Aramaic. The two lower tablets contain the name of the god Amurru.

Assyrian history, the names of foreigners are numerous in the business affairs of the every-day life of the people. The land, as has been said, was a "veritable Babel." In the Murashû documents we find many different nationalities represented: Egyptians, Hebrews, Phoenicians, Arameans, Persians, Cassite, etc. The fact is that more than one-third of the names in the Murashû archives are foreign. Nebuchadrezzar's conquests had brought many captives into the country. Although liberated by Cyrus, many of the influential preferred to remain in that land. The Persian rule which followed not only brought many officials and merchants into the country, but being a foreign rule, it naturally was more agreeable, in general for Gentiles. Then also the great fertility of the country between the two rivers was at all times inviting to the roaming tribes. When such conditions prevail, the process of amalgamation, or an adaptation to the religion of the country is more or less apparent. Persians and Western Semites gave Babylonian names to their children, *e.g.*, the son of Barachel (Hebrew) was named Ninib-êṭir; the son of Baga'data (Persian) was called Bêl-nâdin. And on the other hand we find that persons who bore Babylonian names gave their children Hebrew, Aramean or Persian names, *e.g.*, the son of Bêl-nâdin was named Barachel (Hebrew); the name of the son of Bêl-abu-uṣur was Minyamin (Hebrew). This state of affairs resulted, doubtless, from mixed marriages. In some cases, perhaps, where the names of captives were changed by their masters, they may have given their children names appropriate to their own nationality. We find also names with a Hebrew element compounded with a Babylonian god, *e.g.*, Barikki-Bêl. These facts explain the occurrence of Babylonian names in the lists of Hebrews in Ezra and Nehemiah, such as: Zerubbabel, Sanballat, Sheshbazzar, etc.

In the vicinity of Nippur there were a great many settlements which bore gentilic names, for example: Ashkelon, Gaza, Heshbon, Bît-Tabalai, "the town or house of Tabalites," etc. In other words, the names of towns and of tribes were transplanted to Babylonia with the migration or transference of the peoples, quite similarly as has been done in America by the immigrants from other shores, who introduced in this land the names of their former dwelling places, such as "Berlin," "London;" or their settlements were named after the country whence they came, as for instance in Philadelphia we have "Little Italy."

Of special interest are the Hebrew names from the Old Testament, mostly from the books of Ezra and Nehemiah, that are found in these business documents: *Aḫ-abu* (=Ahab), *Ammashi* (=Amashai) (*Aqubu*) (=Akkub), *Bana-Jâma* (=Benaiah), *Bali-Jâma* (=Bealiah), *Barikki-El* (=Barachel), *Bibâ* (=Bebai), *Biṣâ* (=Bezai), *Bana-Jâma* (=Benaiah) *Barikki-Jâma* (=Berechiah), *El-khadari*

Babylonia in Days of Ezra 405

(=Eliezer), *El-zabadu* (=Elzabad), *Gadal-Jâma* (=Gedaliah), *Gushuru*, (=Geshuri), *Khagga* (=Haggai), *Khanana* (=Hanan), *Khanani'* (=Hanani), *Khananu-Jâma* (=Hananiah), *Khanun* (=Hanun), *Jadikh-Jâma* (=Jedaiah), *Jadikh-El* (=Jediael), *Matanni-Jâma* (=Mattaniah), *Minakhkhim* (=Menahem), *Miniâmen* (=Miniamin), *Nabundu* (=Naboth) *Nadbiia* (=Nedabiah), *Nakhmanu* (=Naaman), *Natanu-Jâma* (=Nethaniah), *Nikhuru* (=Nahor), *Padâma* (=Pedaiah), *Pani-El* (=Peniel), *Pillu-Jâma* (=Pelaiah), *Shabbatai* (=Shabbethai), *Shamakhunu* (=Shimeon), *Shamshanu* (=Samson), *Shilimmu* (=Shillem), *Shullumma* (=Solomon), *Sikha'* (=Ziha), *Tiri-Jâma* (=Tiria), *Tub-Jâma* (=Tobijah), *Zabad-Jâma* (=Zebadiah), *Zabina'* (=Zebina), *Zabudu* (=Zabud), *Zimma* (=Zimmah), *Zuzâ* (=Zaza), etc. The number of these Western Semitic names is especially large in this period, showing that there must have been a large settlement of Jews in and about Nippur at that time.

Of special importance is the identification of the canal, or river, *Kabari*[1] with the river Chebar; on the banks of which Ezekiel, when he was among the captives in Babylonia, saw his famous visions of the cherubim (Ezek. 1:1, 3, 15; 10:15). The identification was first made by Professor Hilprecht.[2]

---

[1] There is another river mentioned in the inscriptions which closely resembles the name, i.e., *Kapiri*, Cambyses 23:2, but the above is more probably the biblical river.

[2] See Introduction to Hilprecht and Clay, Business Documents of Murashû Sons, B. E., Vol. IX. p. 28.

Later Professor Haupt followed by interpreting *Kabari*: "The great river," and said it probably was identical with the present Shatt en-Nil, which ran through Nippur.[1] The former followed by stating[2] that from the beginning it "seemed natural to identify the Chebar" with the Shatt en-Nil which passed through Nippur, but that he preferred to withhold this theory until he could examine the topography of the region. The proof then offered for this identification in brief is as follows. First, the largest canal is often written ideographically as "the Euphrates of Nippur." It is evident that only the Shatt en-Nil could have been designated in this manner. Second, *Nâr-Kabar* is the phonetic pronunciation of the ideographic writing, "The Euphrates of Nippur," and, therefore, is the former Babylonian name of the Shatt en-Nil.

The first argument needs proof, and the second I do not understand, unless it means that as *kabar* means "great," and the "Euphrates of Nippur" ought to be the largest canal, they are identical. Now the fact is, in the same volume of inscriptions four other canals are mentioned more frequently. The canal of *Sin* is found in fifteen texts, the *Kharripiqud* or *Nâr-Piqud* in twelve, while the "Euphrates of Nippur" is only found in two. However, the canal "Euphrates of Nippur" doubtless was a large canal. It may even be the

---
[1] *Ezekiel, Polychrome Bible*, p. 93.
[2] *Explorations in Bible Lands*, p. 412.

Babylonia in Days of Ezra 407

canal which passed through the city. Other inscriptions in time will determine this; but if true, it is not to be identified with the Kabaru. Why not? The text in which the canal *Kabaru* occurs, mentions property, *sha ultu Nippur a-di nâr Ka-ba-ri*, "that which is from Nippur unto the *Kabar* canal" A description of property which mentions that it is situated between a city and a river would be inadequate if the river passed through the city. In brief, the *Kabar* scarcely passed through Nippur, but doubtless is one of the canals that passed close by it.

The ideographic writing of the canal "Euphrates of Nippur" is *Nâr-Sippar*, which means the "Sippar river." The course of the river at the present time is considerably to the west of Sippara, which is represented by the mounds known as Abu-Habba. The river in ancient times doubtless passed through or close by the city. But why is the canal mentioned in these texts, which is far removed from the present bed of the Euphrates, called the *Nâr-Sippar-Nippuru?* Professor Hommel,[1] as well as Mr. C. S. Fisher [2] call attention to the fact that most of the important cities of ancient Babylonia are not along the present rivers, but between them. It therefore appears that what is called at the present, Shatt en-Nil, is the old bed of the Euphrates. In this alluvial plain, which had been covered with a

---

[1] *Geographie und Geschicht des Alten Orients.*
[2] *The University of Pennsylvania Excavations at Nippur*, p. 4

net work of canals, changes of this kind took place. Further, some maps[1] make this canal leave the Euphrates at Babylon. A branch seems to have connected the two bodies of water at that point, but there are excellent reasons for making the chief body of water, now known as the Shatt en-Nil run through ancient Sippara, and pass south to Nippur. That being true the meaning of the ideogram for the river doubtless was the Sippar-Nippur river, which, as stated, may have been the original bed of the Euphrates (*Nâr-Sippar*).

Tel-abîb, the place where the Jews lived in their captivity, and where Ezekiel sat with them, was along the Chebar. Following Tiele, instead of *Tel-abîb*, "mound of the ear of corn," some read *Tel-abûb*, "mound of the flood." Throughout Babylonia large sand dunes are seen. It is supposed that Tel-abûb is one of these hills. It is held that a sand hill within sight of Nippur is the place mentioned in Ezekiel, because[2] Jews lived in the vicinity of that city; that the reports of travellers show that these hills are stationary; the fact that a large number of Hebrew antiquities are found in the small mounds about Nippur; and because the hill "lies about a mile or more to the east of the ancient bed of the Shatt en-Nil, a fact which agrees most remarkably with a statement in Ezekiel 3:15, according to which the prophet went from the

---

[1] *Explorations in Bible Lands.* [2] *Ibidem, p.* 411.

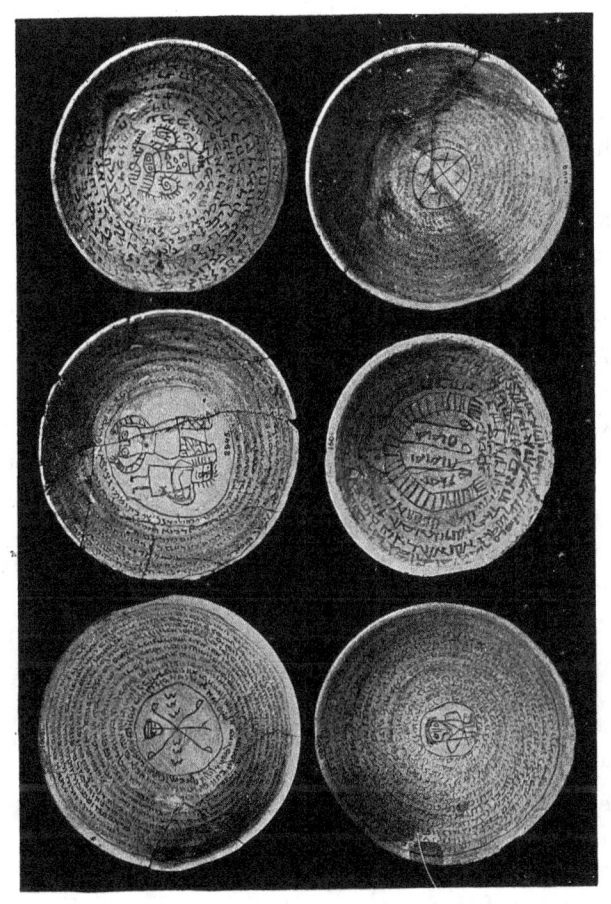

Incantation Bowls in Hebrew and Mandaic. The inscription runs spirally from the center.

Chebar to Tel-abî(û)b, so that this Jewish colony cannot have been situated in the immediate fertile neighborhood of "the great canal." But the Hebrew reads: "Then I came to them of the captivity of *Tel-abîb*, that dwelt by the river Chebar," which would imply that the town lay along the banks of the river. If, as has been stated, *Tel-abûb* is a name by which the Babylonians used to denote the large sand hills scattered over their plain, and there is no stronger evidence in the identification of one of these particular hills as the place mentioned by Ezekiel, than the fact that there are many traces of Hebrews having lived in this vicinity, it seems to me best to say that *Tel-abîb* may have been near Nippur, inasmuch as the *Kabar*, which is identified with the Chebar, may have passed near the city; but at the same time it may have been on the banks of the same river, many miles from Nippur.

The legal and business documents are a very important source of our knowledge of these times. At least ten thousand documents of this character have already reached the different museums, being marriage and dowry contracts; partnership agreements, records of debts, and promissory notes; leases of land, houses, or slaves; records of sales of all kinds of property, mortgages; documents granting the power of attorney; concerning adoption, divorce, bankruptcy, inheritance—in short, almost every imaginable kind of contract. Intensely realistic

Sixty-year lease of lands and buildings, the rent of which was paid in advance.

are the impressions gained from these private and legal documents. Here we become familiar with the doings of the every-day life of the people. We become acquainted with their personalities; we learn their wants; their plans and the things against which they guarded. In their dealings with man-

A jeweler's guarantee that an emerald would not fall out of the setting for twenty years.

kind, we learn how they protected themselves against unseen possibilities, and how they provided in their contracts for the same conditions that are so familiar in these days. Their grasp upon the shekel was just as tight, if not more so, than in the present day. For example we find the broker charging from 20%

Babylonia in Days of Ezra 413

to 50% usury on loans of money and grain. The tablets discussed in the following pages are confined to those found in the archives of the sons of Murashû, which belong to the time of Ezra and Nehemiah.[1] Different kinds of promissory notes are found among the archives, *i.e.*, abstract or interest bearing notes; or notes with mortgage or surety clauses. The following record of a debt which includes a mortgage (always first mortgage) was given as security for the payment at a stipulated time. The location of the estate upon which the mortgage was placed is properly bounded and described.

> 1200 *gur* of dates due to Bêl-nâdin-shum, son of Murashû, are to be paid by Shamash-shum-lîshir, son of Kidin; Shiriqtim son of Nûr-mâti-Sin and Lâbâshi, son of Iqîshâ together with their conscripts of the *khadari* of the *shushanu*. In the month Tishri of the first year of Darius, king, the dates, namely 1200 *gur*, in the measure of Bêl-nâdin-shum in the city Mushêzib-Ninib they shall pay. One is security for the other that the debt shall be paid. Their fields, cultivated and uncultivated, their conscripts; on the Kharipikudu canal, adjoining the field of Ninib-bana and adjoining the field of Bêl-shar-uṣur, which is in the town Mushêzib-Ninib is held as a pledge for the dates namely 1200 *gur* by Bêl-nâdin-shum. No other creditor has power over those fields until the claim of Bêl-nâdin-shum has been satisfied. (Vol. X, No. 14).

---

[1] The translations of several characteristic texts have been reproduced from my introduction to "Business Documents of Murashû Sons, B.E. Vol. X. The translations of the others are here published for the first time from Volumes IX and X.

The names of the scribe and ten witnesses, besides the date (month Airu, of the first year of the reign of Darius) follow also the seal impressions of two witnesses, and the thumb-nail marks (instead of their seals), of the three individuals upon whom the debt rested.

A large number of the documents are in the form of leases. All kinds of real estate, extensive farm lands, canals, and water rights, herds as well as personal effects, were leased. The following interesting lease of fish ponds shows that the lessee, besides agreeing to pay a stipulated amount as rent, agreed to furnish the agent daily with a mess of fish.

> Ribât, son of Bêl-êrib, servant of Bêl-nâdin-shum, of his own free will spoke to Bêl-nâdin-shum, son of Murashû, thus: the fish ponds which are situated between the towns Akhshanu and Gishshu, belonging to Bêl-ab-uṣur, those which are in the fields of the chief of the brokers; [also] the fish pools which are in the field of the prefect of the *khindânu;* and the fish pools which are in the estate Natuel let me have for rent for one year. I will pay for the year, one-half of a talent of refined silver; in addition, from the day I am given possession of those fish ponds for fishing, daily, I will furnish a mess of fish for thy table. Thereupon Bêl-nâdin-shum complied with his request, and rented him those pools of fish for the year, for one-half talent of silver. For the year the silver, *i.e.*, one-half talent, rent for those pools, Ribât shall pay to Bêl-nâdin-shum, and the fish for his table he shall furnish. From the first day of Marchesvan, year first, those pools are at the disposal of Ribât.
> In the presence of Bêlshunu and Umardatu, judges of the Canal Sin.

Babylonia in Days of Ezra 415

Names of six witnesses and the scribe follow; also seal impressions of five witnesses, including that

Lease of Fish Ponds in which the agent required the lessee to give him each day a mess of fish.

of Rîmût Ninib, son of Murashû. It is the only tablet of these archives known to me which contains an impression of the seal of a member of this family. The tablets containing receipts of amounts paid, or obligations resting upon others, contain their seal impressions, or those of the witnesses and judges. In this instance Rîmût-Ninib acted as a witness.

The following is a form of an ordinary lease of a house:

> The storehouse at the Sailor's gate which belongs to Tirakam, the son of Bagapanu he gave for the yearly rent of 2 *gur* of grain to Mannu-lûshulum, the slave of Rêmu-shukun. The bareness of the walls he shall alter; the walls of the house he shall repair. From the first day of Kislev of the thirty-seventh year, monthly 30 *qa* he shall pay (Vol. IX, No. 54).

The names of three witnesses besides that of the scribe follow. The monthly rent, *i.e.* 30 *qa*, would equal 2 *gur* a year. In house-rentals, in addition to the stipulation concerning the replastering of the walls and the keeping of them in repair, is usually found the requirement to cover the beams of the roof, *i.e.* to keep the roof, which was composed of brush, matting and mud, in repair.

The sons of Murashû and those who succeeded them had very extensive flocks of sheep and goats. This is attested by the fact that about the same time in a certain year, a number of leases were drawn up with individuals, in which they received large herds for stock raising. The following will illustrate the manner of drawing up leases for such purposes.

Babylonia in Days of Ezra

Akhushunu, son of Bêl-eṭir, of his own free will spoke to Bêl-supê-mukhur, the overseer of Arsham, thus: Rent me nine male sheep, twenty-seven two year old male sheep, one hundred and forty-four large bearing sheep, thirty-seven one-year old lambs, thirty-eight one-year old female lambs, twenty-five large male goats, nine two-year-old male goats, fifty large bearing goats, seventeen male kids, seventeen female kids, in all three hundred and seventy-three sheep and goats [*Kleinvieh*], white and black, the property of Arsham. In a year, I will give thee, as rent for those sheep: at the rate of one hundred (female) sheep, sixty-six and two-thirds (=66⅔%) offspring; at the rate of one (female) goat, one offspring; for one sheep, 1½ mina of wool; for one goat, ⅜ mina of sheared goat wool; for one bearing sheep, one *dunatum;* for one hundred sheep, one *qa* of butter. Allow me ten dead for every hundred sheep (*i.e.* 10%). For one dead I will give thee one hide and 2½ shekels of sinews. Whereupon Bêl-supê-mukhur granted his request, and gave him for rent nine male sheep, one hundred and forty-four large bearing sheep, thirty-seven one-year old male lambs, thirty-eight one-year-old female lambs, twenty-five large male goats, nine two-year-old male goats, fifty large bearing goats, seventeen male kids, seventeen female kids in all three hundred and seventy-three sheep, white and black, large and small. In a year Akhushunu shall give to Bêl-supê-mukhur at the rate of one hundred female sheep, sixty-six and two-thirds offspring for one female goat, one offspring; for one sheep, 1½ mine of wool; for one goat, ⅜ mina of sheared goat wool; for one bearing sheep one *dunatum;* for one hundred bearing sheep, one *qa* of butter, as rent for those sheep. For one hundred sheep, ten dead Bêl-supê-mukhur shall allow him. For one dead, he shall give one hide and 2½ shekels of sinews. For the shepherding, folding and guarding of those sheep Akhushunu bears the responsibility. From the twenty-first day of Elul, year the eleventh, those sheep are at his disposal. Those sheep shall be obtained from Shabakhtani, the head animal keeper, son of Pashai.

Names of twelve witnesses and the scribe follow. Nine of the witnesses, besides Shabakhtani, left impressions of their seals. Akhushunu made a thumb-nail mark instead of his seal. On the reverse is found the following endorsement in Aramaic, "The document of Akhushunu, son of Bêl-êṭir." The master in the following contract protects his own crop, and that of a servant, by requiring another servant who farmed an adjoining field, to agree to reimburse them in case a breach occurs in his canal whereby their crops are damaged:

> Bêl-nâdin-shum, son of Murashû who to Jâkhulunu and Nâ'id-Shipaq, his servant, spoke thus: Give attention to your canal gates, and your sluices which are in the embankment of the Canal Sin, which in the *kara* are exposed, so that a breach shall not occur in your canals and in your sluices which are in the embankment of the Canal Sin, which reaches you over my grain field and over the rented grain field of my servant Akhu-litia. If a breach in it occurs and my grain, and the grain of the rented field of Akhu-litia are carried off, then as much grain as has been damaged or ruined, from your own, you must pay me. Whereupon Jâkhulunu and Nâ'id-Shipaq to Bêl-nâdin-shum spoke as follows: Our canal gates and sluices that are in the embankment of the Canal Sin which reaches to us we will guard and strengthen in order that a breach will not occur. If a breach develops in it, as much grain as in it is damaged and destroyed, from our own we will refund thee. If a breach [develops and destroys the grain of] Akhu-liti and your servant, from our own we will refund them (Vol. IX, No. 55).

Babylonia in Days of Ezra 419

A contract made with an individual for the gathering of a harvest, with a penalty attached in case the work has not been done at a specified time:

> Unto the second day of the month Ab, year first of Darius, king of countries, the harvest [namely], which had been set apart as the share of Rîmût-Ninib, son of Murashû, he (*i.e.* Rîmût-Ninib) gave to Ninib-iddina, son of Ninib-êṭir, to gather in. If on the second day of the month Ab, year first of Darius, that harvest he has not completely gathered in, the harvest as much of it as should have been delivered, Ninib-iddina shall turn over to Rîmût-Ninib from his own possessions; and there shall be nothing for him, together with the farmers, out of the balance of the harvest. (Vol. X, No. 29).

An agreement to gather and deliver to three agents a certain apportionment of dates which has been made:

> Dates as many as are in the assignment which is made to Bêl-nâdin-shum for the thirty-eight year [of Artaxerxes] to be paid by Shiṭa' son of Nabû-danu. Until Nisan of the thirty-ninth year, the dates in full, in the measure of Bêl-nâdin-shum in Nippur he shall pay to Bêlshunu Shamsham Tadannu and Nâ'id-Ninib. If on that day he has not delivered the dates, he shall pay in full for the dates, as many as there should be. He shall pay at the rate of thirty *gur* per mina. (Vol. IX, No. 64).

A number of contracts refer to partnership or business combinations *i.e.*, two or more persons joined in some enterprise, for mutual gain. In some instances one of the party agreed to furnish the land and seed, while the other became responsible for

The Asiatic water buffalo (*Bubalus buffalus*) used at the present time in the *nartabu* "machines for irrigation." They were doubtless used also in ancient times for the same purpose (see page 225).

Babylonia in Days of Ezra 421

the labor. In the contracts that follow, the son of Murashû furnishes oxen, irrigating machines, and land, while the other furnishes oxen and presumably labor. They agree to divide the crops equally.

> Shum-iddina son of Pukhkhuru, spoke to Rîmût-Ninib, son of Murashû, thus: Let me put two of my oxen with two of thine into thy pasture lands, and everything, as much as in those fields grows, by our work of irrigation, is ours in common. Afterwards Rîmût-Ninib complied with his request, and gave him oxen and seed; ox for ox, seed for seed. They have sworn by the king that whatsoever grows in it shall be divided equally among them. (Vol X, No. 44).

In the following contract one of the servants of Bêl-nâdin-shum, son of Murashû, agrees to farm certain estates, for which he shall receive one-quarter of the crop, and for faithfulness in caring for the property, when the division is made, he shall receive three *gur* of dates and the palm-branches:

> A seed field, cultivated and uncultivated on the banks of . . . . . the fief estate belonging to Zabidâ and Bêlshunû, the son of Iddinâ. [also to] Lâbâshi and Bêl-nâdin, the son of Akh-iddina, to as many parts as there are, which with their conscript, the cultivated field for gardening, [and] the uncultivated for cultivation, they gave to Mushêzib, the servant of Bêl-nâdin-shum. Of whatsoever grows in the uncultivated field, a fourth part of the crop he shall pay. The work under the date-palms he shall perform. Over the premises and the ditches he shall watch. The impost of dates they shall fix for him. When the impost has been established 3 *gur* of dates and the palm branches they shall give to Meshêzib. From Sivan of the 28th year for three years that field is at the

A modern water wheel (or *cered*) in Babylonia, illustrating ox-power machines of irrigation mentioned in the texts. Ox-hides are used to lift the water.

Babylonia in Days of Ezra

disposal of Mushêzib. 5 shekels of silver of the whole amount for their fields, for three years, they received from the hand of Mushêzib. The one who breaks the contract shall pay one-half mina of silver. If he does not guard the premises and the ditches, [if] he does not do the work under the date-palm, [then] dates to the amount of 3 *gur* and the palm-branches they shall not pay. (Vol. IX, No. 10).

The names of seven witnesses and the scribe follow; Also the thumb-nail marks of Zabidâ and Bêl-nâdin, who represented the lessors.

Several bailments are among the contracts found in these archives, *i.e.*, one citizen became surety to another who had an individual imprisoned, that on his release he would not disappear. In one (Vol. IX, No. 57), the condition is made that he shall not leave Nippur without first having obtained legal permission. In violation of this the bailee forfeited the amount agreed upon. The following brief contract will illustrate this class of documents.

> Illindar, son of Iddin-Bêl, of his own free will spoke thus to Lirakamma, servant (*mâr biti*) of Bêl-nâdin-shum: Bring forth from prison Iddin-Bêl, son of Akhu-iddina, and let me become responsible for him. Whereupon, Lirakama hearkened unto him, and brought forth Iddin-Bêl from prison, and gave [him] to Illindar. If he disappears, one mina of silver Illindar shall pay to Lirakamma. (Vol. X, No. 10).

The following document is an agreement to abandon legal proceedings. By it a son of Murashû is granted a release for, and on account of, a claim for damages arising from trespass committed by

Modern water wheel or *nā'ūra* in Babylonia. The river is dammed up and the water made to pass the wheel to which, when in use, paddles were attached and bottles to lift the water to the aqueduct.

Babylonia in Days of Ezra 425

the latter and his servant. The charge of trespass, followed by its denial and payment in consideration for settlement, is quite analogous to similiar transactions of the present day.

Baga'data' the *ustaribari*, son of Bêl-nâdin, who spoke to Bêl-nâdin-shum, son of Murashû, as follows: The town Rabiia, from which silver was taken, Khazatu, and its suburbs, thou hast destroyed; silver, gold, my cattle and my sheep and everything belonging to me, all, thou, thy bond servant, thy messengers, thy servants and the Nippurians carried away. Whereupon Bêl-nâdin-shum spoke as follows: We did not destroy Rabiia, thy town, from which thy money was carried, and the suburbs of Rabiia; thy silver, thy gold, the cattle, thy sheep and everything that is thy property, all I, my bond servant, my messengers my servants and the Nippurians, did not carry away. [But] Bêl-nâdin-shum gave to Baga'data' on conditions that no legal proceedings on account of those claims which Baga' data' and one with the other made, three hundred and fifty *gur* of barley, one *gur* of spelt (?), fifty *gur* of wheat (?), fifty good large jars full of old wine, including the bottles, fifty good large jars full of new wine, including the bottles, two hundred *gur* of dates, two hundred female sheep, twenty oxen, five talents of wool. Baga' data' received from Bêl-nâdin-shum barley, *i.e.*, three hundred and fifty *gur*; spelt (?), *i.e.*, one *gur*; wheat (?) *i,e.*, fifty *gur*; jars, *i.e.*, fifty good vessels full of old wine, including the bottles; dates *i.e.*, two hundred; sheep, *i.e.*, two hundred females; oxen, *i.e.*, twenty; wool, *i.e.*, five talents, he has been paid. There shall be no legal proceedings *in perpetuo* on the part of Baga' data', his bond servant, his messengers, his servants and the men of those cities, and their suburbs, which were entered, *i.e.*, of Rabiia, Khazatu and the suburbs . . . . . . by any of them, against Bêl-nâdin-shum his bond servant, his messenger

A release given for and on account of a claim for damages arising from trespass.

Babylonia in Days of Ezra 427

his servant and the Nippurians. Baga' data', his bond servant, his messenger, his servants and the men of those cities on account of that which they said concerning Rabiia, Khazatu, the suburbs of Rabiia, and everything pertaining to that property, none of them

Wine jar lined with bitumen. Near the center is a hole into which a plug or faucet was inserted, around which bitumen was smeared to make it water-tight.

shall bring suit again, *in perpetuo*, against Bêl-nâdin-shum, his bond servants, his messenger, his servants and the Nippurians. By the gods and the king they have sworn that they will renounce all claims as regards those charges. Baga' data' bears the responsibility that no claims shall arise on the part of the men of those cities against Bêl-nâdin-shum, his bond servant, his messengers, his servants and the Nippurians.

Names of ten witnesses and the scribe; four seal-impressions and a thumb-nail mark of witnesses; also seal of Baga'data' follow.

The further study of these documents will doubtless reveal additional data of interest to the student of life and customs of the ancients who lived in Babylonia at this time, inasmuch as they represented not only the Babylonians but many different nationalities.

The work of uncovering Babylonian cities has practically only been begun. The death-like stillness which brooded over some of these mounds is beginning to be dispelled by the activity of the Oriental with his spade and pick, as directed by the Occidental with his knowledge and skill. Extraordinary results have been achieved in the last few decades, yet it will require several more of continuous labor before either Nippur, where the University of Pennsylvania has worked for a number of years, or Babylon, where the German government has dug for a half decade, will have been systematically excavated; in fact, not a single site has been completely uncovered. Surprise upon surprise awaits the investigator. There is room in Babylonia as well as in Assyria for many more expeditions. Hundreds of ruins remain untouched. Low insignificant mounds,

Babylonia in Days of Ezra 429

unnoticed and unrecorded by the average explorer, may contain antiquities older than any yet known. Interest in excavations is only being awakened. What a decade will bring forth, in opening still wider the vista of those early days, and reflecting additional light upon the Old Testament will only be known at the expiration of that time.

INDEX OF SUBJECTS

ABA-ENLIL, 44
Abaranna, 44
Abijjam, 245
Abdi-Ashirti, 279
Abdi-khiba, 260
Abdi-Ninib, 18
Abi-eshukh, 145
Abil-Sin, 145
Abraham not historical, 126
Abu-Habba, (Sippara) 30
Abu-Hatab, 25, 54
Accad, 131
Accadian language, 90
Adad-'idri, 318
Adad-nirâri, 322
Addu, 19
Adenu, 316
Adoption of children, 212
Agumkakrime, 99
Ahab, 317
Ahaz, 329, 332
Akizzi, 259
Akurgal, 38, 42
Alashia, 18, 257
Alexander the Great, 98
Alluvial plain, 158
Altar, 119
Amarna tablets, 18
Amêlu, 207
Amenenhet I, 271
Amenophis III, 252
Amenophis IV, 252
Ammi-ditana, 17, 86, 128, 137, 145
Ammi-zaduga, 128, 145
Amraphel (Hammurabi), 27, 125 f
Ammurapi, 127
Amurru, 19, 146, 223, 401
Anatomy, Knowledge of, 160
Aner, 143
Anshan, 382
Anshar, 62 f
Antiochus I, 100
Anu, 62
Anunnaki, 81
Apara, 263
Apsû, 60
Arabic, 51
Arachtu, 99
Aramaic language, 51
Aramaic endorsements, 394
Aramaic, the language of diplomacy, 396
Archeology, Credit due, 22
Ardu, 208
Argana, 316
Arioch (Éri-Aku), 131

Arnold, Doctor, 291
Arrian, 100
Aryan, 51
Asharidu, 127
Ash beds in the lower strata of Temple, 119
Ashirta, 18
Ashurbanipal, 27, 49, 77, 100, 109, 116, 120, 135, 356
Ashur-dan, 325
Ashur-etil-ilâni, 358
Ashur-nirâri, 325
Ashur-uballit, 256
Askelon, 274
Asnapper, 127, 356
Assyria, First mention of, 97
Awîl-Nannar, 156
Awîlûtum, 300
Azariah, 327
Azira, 259

BAAL of TYRE, 352
Babal, 95
Babel, 87, 89, 97
Bâbilu, 95
Babylon, 93, 131
Babylonian influences upon Palestine, 18
Babylono-Assyrian, 51
Baby rattles, 195
Bagdad, 19, 102
Baked and sun-dried tablets, 180
Baking furnace, 192
Banks, Doctor, 24
Barga, 316
Barton, Professor, 47, 250, 291
Barzia, 386
Bath-Shar, 274
Bêl, 18, 62
Belias, 199
Bêl-ibni, 341
Bela, 140
Belshazzar, 30, 376
Belshazzar's feast, 398
Ben-Addu-amara, 318
Ben-Addu-natan, 318
Ben-Hadad, 318
Berlin Museum, 164, 175
Berosus, 23, 71 f, 346, 348, 379
Bêth-Ninib, 18
Bezold, Professor, 90
Bibea, 155
Bilhah, 222
Birs-Nimrud, 96
Bismya, 24, 47, 51
Bitiliash, 290,

431

Index of Subjects

Bît-Gimillum, 295
Bît-Nin-ib, 261
Bitumen, Use of, 80, 94
Blau monument, 47
Bliss, Doctor, 26
Blood, Use of, 12
Boat builders, 217
Boissier, Professor, 187
Borsippa, 96
Breaking tablets, 179
Breasted, Professor, 275
Breastplate, 13
Bronze, 54
Brummer, Vincent, 50
Brünnow, Doctor, 91, 189
Bull-colossi, 14
Burna-Buriash, 130, 256, 285, 290
Bur-Sagali, 325
Bur-Sin, 110, 112
Buzur-Bêl, 81

CALENDAR, 151
Calneh, 48
Calno, 327
Cambyses, 379, 386
Canaan, 126
Canephorus, 164
Cardinal points, 106
Case tablets, 177
Cassites, 283
Causeway, or means of ascent to top of tower, 108
Cave of Machpelah, 221
Chaldean Account of Genesis, 59
Chaldeans, 196
Check-marks, 309
Chedorlaomer, 125, 131 f
Cherubim, 14
Children's toys, 195
Circumcision, 6
Clay as writing material, 167
Clay images, 193
Codes compared, 233
Colossi of Memnon, 252
Concubinage, 209
Confederation of powers, 136
Constantinople, 19
Cope, Professor, 42
Corporal mutilation, 219
Cosmological ideas of the Hebrews, 123
Craftsman, 52
Craig, Professor, 187
Creation, 68, 87
Ctesiphon, 102
Curb for an enclosure, 119
Cyprus, 18

DAGON, 19
Damascus, 125
Dan, 125
Dapur, 274
Date of Hammurabi, 130
Dating of tablets, 153

David, 5
Death penalty, 219
Debris, Accumulation of, 33, 110
Delitzsch, Professor, 25, 59, 77, 91, 204
De Morgan, M., 46, 201, 288
De Sacy, 247
De Sarzec, M., 24, 164
Desertion, 211
Diarbekir, 314
Divergencies of the deluge stories, 85
Divination, 10
Diodorus, 120
Disease of a slave, 214
Divorce, 210
Djocha, 47
Dragon, 69
Drainage systems, 191
Driver, Professor, 95, 121
Dungi, 164, 285
Dungur, 43
Dur-an-ki, 124 f
Dûr-Kuri-Galzu, 288
Dûr-Sin, 155
Dûr-sir-ilâni, 132
Dushratta, 256

EA, 62
Eannatum, 38
Earliest inscriptions, 47
Ebarra, 30 f
Eclipse of the sun, 325
Eden, 14, 87
Edingiranagin, 38
E-dur-an-ki, 123
Ethiopic language, 51
Egibi, 393
E-gigunu, 120
E-gishshir-gal, 197
E-gubba-an-ki, 123
Egypt, 5, 126
Ekron, 348
Ekur, 112
El-Hibba, 119
Elam, 42, 125
Ellasar (Larsa), 131, 133
Eltekeh, 343
E-mu-ri-a-na-ba-ak, 197
Emutbal, 135
Enannatum, 38
Enlil (Bêl), 92
En-mishpat, 140
Ennugi, 78
Enshagkushanna, 38
Entemena, 38, 43, 52
Envelopes inscribed, 179
Epilogue, to code, 205
Eponym Canon, 327
Erech, 42, 97, 115
E-ri, 133
Eri-Aku (Arioch), 133
Eridu, 49, 115
Eri-Eaku, 132
Esar, 47

Index of Subjects 433

Esarhaddon, 100, 351
Eshcol, 143
E-shu-gan-du-du, 197
E-temen-an-ki, 89, 102, 123
Euphrates of Nippur, 407
E-ur-imin-an-ki, 96, 123
Exodus, 126

FARA, 25, 51, 54, 84
Fees of surgeons, 216
Fight of Marduk and Tiâmtu, 65
Fisher, Mr. C. S., 32, 35, 102, 108, 113, 182, 407
Fish-pond lease, 415
Foote, Doctor, 14
Foreign names in Babylonia, 404
Frederick, Doctor, 221

GAGA, 63
Gamâru, 15
Gate of temple, 109
Gazri (Gezer), 261
Geere, Mr. V., 84
Genesis, 14th Chapter, 126
Geography of Palestine, New, 263
German Oriental Society, 25
Gezer, 265
Gilgamesh, 49, 56, 77, 86
Gilukhepa, 252
Gimil-Marduk, 155
Gimil-Sin, 197
Gimti (Gâth), 261
Girsu, 89
Gomates, 386
Gray, Doctor, 245
Greece and Rome, 2
Gudea, 17, 62, 113, 116
Gunkel, Professor, 59, 69, 71
Gutters around the ziggurrat, 160

HABBATU, 264
Habiri, 258
Habiraeans, 265
Halevy, Professor, 90
Halqat, abada, 263
Hammu, 128
Hammurabi, 17, 97, 127; Date of, 130; Letters of, 151; Piety of, 152
Hammurabi-il(u), 129
Harran, 195, 199 f
Harper, Professor R. F., 221, 222
Harri, 263
Haupt, Professor, 10, 13, 90, 91, 406
Haynes, Doctor, 30, 34, 38, 56, 104, 106, 108, 115, 120, 183, 290, 289, 294
Hazael, 34, 319
Hazatu, 266
Heber, 265
Helm, Professor, 54
Herodotus, 102, 104, 106
Hezekiah, 241, 339
Hillah, 96, 102
Hilprecht, Professor, 35, 42, 44, 84, 108, 115, 120, 187 f, 192, 242, 284, 405
Hinke, Professor, 121
Hirom, 328
Historical geography, 5
Hit, 95
Hittites, 21, 261
Hommel, Professor, 47, 90, 91, 120, 142, 196, 407
Hobah, 125
Hoffman, E. A., Collection, 47, 187
Horam, 280
Hoshen mishpat, 13
Hronzy, Dr., 244
Humbani-gash, 337
Humri, 266
Hyksos, 283

IBADID, 338
Ibni-sharru, 56
Incantation tablet, 50
Inner-court of temple, 112
Inscriptions, 147
Ipira, 263
Irkhuleni, 315
Isaiah, 314
Ishmê-Dagan, 19
Ishtar, 18
Isin, 115

JACOB, 9
Jâma, Names with, 244
Japakhi-Addi, 259
Jastrow, Professor, 10, 49, 59, 60, 62, 91, 242
Jau-bi'di, 338
Jau(m)-ilu, 239
Ja-ve-ilu, 235
Jensen, Professor, 59, 77, 90, 401
Jeremias, Dr. A., 59, 77, 257
Jeroboam II, 324 f
Jethro, 231 f
Joel, 238
Johns, Rev. C. H. W., 166, 221
Joseph, 10
Jeweler's guarantee, 412
Judge, Office of, 217
Judgment, 13

KADASHMAN-BÊL I, 254, 284, 288, 290
Kadashman-Turgu, 33 f, 27 f, 116, 285, 288
Kadesh, 140
Kalbia, 295
Kaldu, 196
Karnak, 272
Khabour, 337
Khani, 99
Khanni, 260
Khayâpâ, 338
Khu-en-Aten, 253
Khunnubi, 295
Kimtu, 128
Kinahni, Kinahhi, 264

Index of Subjects

King, Mr. L. W., 57, 59, 68, 149, 187
Kingu, 61, 65
Kish, 38, 42, 45 f
Ki-shag-gul-la Bur-Sin, 110
Kissians, 283
Koldewey, Doctor, 119, 120
Kudur, 131
Kudur-Bêl, 290
Kuri-Galzu, 256, 284 f, 290
Kudur-Lakhgumal, 132
Kudur-Mabug, 17, 132 f, 136 f, 164
Kudur-Nankhundi, 115, 132, 135, 199, 286

LACHISH, 26
Lagamar, 132
Lagash (Telloh or Shirpurla), 92
Lapidaries, 55
Larsa (Ellasar), 42, 123 f, 131, 133
Lathe, 162
Layard, 321
Leave of absence, 304
Legal documents, 410
Lehman, Professor, 32
Lenormant, Professor, 90
Letters, 154, 179
Lex talionis, 219, 224
Leviathan, 69 f
Library of the Temple School, 186
Limmu-Bêl-illatua, 154
Literature, The great antiquity of Babylonian, 48
Loftus, 25
Lot, 126
Love letter, 155
Lugal-ezen, 44
Lugal-kigubnidudu, 44, 196
Lugal-kisalsi, 44, 196
Lugal-shag-Engur, 38
Lugal-zaggisi, 44, 138, 196
Lyon, Professor, 205

MAGAN, 160
Mamre, 143
Manasseh, 354
Manishtusu, 46
Marduk, 60
Marduk-zâkir-shum, 339
Marriage contract, 209
Marriage portion, 210
Marsiman, 338
Medicine, 216
Medina, 162
Melchizedek, 125
Melukhkha, 162
Memphite sculptor, 160
Menahem, 325, 328 f
Merneptah, 275
Merodach-baladan, 339
Merom, 274
Mesilim, 46
Messerschmidt, Dr. L., 172
Meyer, Edouard, 92, 119
Milkilu, 261

Minaean, 147
Moore, Professor, 10
Moritz, 119
Moses, 238
Moabitic dialect, 147
Money-lenders, 151
Montgomery, Professor, 241
Mt. Nebo, 18
Mt. Sinai, 18
Mugayyar, 196
Müller, Professor W. Max, 257, 275
Multiplication tables, 118
Murashû Sons of Nippur, 394
Museum of the University of Pennsylvania, 138
Musical instruments, 164
Muskhênu, 207

NABONIDUS, 30 f, 130
Nabopolassar, 100, 123
Nabû-balatsu-iqbi, 276
Nahum, 356
Narâm-Sin, 16, 30 f., 117, 119, 156, 204
Narima or *Nakhrima*, 264
Naville, Mr. Edouard, 267
Nazi-Maruttash, 287, 290
Nebo, 96
Nebuchadrezzar, 30, 96, 100, 123
Nejd, 162
Nergal, 18
Nibmare, 252
Nibmuaria, 252
Niebuhr, 96
Nimmuria, 252
Nimrod, 401
Ninâ, 92
Nineveh, 97
Nin-girsu, 52
Ninib, 78, 299
Nin-kharsag, 43
Ninos, 120
Nippur, 24, 97, 104
Nizir, 82
Nöldeke, Professor, 125 f
North American Indian, 232
Nukhashshi, 259
Numerals, 180
Nûr-Rammân, 135

OATH, 218
Office of judge, 217
Oppert, Professor, 90
Outer-court, 112

PADI, 341
Pahil, 274
Pa-Kan'ana, 274
Palestinian language, 51
Parthians, 26
Passover, 12
Pay-rolls, 299
Peiser, Professor, 204, 401
Pekah, 330

Index of Subjects 435

Penates, 193
Peters, Doctor, 110, 115, 186, 197, 284, 289
Persia, 5
Pinches, Doctor T. G., 15, 59, 132, 124, 222
Pithom, 266
Poeble, Dr. A., 222
Political influence of Babylonia, 16
Pottery objects, 190
Post system, 156
Pre-Sargonic kings, 44
Prince, Professor, 91
Priest Code, 14
Pulu, 326
Pupil exercises, 187
Purpose of the tax, 292

Quti, 382

Ragia, 123
Rahab, 69 f
Rameses II, 268
Rammân-shum-usur, 284
Ranke, Dr. H., 141, 222, 238
Rassam, Hormuzd, 25, 30
Rawlinson, Henry, 130, 133, 195
Red Sea, 70
Reisner, Dr., 49, 187
Remaliah, 330
Rezin, 329
Rib-Addi, 259, 279
Rim-Sin, 131, 133, 148, 164, 207
Rogers, Professor, 91
Ruling of tablets, 180

Sabara'in, 333
Sabbath, Babylonian, 15
Sacrifice, 13
Sa-ga-as, 264
Salem, 125
Samaria, 333, 336
Samsê, 337
Samsu-ditana, 145
Samsu-iluna, 145, 283
Sarah, 198
Sargon I, 16, 31 f, 46, 98, 110, 117, 156
Sargon II, 334
Sarpanîtum, 98, 153
Sayce, Professor, 59, 90, 236
Scheil, Father, 46, 155, 184, 187, 222
Schoolboy exercises, 186
Scribes, 166
Scribes' libraries, 189
Seal cylinders, 171
Seal impressions, 296
Seals, 171
Sepulcher of Bêl, 120
Semitic languages, 51, 146
Sennacherib, 99, 330, 397
Seleucia, 102
Septuagint, 129

Sety I., 275
Shabat, 15
Sha-bat-tum, 15
Shadî, 263
Shagarakti-Shuriash, 290
Shargâni-shar-âli, 334
Shar-kênu, 334
Shar-ukîn, 334
Shalam, 274
Shallum, 325
Shalmaneser II, 314
Shalmaneser IV, 332
Shamshi-Adad, 322
Shasha (Shushan), 285
Shasharû, 218
Sheep's liver, used for divination purposes, 312
Shimti-Shilkhak, 133
Shinar, 73, 93, 127, 131
Shirpurla, see Lagash and Telloh
Shishak, 313
Showbread of the Babylonians, 11
Shuardatum, 261
Shumer, 93, 115, 131
Shunagargid, 156
Shurippak (Fara), 78
Shurpu-Maklu, 49
Shushan, 285
Sib'e, 333
Silversmith, 52
Silver standard in Sargonic age, 46
Simyra, 259
Sippara (Abu-Habba), 93, 49, 124, 182
Sinaitic peninsula, 162
Sin-idinnam, 135, 149
Sin-imguranni, 298
Sin-muballit, 135, 145
Sin-shar-ishkun, 358
Sin-shum-lîshir, 358
Sin-uzili, 298
Sisiktu, used instead of a seal, 175 f, 296
Sive, 333
Slavery in the Code, 213
Slime (bitumen), 94
Smith, 162
Smith, Mr. George, 59, 77, 133
Smith, Professor G. A., 141
So, 333
Sodom, 125
Solomon, 5, 20
Stevenson, Dr. J. H., 397
Strabo, 120
Strassmaier, Father, 291, 378, 391
Statues of gods, 193
Stone statues, 158
Stylus, 168 f
Syllabaries, 182
Sumerian question, 90
Sumerians, 90, 92
Sumu-abi, 145
Sumu-la-ilu, 98, 145
Surgery in the Code of Hammurabi, 216

436 Index of Subjects

Suti, 279
Sutruk-Nakhundi, 204
Sutu, 155

TABLETS, Shape of, 180
Tablet Hill, 183
Tabor, 274
Tags and labels, 158
Takalta, 13
Talmud, 47
Taylor, 25
Taylor cylinder, 341
Taxes, 291
Tehenu, 275
Teispis, 382
Tel-abîb, 408
Telloh (Shirpurla and Lagash), 116
Temple A-E, 99
Temple, Plan of the Babylonian, 113
Temple Belos, 102
Terah, 200
Teraphim, 193
Terhatu, 208
Text-book, 189
Thebes, 358
Theodoret, 241
Thothmes III, 258, 271
Thumb-nail marks, 174
Thummin, 13
Thureau-Dangin, Professor, 43, 44, 47, 91
Tiâmat, 60, 74
Tidal, 125, 132
Tiglath-pileser III, 326
Tihom, 69 f, 72
Tirhakah, 352
Topographical map, 294
Trumbull, Dr. H. C., 12
Tukulti-Ninib, 99, 314
Turanian languages, 51
Turkish Government, 182

UBAR-TUTU, 78
Ugarit, 259
Ukîn-zêr, 326
Umliash, 153
Umman-manda, 382
Ummu-Khubur, 61
Um-nûh libbi, 15

Umu-limnu, 15
Ungnad, Doctor, 175
University of Pennsylvania, 104
Ur-Mama, 44
Ur, 8 f, 42, 87, 195
Ur-Engur, 27, 105, 109, 113, 117, 192
Ur-Enlil, 41
Urim, 13
Urfa, 195
Ur-Ninâ, 38 f
Ur-Ninib, 33 f, 115
Urukagina, 38, 43
Urumush, 45, 92
Urusalim, 263
Urzage, 38
Use of the seal, 173
Ussher, 23, 129
Ut-napishtim, 78
Utug, 44
Uzziah, 324

VALE OF SIDDIM, 125
Vases, 162
Vaults, 112
Virolleaud, Dr., 291
Votaries, 214
Verterinary surgeon, 216
Walls, Temple, 109
Ward, Dr. W. H., 172
Weights, 46
Why tablets were encased, 178
Winckler, Professor, 32, 222, 259
Wine jar, 427
Wine shops, 215
Winkelhaken, 178

XERXES, 100

YABIM, 280
Yaphi, 280

ZABIUM, 98, 145
Zachariah, 325
Zeus, 104
Zidka, 342
Ziggurrat Bâbili, 89, 102
Zimmern, Professor, 14, 49, 5″, 90, 187
Zimrida, 280
Zoan, 271

INDEX OF SCRIPTURE REFERENCES

GENESIS
TEXT	PAGE
1 : 2	72
1 : 6, 7	123
2 : 3	16
10 : 10	48, 97
11 : 9	95
14 : 4	137
16 : 1, 2	222
23 : 14-20	222
24 : 4	221
30 : 1-4	222
44 : 5	10
46 : 17	265
47 : 11	271

EXODUS
TEXT	PAGE
18 : 14-27	231
21 : 2	227
21 : 7	227
21 : 12, 13	229
21 : 15	228
21 : 16	225
21 : 18, 19	229
21 : 22-25	229
21 : 24, 25	229
21 : 26, 27	229
21 : 28	230
21 : 29	230
21 : 32	231
22 : 1	225
22 : 2-4	225
22 : 5	227
22 : 7-9	227
22 : 12	227
22 : 14, 15	230
29 : 13	10

LEVITICUS
TEXT	PAGE
3 : 4	10
6 : 2-7	224
9 : 10	10
18 : 3	7
20 : 10	228
20 : 11	228
20 : 12	228
24 : 5 ff	12
24 : 20	229

NUMBERS
TEXT	PAGE
13 : 22	271

DEUTERONOMY
TEXT	PAGE
18 : 3	12
19 : 21	229
26 : 5	9

JOSHUA
TEXT	PAGE
10 : 1	280
15 : 41	343
19 : 28	342
19 : 29	342
19 : 44	343
19 : 45	343
24 : 2	200

JUDGES
TEXT	PAGE
1 : 31	342

I KINGS
TEXT	PAGE
6 : 1	278
14 : 25	313
16 : 31	342
17 : 9	342

II KINGS
TEXT	PAGE
8 : 15	319
10 : 32 f	321
13 : 5	322
15 : 19	328
15 : 20	329
15 : 29, 30	330
16 : 5	328, 329
16 : 7	331
16 : 9	330
16 : 10	332
17 : 3-5	332
17 : 6	333, 337
17 : 24	337
18 : 8	341
18 : 13 ff	344
18 : 26	396
19 : 9	346, 352
19 : 37	400
20 : 12-19	339
20 : 20	341
23 : 29, 30	362
23 : 31-35	362
24 : 1	362
24 : 7	362
25 : 6 f	364
25 : 28 ff	371

I CHRONICLES
TEXT	PAGE
5 : 26	326

II CHRONICLES
TEXT	PAGE
33 : 11 ff	356
36 : 6	362

EZRA
TEXT	PAGE
1 : 1, 4	384
1 : 2 f	386

TEXT	PAGE
1 : 7	384
1 : 7-11	381
4 : 7	396
4 : 10	356
4 : 21-24	389

ESTHER
TEXT	PAGE
1 : 2	388
3 : 7	388

JOB
TEXT	PAGE
26 : 12	70

PSALMS
TEXT	PAGE
74 : 13	71
83 : 7	259
89 : 9	70

ISAIAH
TEXT	PAGE
10 : 9	327
20 : 1	334
30 : 1-4	341
36 : 1 ff	344
37 : 38	351
51 : 9	70

JEREMIAH
TEXT	PAGE
37 : 5 f	364
39 : 3	371

EZEKIEL
TEXT	PAGE
1 : 1, 3, 15	405
3 : 15	408
10 : 15	405
21 : 21	10
27 : 8	342
27 : 9	342

DANIEL
TEXT	PAGE
2 : 4	399
4 : 30	371
5	376

AMOS
TEXT	PAGE
8 : 9	325

NAHUM
TEXT	PAGE
3 : 8	358
3 : 18, 19	360

MATTHEW
TEXT	PAGE
5 : 38	229

www.ingramcontent.com/pod-product-compliance
Lightning Source LLC
Chambersburg PA
CBHW071232300426
44116CB00008B/1007